Australian Politics

124-129 !

Australian Politics
Theory and practice
BILL BRUGGER AND DEAN JAENSCH

GEORGE ALLEN & UNWIN
SYDNEY LONDON BOSTON

© Brugger and Jaensch 1985
This book is copyright under the Berne Convention. No
reproduction without permission. All rights reserved.

First published in 1985
George Allen & Unwin Australia Pty Ltd
8 Napier Street, North Sydney NSW 2060 Australia

George Allen & Unwin (Publishers) Ltd
18 Park Lane, Hemel Hempstead,
Herts HP2 4TE England

Allen & Unwin Inc.
Fifty Cross Street, Winchester Mass 01890

National Library of Australia
Cataloguing-in-Publication entry:

Brugger, Bill
Australian Politics

Bibliography
Includes index
ISBN 0 86861 679 6
ISBN 0 86861 711 3 (pbk)
1. Australia – Politics and government

320 994

Library of Congress Catalog Card Number: 85-70670

Set in 10/11 Times by
Setrite Typesetters Ltd, Hong Kong
Printed by Bright Sun Printing Co. Ltd., Shenzhen, China

Contents

Tables vi
Abbreviations vii
Acknowledgements viii
Introduction ix

PART I IDEOLOGY
1 Political ideologies in Australia   3
  The first thirteen decades
2 Political ideologies in Australia   24
  1918 to the present

PART II POWER
3 Inequality and power   55

PART III INSTITUTIONS
4 Parliament, party and political practice   87
5 Commonwealth bureaucracy   130
6 Federalism in Australia   164
  '*E pluribus plura*'

PART IV ELECTORAL SYSTEMS
7 Electoral politics   199
  The roots of apathy and cynicism
Notes   226
Bibliography   244
Index   255

TABLES

3.1 Elite typology   72
7.1 First preference votes, Macmillan Victoria 1972   206
7.2 Preference distribution, Macmillan   206
7.3 Actual and estimated results, House of Representatives, 1977, 1983   207
7.4 Indices of malapportionment   210
7.5 Gini index of malapportionment in Upper Houses   210

ABBREVIATIONS

AGPS	Australian Government Publishing Service
AIDC	Australian Industries Development Commission
AIPS	Australian Institute of Political Science
ALP	Australian Labor Party
AMA	Australian Medical Association
ANU	Australian National University
ANZAC	Australian and New Zealand Army Corps
APCOL	Alternative Publishing Co-op Ltd.
APSA	Australasian Political Studies Association
ASP	Australian Socialist Party
AWU	Australian Workers Union
BP	British Petroleum
CIS	Centre for Independent Studies
CP	Country Party
CPA	Communist Party of Australia
CPA(ML)	Communist Party of Australia (Marxist-Leninist)
CSIRO	Commonwealth Scientific and Industrial Research Organisation
DLP	Democratic Labor Party
DURD	Department of Urban and Regional Development
EPAC	Economic Planning Advisory Council
FPP	First-Past-the-Post
GNP	Gross National Product
ILO	International Labour Organisation
IWW	Industrial Workers of the World
NONGO	Non-government Organisation
OBU	One Big Union
OECD	Organisation for Economic Co-operation and Development
PR	Proportional Representation
QUAGO	Quasi-government Organisation
QUANGO	Quasi-non-government Organisation
RCA	Review of Commonwealth Administration
RCAGA	Royal Commission on Australian Government Administration
TAA	Trans Australia Airlines
UNESCO	United Nations Educational Scientific and Cultural Organisation
VSP	Victorian Socialist Party
WEA	Workers Educational Association

ACKNOWLEDGEMENTS

Special thanks are due to Hugh Stretton, without whose mediation this book would never have been completed. Thanks are also due to many students and staff of the discipline of politics at Flinders University. Some of the latter were extremely helpful in their criticisms, whilst others at least ensured that the book was delayed sufficiently to allow some assessment of the Hawke Government to be included. Much of the criticism was sharp; yet there was also much encouragement. This encouragement was necessary to two authors from different backgrounds who were not always sure whether their co-operative efforts would bear fruit. Commenting on the original proposal, Suzanne Brugger made the point that 'even an ox and an ass harnessed together sometimes walk in step'. We never found out who was which. It now does not matter. We now realise that walking in step is irrelevant in getting a load to market. What is important is the stimulus given to the animals. But Helen Jaensch made the point that the gestation time for the book was more akin to that of elephants. Thanks are due to the patience of both spouses. Finally for word-processing, sincere thanks are due to Anne Gabb and Judy Stewart.

January 1985

INTRODUCTION

The title of this book, *Australian Politics: Theory and Practice*, suggests a methodology: give an account of the theory and show how practice conforms with or departs from it. But where is the theory? In case the British or American political scientist should express incredulity at that question, let us state the case baldly; one can think of few text books which deal with Australian political theory and few courses where the concept is ever raised at all. Why should this be so? True, there is no Australian John Locke, John Stuart Mill or Karl Marx; but there have been many interesting and seminal works produced in Australia which raise questions at the heart of political theory: what is the nature of the good life, what is the state for, where do rights come from, etc? That these contributions have rarely been collected together, within the discipline of politics, reflects the dependent nature of the discipline on foreign sources. The discipline of history has done much better. Take for example the work of Manning Clark who, for all his adherence to the view that history is best described as the biography of great people, is concerned to show the interplay of the ideas of Enlightenment, Protestantism and Catholicism upon Australian history. There are also interesting Australian contributions to jurisprudential thought. In contrast, the academic discipline of Australian politics is pretty dull!

Much work is required to rectify the deficiency. This book may only serve to provoke those Australian political scientists who seem to consider an atheoretical approach as a profession of virtue. One is reminded here of the point made long ago by Immanuel Kant:

> No-one can pretend to be practically versed in a branch of knowledge and yet treat theory with scorn, without exposing the fact that he is an ignoramus in his subject. He no doubt imagines that he can get further than he could through theory if he gropes around in experiments and experiences without collecting principles (which in fact amount to what we term theory) and without relating his activities to an integral whole.[1]

This book wishes to stir most Australian political scientists out of a situation in which all that passes for theory is an implicit utilitarianism. It seeks to provoke but not to condemn. One may understand the academic distaste for the crude and often silly rhetoric which passes for political debate in Australia. Moreover, some of the institutional and behavioural work on Australian politics clearly measures up to the highest international standards. In addition, some political theorists in Australia deserve the highest respect, but one may wonder why few combine their study of theory with considerations of Australian practice.

But where does one start? If this were to be a rigorous academic study, it should begin by studying history—the ebb, flow and clash of classes, groups and individuals, and the framework of ideas in which those processes took place and to which the processes gave rise. The result might be good scholarship, but it would be at the expense of this book's polemical purpose. Alternatively, this book could examine the works of those Australians who achieved some status as theorists and subject them to philosophical analysis. This again might illuminate but it would not provoke.

By way of introduction, therefore, Part I of this book will do something which, one predicts, reviewers will consider unscholarly. It will present a selective, and necessarily over-simplified, view of the ebb and flow of a number of systems of ideas in Australian history. Those systems will be referred to as *ideologies*, though one knows full well the complexity of interpretation which that word evokes. As far as this book is concerned, ideologies are simply sets of symbols which render social situations meaningful and impart to social actors a sense of identity. This definition sounds Eriksonian, though this book will avoid Erikson's Freudian methodology and his unsociological reductionism.[2] The definition also sounds idealist; and doubtless the broad strokes of the brush will prevent any detailed treatment of the social forces from which those ideologies arose. This is not to imply that ideas alone cause historical events to occur any more than ideas are simply epiphenomena of material forces. The approach should be consistent with a number of positions including the historical materialist.

This book is concerned not with all ideologies but merely with political ideologies—the sets of symbols which give identity to people as political actors. At the risk of oversimplification, Part I will look at ideologies which define politics in two very different ways. First, taking politics in Lasswell's sense of 'who gets what, when and how', an ideology may be seen as a system of ideas which locates citizens within the struggle for scarce resources and rationalises their interests or the interests of a wider social group, organisation or class. Alternatively, if one takes politics in the sense of activity appropriate to an ideal *polis* (the vehicle through which to achieve the common good and the full potential of the individual), ideology locates the citizen within a potentially rational, organic whole. According to this view, ideology is not a process of rationalisation but an aspect of reason. Both of these uses of ideology will be found in the Australian political tradition and both will be considered here.

INTRODUCTION

In discussing ideology, one could proceed in one of two directions. One could move from the individual to the state or vice versa. The first approach leads to psychologism (where 'social facts' are reduced to individual predispositions). This book, therefore, will start with diagnoses of, and prescriptions for, the relationship between the state and civil society. What is the state for? As the classical liberal sees it, the state should exist to preserve fundamental human rights (usually some variant of Locke's 'life, liberty and estate'). For the utilitarian liberal, the state should exist to monitor the competition between utility-maximising individuals and to set the rules of the game. In the Hegelian tradition (liberal or otherwise) the state should embody 'social ethics' and provide the forum for the attainment of reason and freedom. An extension of this is the view of the social liberal which advocates a state, providing the opportunities for individual self-development and the attainment of positive freedom. For the conservative, the state embodies and should continue to maintain a national tradition or a historical social-contract. On the other side of the political spectrum, the Marxist believes that the state must be transcended because it represents structures which maintain class oppression, whilst the anarchist believes the state must be destroyed because the state itself is the structure which *causes* oppression. All of these approaches might be found in Australia, but there is one peculiarity in the Australian situation which must influence every diagnosis. In Australia, the state played an extraordinarily important role in actually creating civil society in the first place.

Chapter 1 will chart ideas about the creation of that civil society and its relation to the state down to the First World War, and Chapter 2 will continue to the present. The aim of these chapters will be to set the scene chronologically for later discussions of power, parliament, political parties, bureaucracy, federalism and voters.

Chapter 3, which alone constitutes Part II, will argue that it is not meaningful to talk about power in society outside some theory of social integration and that there are many such theories. The picture of power in Australia will differ considerably depending on whether the starting point in social analysis is the individual or the totality. The utilitarian framework assigns priority to individuals, and this goes a long way to explain the continued dominance of pluralist views in Australia, long after pluralism waned in the United States. Pluralism, it will be argued, does not answer the question as to how social order might be possible. The thesis, moreover, that pluralist group competition diffuses power will be challenged from a number of perspectives. This has been done many times before but some claim to novelty, in Australian writing, might be advanced for the (Theodore Lowi-type) proposition that a focus on groups, classes or elites might each be valid *at different levels of analysis*. Contradictions arise when the wrong approach is applied to a particular level; and often the tendency to do this stems from a clear ideological purpose. Long-term historical processes can no more be explained simply in terms of the interaction of groups (pluralism) than the internal operation of the Department of Transport can simply be explained in terms of class struggle.

Part III will deal with institutions. Chapter 4 will again cover ground traversed by many—the thesis of the decline of parliament. Much has been written on the harmful effects of a model of government which derives from two contradictory sources—Britain and the United States. Much, too, has been written on the limitations of parliamentary sovereignty, the growing irresponsibility of government, the failure of government to represent the people and the problems arising from having two houses of parliament with almost equal power. Chapter 4 differs from much writing on Australian politics, however, in its emphasis on the effects of the Australian party system—a point stressed elsewhere by one of the authors.[3]

Chapter 4 contends that the problems afflicting parliamentary government in Australia stem not only from party conflict, but also from the limitations of outdated constitutional provisions and, above all, the 'Westminster myth'. That myth should be seen not as the product of centuries of constitutional development but as an invention of the late nineteenth century. Adherence in rhetoric to the myth has masked the practical realities of politics in Australia. This is of particular relevance to the discussion in Chapter 5 of the Commonwealth bureaucracy which is clearly much more than a neutral instrument to be used by whatever government happens to be in office. Neither is the Commonwealth bureaucracy simply an outgrowth on society, the inefficiency of which is guaranteed by the egalitarian myth which sustains it. That chapter will dwell, at length, on the weaknesses of the bureaucratic machine as diagnosed by the mid-1970s Royal Commission on Australian Government Administration. It will examine also the recommendations of that body for reform. Few of these have been acted on up to the present, though the election to office of a Labor government in 1983 has led to its proposals being reconsidered.

Chapter 6 deals specifically with the rigidity of the Australian Constitution and the need for reform of the federal structure. It will note the continued influence of a myth of co-ordinate federalism in a situation characterised by what has been called co-operative federalism. The mechanics of co-operative federalism themselves have led to a situation where the very word 'co-operative' is often more an expression of hope than an accurate description. That chapter will argue unequivocally for constitutional change and the establishment of a unitary state—decentralised maybe but not possessing any notion of dual sovereignty. Considerations of economic efficiency, legal equity and human rights all point to the need for change in a unitary direction.

The inertia caused by a federal structure has interacted with a partisan political process to create a society which is far from rational, efficient and democratic. Chapter 7, Part IV of the book, will consider the effect of that partisan political process on the electoral system. A few proposals will be offered for its democratisation.

Throughout, the book will examine the divergence of practice from theory—not only the theories which legitimise the Australian polity, but also academic theories designed to explain rather than justify. It might be the case, as Habermas maintains, that a growing crisis will force governments to act against the theoretical supports of their own legitimacy.[4] That hypothesis will not be tested here. The first aim of the book is simply to point out the areas where those theoretical supports are already rather weak and to suggest ways of reform which will prevent, or at least delay, the authoritarian future which Habermas fears. Secondly, the book aims to interest Australian political scientists a little more in the beliefs which sustain or undermine the polity about which they write. The first aim is particularly timely as the clamour for reform heralds Australia's bicentenary. That so many Australians see that bicentenary as the 'New South Wales bicentenary' is a symptom of the problem this book urges should be corrected. The second aim is put forward with considerable self-interest—students of Australian politics should cease to be seen as purveyors of dullness under the guise of 'realism'.

PART ONE
Ideology

ONE
POLITICAL IDEOLOGIES IN AUSTRALIA
THE FIRST THIRTEEN DECADES

The significance of the early Australian state

DURING THE EARLY days of the convict settlement of New South Wales, there existed two strands of thought on the nature of the state. One conceived the state as a penitentiary whilst the other saw it as a source of cheap labour. Though these views were often combined they could be seen as representing the different positions of emancipist and exclusivist. Such groups survived for only a few decades but the same two strands of thought on the state continued to inform Australian politics. Instead of the state as penitentiary there grew up the notion of the state as a potential instrument of moral transformation and the creator of citizen rights, and instead of the state merely as a source of cheap labour there grew up the view of the state as an instrument to be dominated by different kinds of capitalist. The first view sought to create a civil society in ways as diverse as an idealised new Britannia or an even more idealised new Jerusalem. The second view sought to create a civil society where the market was stacked in favour of its advocates' notion of the common good.

Political argument in the early nineteenth century, therefore, turned more on the nature of future civil society than, as in Europe, on the relative strength of the state and civil society. The classical liberal view of the minimal nightwatchman state was not an option. In Governor Burke's view, civil rights could only be created by strengthening executive power in the face of exclusivist oligarchs. But even the conservative oligarchs, who were frequently at odds with colonial governors, affirmed the need for a paternalist interventionist state. Notable here was James MacArthur, that 'sophisticated political theorist'[1] who, whilst reproducing in Australia a Burkean view of politics, went way beyond Burke in drawing upon the more recent works of Sismondi.[2] Sismondi was attractive because he combined a distaste for democracy with the advocacy of a broadly-based system of property ownership maintained by a paternalist redistributor state. As for those who did press for greater democracy, there was similarly the recognition of the need for a strong state. Thus, the Australian Patriotic Association associated its advocacy of representative institutions with a strong executive. All this was the converse of British classical liberalism which sought to limit executive power and thus safeguard individual rights. Classical liberalism was not on the agenda and free trade was usually modified by a criticism of unrestricted *laissez faire*.

Though the classical liberal doctrine of the state was to have little relevance in early nineteenth century Australia, there was one aspect of classical liberalism which was often apparent. This was the belief that ownership or possession of a scarce resource might be justified by productivity. The slaughter of Aborigines was often rationalised in terms of their failure to use land productively. Similarly the long struggle against squatters was couched in terms of the inefficiency of that form of pastoral farming. These were liberal rather than conservative arguments. In the long run, liberal arguments about productivity were more important than Burkean notions that the 'landed gentry' (who had received grants of land in the early days) embodied a national tradition which overrode claims about productivity. Ward's magisterial study of James MacArthur does indeed demonstrate the attempt to transplant conservative ideas into Australia, but such ideas were not to survive the discovery of gold. By the second half of the nineteenth century, the descendants of the exclusivists rarely mounted a sophisticated Burkean defence of their position. A view of the state as the embodiment of a tradition had been replaced by that of the state as an instrument to serve their own ends.

Early utilitarianism in Australia

If classical liberalism was not on the agenda and if Burkean conservatism was short-lived, what were the dominant ideological streams of nineteenth century Australia? Clearly they were utilitarian liberalism and populism. Let us first consider the utilitarian current which was dominant both in Britain and Australia. The utilitarian takes as an axiom the universal tendency of all individuals to pursue pleasure and avoid pain. The function of the state should be to monitor the competition between individuals for the realisation of those pleasures and to set the rules governing that competition in the interests of the greatest good of the greatest number. Those rules should, as far as possible, secure equality of opportunity and ensure that there is some equivalence between the pain inflicted by punishment and the pleasure derived from getting away with a crime. According to the original version of the doctrine, all pleasures and pains had to be seen as qualitatively the same, and thus democracy might be promoted in the interest of enlarging consumer choice.

When first advocated in Britain the utilitarian doctrine was known as 'radical'. And radical it was in every sense of the word. At the root of society there were no basic human rights. There was merely self-interest. One could, of course, not fail to reflect on the class division of society but the development of that society depended less on the outcome of class struggle than on the competition of atomised individuals. A good state, moreover, was one which sustained that competition. Implied here was a state much more interventionist than the nightwatchman state of the classical liberals. The state was increasingly portrayed as a regulator.

The regulating role of the state could be seen most clearly in the utilitarian views on colonisation.[3] Mercantilism had long since been rejected by all liberals and that rejection was enshrined in the works of Adam Smith. After all, mercantilism favoured the interests of colonial oligarchies who enjoyed a disproportionate share of pleasure. The early settlement of New South Wales had produced such an oligarchy, though under the peculiar circumstances of a convict settlement. For all those peculiarities, however, New South Wales did seem to point out a flaw in Smith's classical liberal views. The abundance of land did not necessarily produce prosperity for all. On the contrary, it produced a labour shortage which was normally solved by slavery or quasi-slavery—a situation far from the greatest good of the greatest number. Clearly transportation should be opposed because it violated the utilitarian belief that there should be some equivalence between crime and punishment. Yet the end of transportation could only exacerbate the shortage of labour. The transportation system, moreover, continued the centralising tendency in imperial administration which had provoked the rebellion of the American colonists. Utilitarians were united in their commitment to colonial self-government, but this would only result in the greatest good for the greatest number by more rather than less central (imperial) control over the relationship between labour and land.

A solution to the above problems was proposed in what eventually became known as the Wakefield scheme.[4] There is much controversy as to the origins of that scheme. Various writers have located its origins in the advocacy of the physiocrat Mirabeau Père, Colonel Torrens, W.C. Wentworth or Robert Gourlay, with Edward

Gibbon Wakefield merely as the synthesiser. All that need be said here about its origin is that it grew out of the utilitarian liberal body of thought and found favour with its most vigorous exponents—the followers of Jeremy Bentham. The argument was very simple. Centralised control over the Australian colonies should be replaced by centralised regulation of the price of land. Land should be priced sufficiently high to allow for a pool of landless labour to work it, but not so high as to choke off upward social mobility. Secondly, all or part of the proceeds of land sales were to be used to finance immigration. The aim was to recreate part of the English class system in Australia (the transplantation of the 'fully grown tree' and not 'the planting of saplings'). Together with this went a scheme for self-government. This was said to be a return to the economical form of administration which applied to some of the original American colonies before the eighteenth century imposition of central control. It was infinitely cheaper, Wakefield pointed out, than the latest example of centralised colonisation, the Swan River Colony in Western Australia, and could be expected to relieve the imperial government of excessive defence costs. Such self-government would encourage a 'better class' of emigrants and was consistent with the utilitarian belief that the greatest good for the greatest number is best achieved when the greatest number have a say in determining the appropriate mixture.

The above package was implemented in a rather piecemeal fashion and the political elements were often separated from the economic elements. The two economic elements, moreover (the price of land and assisted immigration), were not always complementary. The vagaries of implementation, however, do not detract from the main point. The dominant form of liberalism in the early nineteenth century was one which saw a connection between democratic forms of government and regulation of the labour market. There was a contradiction between this form of liberalism and that based on *laissez faire*. Such a contradiction was to find its earliest expression in the troubles the Wakefieldians had with land auctions and was to remain salient throughout the century and a half which followed. Throughout the debates, it was clear that the state would remain important in economic management and in the control of key prices. In its creation of civil society, moreover, the state was required to provide infrastructural investment far in excess of its British prototype. On this score Gawler, the governor of the most Wakefieldian of colonies—South Australia—was to come to grief. Yet what Gawler tried to do was later seen to be an absolute necessity.

By the time responsible government was achieved in most colonies in the mid-1850s, the idea of the regulator state based on utilitarian principles was dominant. The classic flaws in utilitarian doctrine, however, were quite apparent. People do not pursue pleasure but the objects which give pleasure and no-one could be persuaded that all those objects should be treated as equivalents. Faced with this problem the most famous of all the liberals, John Stuart Mill, attempted to distinguish between the objects of pleasure, leaving himself open to the charge that he thereby implied a yardstick of worth outside the utilitarian framework. Mill's qualification, therefore, effectively destroyed the doctrine he sought to defend. Yet Mill was only being explicit about what most utilitarians did implicitly. The utilitarian calculus was meaningless without some moral code which ordered values. In Britain the utilitarian doctrine was usually accompanied by moralism directed against drink, vice and sexual promiscuity. Here the uncompromisingly secular code of the utilitarians merged with the work of various Christian sects. In Australia this was even more the case. South Australia, the most utilitarian of all the colonies, was also the most moralistic.[5] The utilitarian doctrine co-existed with views on the redemption and perfectability of humankind.

The origin of the populist mood

The moralism of mid-century South Australia was a trifle smug. In the Eastern colonies, on the other hand, where the contradictions between types of land ownership were more acute, moralism was often pressed into the service of advocates of fundamental change. Such people are sometimes called radicals, though that term will not be used here since the utilitarians themselves were also described as radicals. It is better to see them as outraged liberals on the way to becoming what will be described as populists. Of course there was outrage in South Australia, but that was merely directed against the consequences of the Wakefield scheme which did not offer the scope for upward mobility (after four of five years) as had been envisaged. In New South Wales and what had recently become Victoria, outrage was directed at the consequences of that other view of the state from which the utilitarians had dissented. The enemy was the squatters whose claim to land occupation seemed based on no known political or moral principle. Yet there the attack went beyond the Wakefieldian framework. The Wakefield scheme depended on the imperial connection and sought to create a moderated version of the English class system. Now, in the Eastern states, orators such as John Dunmore Lang denounced the imperial connection and put forward programmes which were both nationalist and republican.[6] Whilst professing respect for Wakefield, Lang repudiated the transplanting of the mature English tree to Australian soil. The imperial authorities were not just incompetent but were positively evil. Lang, the Presbyterian clergyman, was ever the moralist. Earl Grey, the Colonial Secretary, was cast as a latter-day Lord North repeating all the old mistakes concerning the treatment of the American colonists. Yet strangely enough, there was a parallel between Lang, who denounced the imperial government for letting in too many Irish Catholics, and the views of Irish immigrants who had even less cause to admire the imperial administration. The Eureka Stockade may have just been a tax revolt but it remained as a powerful symbol for republican Australia.

The polemics of the 1840s and 1850s were largely carried on within the framework of utilitarian liberalism interlaced with both Protestant and Catholic moralism. Nevertheless, the republicanism of the 1850s was the harbinger of a populist myth which supposedly reached its apogee at the end of the century. The term populism has many meanings and covers movements as diverse as the Russian *Narodniki* and the American People's Party.[7] It is fruitless to distil the essence of such diverse movements, but one may outline a number of features of Australian political ideology in the second half of the nineteenth century which seem to fit that label better than any other.

The first feature of populism is the belief that virtue resides in the loosely-defined category of the common man (the people versus 'the classes'). This differs from utilitarian liberalism, which has nothing to say about the carriers of virtue but owes something to the religious moralism of the mid-nineteenth century. Secondly, populism maintains that the virtue of the common man is not being realised because of the domination of parasitical interests which achieved and maintain their position by conspiratorial means. Thirdly, populism believes that a new order of society might be brought about by a single act of redemption which, in Australia, need not be revolutionary. This is because the state has no inherent class nature and is merely the instrument to be used by whichever group or class is dominant. Once again this differs from the utilitarian view which, it will be remembered, recommends that the state be a regulator of conflict in the common interest rather than in the interest of any group or class. Fourthly, because the populist mood is profoundly jealous of its virtue and suspicious of foreign conspiracies, it advocates isolationism and often gives rise to a distrust of foreigners and to overt racism. Such a mood is a long way from Wakefieldian liberalism.

In Australia, the origins of the ideology of the common man were predominantly rural. This is true of most forms of populism, though some writers have pointed to a particular variety which draws on urban origins.[8] It was initially described as 'radical' in that it developed as a response to attempts by urban-based legislatures to break the power of the squatters by the introduction of land legislation to benefit the agriculturalists. At first sight, the rationalisation of the interests of those agriculturalists was couched in liberal terms. Locke, for example, was pressed into service in the claim that land was the common stock of society to which every person has a right. Title to that land, moreover, should be vested in all those who 'mixed their labour with it' (Locke's labour theory of value). The function of the state was to protect the right of the individual to landed estate. To this classical liberal notion was added John Stuart Mill's utilitarian views on the state as the trustee controlling land distribution in the interests of the greatest good of the greatest number.[9] Yet there were strands in the justification of agricultural interests which went far beyond liberalism. One influence was John Dunmore Lang who, as has been noted, was a precursor of the populist mood. For those who sought to promote free agricultural settlement the health of society and its advance towards civilisation depended on self-sufficiency, rural equality and the enobling quality of country toil.[10] To the liberal notion that the importance of the farmers depended upon their contribution to social wealth was added the populist notion that farming interests were the carriers of virtue. Virtue resided in the rural areas not because they contained institutions which embodied a tradition (Burkean conservatism) but because the farmers were in some way the chosen people. Thus the rural interest was basic to the national interest, not just because the farmers fed the cities and provided the greater part of the national income, nor because of some historical social contract, but because that was the way God had created the human condition.

The agrarian populist appeal of the late nineteenth century was not, it must be stressed, an appeal to class.[11] The appeal was to the people of the country town as a whole who benefited from the expansion of agriculture in the 'Long Boom' and who suffered together in the depression of the 1890s. By that time what had started out as a movement extolling the virtues of the agriculturalist as opposed to the pastoralist underwent a transformation. Gradually a fusion began to develop between agricultural and pastoral interests in the face of the growth of a rural labour movement. In such a situation rural populism split into a left and right-wing tendency.[12] The former sought common cause with the itinerant rural worker, whilst the latter began to see the interests of labour as identical with the interest of the cities. For the right-wing populist the growth of the cities had swamped the influence of the small farmer and had encouraged decadence, selfish competition, mob rule and financial speculation which profited from the labour of others. In right-wing populist views hostility towards the cities was extended to hostility towards other colonies (spurred on by the need to protect grain producers against competition), to other parts of colonies and to the international environment (since the fall in international prices was a major factor in the rural crisis of the 1980s). The act of redemption required was the attainment of state power to give the rural influences their proper due (by electoral 'reform' away from the idea of 'one vote, one value'), to control the growth of cities, to settle the sparsely populated land and to regulate the currency in the interests of stimulating agricultural exports.

In the above right-wing populist ideology, one sees the kind of thinking which eventually was to result in the formation of the Country Party.[13] It was right-wing in its growing opposition to organised labour and in that it served the interests of the big farmer whilst appealing to the embattled cocky. Under such conditions the left-wing variant of populism represented less and less the interests of the small farmer, though a rural collectivist orientation remained in what was to become the Country Party for several decades.[14] By and large left-wing populism took as its core the rural worker symbolised by the shearer who had played such a major role in the strikes of 1890. But again the appeal was not to that particular class but to the 'people' as opposed to the 'classes' (increasingly coming to include all farmers and graziers). At the core of the left-wing populist view was a personality type very different from the honest yeoman. Idealised was a person tall yet robust, sardonic in temperament, daring in action, idealistic without being romantic, chauvinistically male and dedicated to his 'mates'. Though born in the early days of white settlement, the legend maintains, the type was reborn in gold rush days and celebrated his reincarnation at the Eureka Stockade which was transformed from a petty-bourgeois tax-revolt into a national symbol. By the 1890s the legend had jelled as a celebration of the bush-myth—the Australian equivalent of the myth of the Russian *obstchina*. But, instead of peasants tilling their traditional communal property to the sound of Slavic songs, there was the mateship of the shearing shed, the ballads of the perpetual 'smoke-o' and the romantic nostalgia of Banjo Patterson.[15]

According to the right-wing populist view, the achievement of responsible government in most of the colonies in the 1850s should have created a balance between rural virtue and urban numbers. Instead it created an electoral system which increasingly discriminated against rural people who were declining in numbers. According to the left-wing populist view, responsible government should have provided the institutional framework for the basic democratic temper of the common man to find realisation. Instead, government was in the hands of self-seeking scoundrels who maintained control of opportunistic political groupings which were no more than patron-client networks representing pastoral or finance capital. For the left-wing populist, opposition to those scoundrels and those interests resulted in an idealisation of the bushranger and even the urban larrikin (long after the original prototypes had disappeared).

The 1890s, therefore, were crucial in the growth of both sorts of populism. Until then the right-wing populist might believe that the 1860s legislation, aimed at creating a yeoman class, would yield some fruit and that the diversification of mineral development might help revitalise new rural areas. Until then the left-wing populist might believe that the rural-based general trade unions would continue to grow in strength. In the slump of the 1890s, however, it was clear that patterns of land ownership were not benefiting those who considered themselves the most productive groups in society. The drastic fall in wool prices showed that Australia had not much control over its economic destiny and that many of its leaders were abjectly subservient to the imperial economy (a left-wing complaint) or insufficiently attentive to its rural producers (a right-wing complaint). The result was a wave of isolationist sentiment and the organisation of farming interests to protect their position. The much more spectacular organisation of labour to protect its interests, moreover, led to a savage and successful counter-attack on the part of employers and the birth of the labour movement.

It is now the conventional wisdom that the labour movement, which emerged in the 1890s, was not particularly socialist. The appeal was not to the working class *per se*, or to an alliance of classes led by a clearly identified working class, but to workers as part of an undifferentiated mass of people affected by the economic crisis. A number of reasons are advanced for this. The first set of explanations centres on the leadership of the movement and notes the domination of liberal politicians. Such accounts tend to focus only on the growth of the parliamentary Labor Party and to ignore those many leaders, both outside and within that party, who were left-populist (William Lane) or clearly socialist (Tom Mann). They do not explain the growth of bodies such as the IWW or the Victorian Socialist Party. In any case, in so far as the labour movement was dominated by liberals, what were the social conditions which allowed this to come about? A second set of explanations focus on the fragmented nature of the labour force. Again such explanations do not get us very far. The French labouring people who took part in the Commune were most fragmented but that did not stop the radical Proudhonist leadership (hardly liberal) coexisting with various groups which were quite socialist. An allied set of explanations talks about the growth of a reformist working class which enjoyed considerable upward mobility in the late nineteenth century boom. Wages were high and there was a significant degree of home ownership. Such explanations are also unsatisfactory. It is not at all clear that upward mobility was so very much higher in Australia than elsewhere and, if one shifts the explanation to a working class belief in high mobility, one has to ask what were the conditions which brought that belief into existence and why liberal leadership would ensure its continuance. As for high wages and security of home ownership, they were the first things to be threatened in the depression of the 1890s and that threat, in other societies, could lead to a right-wing radical response which would have little time for liberal leadership.

An alternative explanation returns to the peculiar nature of the Australian state. By the last decade of the nineteenth century, it is argued, the Australian state was a huge employer and entrepreneur. It had thrived on maintaining the conditions where wool and gold provided easy profit; the state, moreover, was not particularly interested in 'screwing out more surplus value from *factory* workers'.[16] In Australia, there were no Junkers nor House of Lords which maintained control over key state institutions. The institutions of liberal democracy had been established with relative ease and the state seemed already to have created the institutional framework whereby working class interests could come to power and could use the already highly socialised institutions in their own interests. Such an argument is persuasive but does not demonstrate why liberal politicians were so influential in the early Australian labour movement. After all, the idea that the state should be no more than an instrument to be used by whichever group can come to dominate it is not a *liberal* way of thinking. Liberals maintain that the state should not be a vehicle for the domination of a particular class and, as has been noted, the utilitarian variant prescribed it as a regulator acting for the general welfare. In fact, the idea that the state is, and should be, an instrument to be used by the dominant class can be a socialist view. A more accurate picture of late nineteenth century labour movement views of the state, however, was not that the state should be used in the interests of a new dominant class but in the interests of 'the people' as opposed to 'the classes'. After all had not much of Australian politics in the past century been the cynical struggle of pastoral and mercantile interests for control of the state?

The left-wing populist response was to wish a plague on both their houses.

However much liberal politicans might have recourse to gradualist ideas, the rhetoric of the labour movement at the end of the nineteenth century was apocalyptic. Whatever Henry George might have meant[17] his ideas were used as formulae to regenerate the world through a single tax on land. To be sure, land concentration was a major contemporary problem, but who but a left-wing populist would agree with the Fourth Intercolonial Trade Union Congress that abolishing all taxes save that on land values would:

> raise wages, increase and give remunerative employment, abolish poverty, extirpate pauperism, lessen crime, elevate moral tastes and intelligence, purify government and carry civilisation to a yet nobler height(?)[18]

The liberal David Ricardo, who spent much of his life campaigning against landlords, would have been amazed at the simplicity of the vision. Marxists, moreover, would concur that the simplicity of the remedy revealed a poor grasp of political economy. Indeed, for the left-wing populist, political economy was replaced by the belief in a single act of redemption which might be pursued neither by gradualist nor revolutionary means. Populists were attracted to simple blueprints and instant glimpses of the future. In this lay the attraction of Edward Bellamy's picture of Boston in *Looking Backward*,[19] of the advocacy of the early *Bulletin* for an isolationist democratic republic and of the literature of Henry Lawson who envisaged a future only of common men. In this also lay the appeal of William Lane whose message was clear—throw over the old world, its vices and its decadence (be it British or Chinese) and let the pure elemental virtues of the Australian common man have free reign; if this could not be done in Australia then it could be done in Paraguay.

The state, therefore, was there to be used by good and honest men. The immediate task was to break the power of British institutions and British capital. It is when one considers the nature of these enemies of the labour movement that one understands the leading role of liberal politicians, anxious that they should have control over the boundaries in which the 'common good' might be pursued. Here was the coincidence of interest which eventually culminated in the New Protection in the early days of the Commonwealth. In the heyday of left-wing populist fervour, however, the labour movement was as divided on the tariff as it was on most national institutional issues. Labour support for compulsory arbitration, for example, was only effected after a partial merger had been brought about between liberals and populists. When compulsory arbitration was proposed first for New South Wales a typical populist response was to bemoan the fact that it gave legal recognition to a class-divided society.

Discussion of the partial reconciliation of liberal and populist ideologies must wait upon a discussion of the transformation of liberal thought in the late nineteenth and early twentieth centuries. But before undertaking such a task one must consider the racist theme which was always a major element of Australian populism. The populist racism of the late nineteenth century was very different from the racism of the early nineteenth century, which wiped out Aborigines either unreflectedly or as a result of sheer greed. A justification for genocide might be advanced by late nineteenth century racists as necessary for land productivity. Clearly, though, the ends of those who wished to expel the large number of Chinese immigrants could not be served by the same ideological rationale. Here two sorts of arguments were advanced. First was the left-wing populist notion (opposed strongly by right-wing populist rural interests) that the high price of labour in Australia was directly attributable to its scarcity and that scarcity had to be maintained by state action. Such inversion of the Wakefieldian views was hardly liberal. This left-wing populist view tended to become mixed with arguments about racial purity. In Australia these took the form of domestic symbols depicting the 'hordes to the North' which were first Chinese then, after the Treaty of Shimonoseki, Japanese. Such was the typical response of a rich, white, selfish island in a poor environment.

The social liberal vision

This chapter has argued so far that the utilitarian liberal and populist ideologies in nineteenth century Australian politics stemmed from two prescriptions for the state—the state as regulator in the public interest and the state as instrument to be captured by the common man. By the foundation of the Commonwealth at the beginning of the twentieth century, two further prescriptions for the state became salient. The first of these, encouraged by overseas influences and nourished domestically by the class confrontation in the depression of the 1890s, was the socialist view that the state was the instrument of the capitalist class as a whole and thus should be captured by the working class. The late development of that view was probably due to the fact that it was not until late in the century that the struggle between mercantile interests and pastoral interests was decided in favour of the former and, indeed, it was not until the First World War, when manufacturing interests had sufficiently developed, that anything like a socialist movement appeared in Australia. Until that time there was probably a much greater appeal in the old populist view of 'the people against the classes'. By the time the socialist movement developed a head of steam conditions had been created where it could be branded as unpatriotic.

The second prescription for the state, which developed at the turn of the century, was the New Liberal, or social liberal, view of the ethical state. A number of explanations for the rise of social liberalism at the turn of the century may be offered. First it may simply be seen as a response to developments in Britain where Green, Hobson, Hobhouse and others had sought to replace the theoretically-defective utilitarian social calculus with a new moral calculus and a theory of progress which derived, in part, from a rereading of Hegel. The good life, it was believed, might be achieved by citizens developing their ethical personality by participating democratically in the life of a state which embodied social ethics. To this was added the view that such development was in accord with the progress of the Hegelian Mind toward greater rationality, greater commonality between citizens, greater co-operation between interests and greater *positive* freedom (freedom to realise one's potentiality as opposed to freedom from restraint). Such a view was in accord with the new British version of sociology, which Hobhouse had rescued from its earlier positivist origins in a sophisticated attempt to solve the eternal contradiction between individualism (the premise of liberalism) and social determination (the premise of sociology), and the eternal contradiction between what Durkheim called 'social facts' and specifically human values. Social liberalism was indeed an impressive package. But why was the new social liberalism so attractive to Australian intellectuals?[20] Perhaps, following Rowse, one might argue that it represented a powerful liberal response to the growing challenge of labour.[21] Perhaps also it constituted a new theoretical framework which could inform those who were creating the new Australian Commonwealth; though the uninspiring Constitution for that Commonwealth was based largely on classical liberal theory (without its natural law and consequent rights) that would inhibit rather than advance the realisation of social liberal aims. This point will be explored in some detail in Chapter 6. Finally, perhaps the answer lay in the fact that social liberalism suited the needs of those who countered the populist demand for a single act of redemption, by claiming that human salvation lay in a long process of mass education to be conducted by the 'secular evangelists' of the WEA—which to its advocates appeared as both church and democratic prototype.[22]

The most important appeal of social liberalism in the days of the early Commonwealth, it may be argued, lay in its historicity. At its core was a theory of progress. This was lacking in utilitarianism which was based on the ahistorical postulate of individuals universally pursuing pleasure and avoiding pain. It was lacking also in populism which was based on the unchanging virtues of the common man to be made potent in a single act of redemption. It is true that the faith in progress had been damaged somewhat in the depression of the 1890s but, in the new century, it seemed that evolution was on the side of the newest nation. And there was something for everyone in the new notion of progress. It was British in origin yet anti-imperialist (Hobson was the most eloquent opponent of the Boer War). It was moral without being sectarian. It showed the way to greater organisational efficiency, which appealed both to the new manufacturing interests and to the populists who wondered how Bellamy's efficient and egalitarian society might come about. It was also sanctimonious without being dogmatic and could thus appeal to the wowserism of the populists without generating too much hostility about its intellectual origins.

How then does one explain the incorporation of populist elements into social liberalism? One answer suggests that there occurred an extension of bourgeois hegemony to encompass two strands of thought which both took 'the people' as its base. Populism, directed originally against the urban bourgeoisie, was redirected against a mythical upper class.[23] It could thus be incorporated by social liberalism which had developed in England during a struggle against a real upper class. Such explanations are not totally convincing. Chapter 3 will return to the question of hegemony. It is enough to note here that, so formulated, hegemony tends to explain anything which has not been reshaped by a dominant ideology as either residues of the past or germs of a new counter-ideology. One may suggest an alternative way of looking at the problem. Of course, subordinate ideologies are always reshaped by dominant ideologies and Australia's 'Whig' historians, such as Ward, have a point in noting that change in the reverse direction may also occur.[24] But such observations should not ignore the fact that a more common way of dealing with challenge is for a dominant ideology to swallow the challenge whole, to preserve it intact whilst showing that the new subordinate ideology depends for its existence on the dominant ideology. For example, the authority of Imperial Rome swallowed the subversive creed called Christianity and showed that the doctrine whereby the meek should inherit the earth depended on papal hierarchy. The sociologist W.F. Wertheim referred to this process as the 'institutionalisation of counterpoint values'.[25] For every dominant ideological value there is a counterpoint value which may challenge the dominant value. However, the counterpoint value is usually institutionalised to the point where it adds strength to the dominant value. From time to time, however, external conditions are such that a process of deinstitutionalisation occurs; and in extreme cases that deinstitutionalisation results in a total substitution of counterpoint values for dominant values. Such is the essence of revolution. Nothing like a revolution has happened in Australia but what occurs from time to time is the uncoupling (or deinstitutionalisation) of the subordinate populist values. Such uncoupling can never adequately be explained by theories of hegemony but Wertheim's scheme does offer us the basis for a fuller explanation.

The social liberalism of the early Commonwealth, with its populist admixture, was to appeal to national leaders as diverse as Hughes, Deakin, Higgins and Holman. It embraced the whole spectrum from the Protectionist Liberals to the majority of the parliamentary ALP. Indeed, there was no fundamental difference in principle between those early parties. As Alfred Deakin saw it:

> Now we are confronted by a third party—a Labor Party, which is not distinguished from the Liberal Party in regard to its main principle of seeking social justice. It is not divided from the Liberals when we trust the people with the powers of self government. It is not divided from us in our use of the powers of the state.[26]

Indeed, for Deakin, the only difference between the two parties were arguments about the speed of change put forward by the extremist wing of the ALP. But, for most practical purposes, arguments about speed were not particularly important. For the social liberal it ought to be possible to monitor the unfolding of the rational mind and objectively to determine an optimum pace of change towards the co-operative goal. With such a view there was little room for revolutionary socialism. In the words of the preeminent leader of organised labour W.G. Spence:

> As to whether Labor will nationalise the land, the means of production, distribution and exchange, the question is hardly worth discussing at this stage, except as an abstract proposition. Every intelligent student of our social system agrees that universal co-operation must come... Revolutionary Socialism is an impossibility. No practical man can conceive it possible.[27]

To Spence it was obvious what needed to be done. The new institutions of the Commonwealth (such as the arbitration system) should be perfected to ensure the attainment of the common good, and institutions which protected selfish sectional interests (such as State upper houses wrongly referred to as Tory) cleared away. The major determinant of the speed of that process was the extent to which people's consciousness had awakened. The function of Labor leaders was to keep one step ahead of the people's aggregate intelligence and to promote general education in the interests of the common good.

It was as if Australia was in the vanguard of a movement which ensured the self-realisation of the co-operative and rational spirit. There was indeed no contradiction between the principles of co-operation and scientific management for those who believed that history was on their side. Spence was to quote approvingly the view of the new rationalist Carl Snyder:

> The scientific organisation of industry, illustrated in the great trusts, is going on under our eyes. It should give no alarm. When the work is complete public utility will necessitate governmental control, and from this to the complete unification of the whole machinery of production and distribution will be but a step. With this will come, too, the disappearance of the leisured and parasitic class generally. The invidious distinctions of wealth with their attendant vulgarity and their inevitable debasing influence will disappear. Under a rational regime men and women will satisfy their instinct for activity and work, while they will have ample time for that recreation and change which alone make life agreeable or supportable. Ostentatious riches and depressing poverty, greed and want, crime and prostitution will cease to exist and with them the physical and moral maiming and stunting of the children of the poor.[28]

Such was the creed of the believers of rational industrialism which in Europe had developed over the past three-quarters of a century. Starting from the belief that the fundamental cleavage in society lay not between capital and labour but between, on the one hand, productive capital plus labour and, on the other, the unproductive leisured classes, this view had developed along lines variously described as socialist, liberal or positivist. It had found its earliest expression in the work of Saint-Simon, whose ideas were remarkably similar to the promoters of modern efficiency and whose future society looked remarkably like that described by Bellamy. It might be found also in the works of Robert Owen, whose Grand Consolidated Trades Union based on the fundamental unity of the productive classes was a prototype for the Australian Workers Union. It could be found in the works of John Stuart Mill, who was at one time highly influenced by the 'positivism' of Auguste Comte. In more recent times it found expression in the managerial ideas of the British Fabian Society and, of course, was celebrated in that very British reconciliation of liberalism and sociology which followed the establishment of the London School of Economics. Social liberalism, it seemed, was able to bring all these strands together, but that unity was somewhat superficial and in the Australian context highly illusory.

The first collapse of the social liberal vision

First of all, it was abundantly obvious that the doctrines of managerial co-operation would have little chance of success in a federation which gave the central government very little power over economic policy within the individual States. The doctrine of Fabianism, for example, won some Australian adherents. But how was it possible in Australia to construct a co-operative managerial system based on the combination of strong central and strong municipal governments? The eventual scheme of the Webbs for a national economic parliament[29] seemed a long distance away from the Australian reality.

Second, it should be borne in mind that a powerful factor in the formation of the Commonwealth was the fear of expansion of foreign powers into the region. Events on the Afghan frontier, in the Crimea and in the Balkans had been sufficient to produce a feeling of paranoia in earlier decades. How much more important was the German imperial design in New Guinea and the Japanese expansion after the Treaties of Shimonoseki and Portsmouth? In academic circles the new social liberals such as Francis Anderson might be influential, but in practical politics the populist appeal was much more persuasive. There was, therefore, a fundamental contradiction between the universalism of the new social liberals and the outright nationalism and racism of both Labor and non-Labor. Labor demanded 'the cultivation of an Australian sentiment based upon the maintenance of racial purity and the development in Australia of an enlightened and self-reliant community'.[30] For his part, Alfred Deakin had no illusions about liberalism and racial purity:

> A united race means not only that its members can intermix, intermarry and associate without degradation on either side, but implies one inspired by the same ideas, and an aspiration towards the same ideals, of a people possessing the same general cast of character, tone of thought—the same constitutional training and traditions—a people qualified to life under this Constitution—the broadest and the most liberal perhaps the world has yet seen reduced to writing—a people qualified to use without abusing it, and to develop themselves under it to the full height and extent of their capacity. Unity of race is an absolute essential to the unity of Australia...[31]

And in case any illusions existed that Deakin's argument was based on an evolutionist liberal view concerning 'levels of civilisation', it must be noted that even the 'high spirited' and 'civilised' Japanese should be excluded, through this time 'with courtesy', unlike the treatment meted out to 'untutored savages who visit our shores'.[32]

A third factor in the disillusionment with the social liberal vision concerns the popular view as to the probity of the carriers of the new vision. For a time Deakinite liberalism was seen as an Australian synonym for the social liberal vision and it was a view which most Labor leaders shared. The fusion of 1909, however, left many Labor supporters disillusioned. The leader of the social liberal cause had formed an alliance with the atheoretical opportunist defenders of privilege who had previously been united behind the Free Trade banner. Credibility was difficult to maintain once an alliance was concluded with people who had previously been branded as the real enemies of social liberalism. The need for the fusion, it was said, was to offset the power of 'the party of revolution'.[33] However ludicrous such an attribution of revolutionary intent might be, it was clear that the thrust of much press comment cast a severe doubt on those who sought to lead the people against 'the classes'. As time went on it became quite clear that the ALP was not short of 'rats', and the general disillusionment with politicians reached a new height over the conscription issue. This split the ALP and demonstrated ethnic and religious cleavages denied by the social liberal rhetoric. Interesting in this regard is the fact that in Queensland, where the ALP did not split, the social liberal reformist vision was to achieve more than in any other part of Australia. For a time, the corrupt and opportunist politicians could be demonstrated as being outside Queensland. Wasn't Ryan standing up to Billy Hughes, the symbol of that opportunism?[34] At this point a populist appeal could be pressed into the service of social liberalism. It was the Federal Government which symbolised conspiracy and the State Government which promised redemption.

Early socialism

Perhaps the most important reason why the social liberal vision came to grief in the First World War lay in the field of industrial relations. In the face of widespread strike activity, it seemed fairly clear that the unity of the people against the 'classes' was illusory. Such a situation was to give rise to a small but significant socialist appeal. At this point, therefore, one must decide what is meant by socialism.

Socialism, as used here, is simply the belief that the fundamental contradiction in society is between capital and labour and that, in the long run, social cleavage may only be ended by the exercise of workers' power. In the short-run, all class alliances are merely tactical; there can be no fundamental unity among 'the people' as opposed to 'the classes' nor among the productive (defined here in a non-Marxian sense as entrepreneurs plus workers) as against the parasites. This definition excludes a large number of people who think of themselves as socialists, including the large body of people who talk of the transition to industrialism. Furthermore there can be no *socialisme sans doctrines*.[35] Socialism, like conservatism or liberalism, is not a behavioural disposition but an ideology and a programme of action.

To define socialism more narrowly than this would lead to analytical confusion. If one took every Australian who called himself or herself a socialist one would have to include social liberals and populists along with Marxists and anarchists. Think, for example, of the confusion generated by the following quotation from W.G. Spence:

> Australians generally are Socialistic, most of them as yet unconsciously so. The most Socialistic in their demands are those calling themselves 'Anti-Socialists'. They are great in asking for State assistance for practically everything they are connected with. The Victorian farmer declares himself against Socialism, yet he escapes much local taxation by securing Government subsidies for roads, bridges, parks and gardens, and other public utilities which, were he a true individualist, he would scorn to ask aid in supporting. Likewise he gets money for agricultural shows, and experts of all kinds are sent around to teach him how to grow things in the most profitable manner.[36]

According to this quote, what is a socialist—a person who seeks state aid, a tax-avoider, an anti-individualist or what? Indeed Spence's quote would fit almost any of the ideologies mentioned so far, with the exception perhaps of the classical liberal. It could even be consistent with the doctrines of those who uphold the utilitarian regulator state.

Using the above restricted definition, one has to conclude that there were not many socialists in Australia before the First World War. A few parties influenced by Marxism and anarchism, such as the Australian Socialist Party and the Socialist Labour Party, appeared at the turn of the century. A few individuals appeared as socialist both within and outside the ALP, but the main socialist organisations were the Victorian Socialist Party and the IWW. Both of those bodies were explicitly anti-liberal and anti-populist in the sense that they saw no fundamental unity among 'the people' and believed that the common good would only be achieved when the particular good of the working class became generalised. They were also anti-populist in the sense that they condemned nationalism, and saw class oppression as systemic rather than the result of conspiracies. Virtue, moreover, was not the property of any class or class grouping. More important by far was class consciousness which was the result of both structural conditions and sheer hard work on the part of the IWW and VSP.

The First World War was to see a spectacular growth of the IWW which managed to combine two strands of thought which in Europe were usually separate: syndicalism and Marxism. In Europe most forms of syndicalism derived from the anarchist thought of Proudhon who predicted the transcendence of the state and its replacement by self-governing syndicates of workers integrated through the market with independent peasants and artisans. In such a system the only form of regulation necessary could be performed by the banking system. Since market integration was the norm, one suspects that Proudhonist society would take the form of simple-commodity capitalism. The co-existence of peasants and workers' syndicates was, it seems, another form of the fundamental unity of the people. The IWW programme, on the other hand, rejected that unity, preferring the organisation of the whole of society into one big economic union divided into various departments. Implied here was a redistributive rather than a market form of integration[37] and a transitional state similar to the Marxists' dictatorship of the proletariat. It is for this reason that one should be wary of considering the IWW under the usual rubric of anarchist.

The growth of the IWW in the first and second decades of this century was to take place amongst the unskilled rural workers, which is quite surprising in that this was also a major source of populist influence. It took place, however, at a time when people considered to be Labor 'rats' seemed to be demonstrating that control over the existing state could not bring about the single act of redemption in which the populists believed. In affirming nationalism (soon to be enshrined in the Nationalist Party) those rats had given nationalism something of a bad name, causing it to change from an affirmation of Australian self-reliance to support for one side in a war between capitalists for a redivision of the world. Now that Kanaka immigration and the fear of 'Chinese hordes' had diminished, internationalism was much more acceptable.

Some of the old populist belief in a single act of redemption remained in the IWW belief in the efficacy of the general strike, though this time the advocacy was revolutionary. So also was the propaganda by the deed, deemed necessary to raise workers' consciousness, though it is impossible to assess just how effective such action was. For commentators such as V.G. Childe, the IWW played the major part in defeating the moves for conscription advocated by Hughes[38], though perhaps this is going too far. One is indeed struck by the relative ease with which the movement was suppressed following the Unlawful Associations Act and the big strike of 1917. Perhaps the roots of the IWW were not very deep. After 1917 all that remained of the IWW programme was the movement to create One Big Union (OBU) which was soon to founder on the rocks of established union opposition (especially the AWU). Yet the labour movement which emerged from the First World War was much more militant than the one which had entered it. By 1920 there were a number of clearly socialist organisations in existence and a significant socialist presence in the ALP. The presence of socialist elements was to result in the adoption of a moderate socialisation objective for the ALP though this was tempered by the liberal belief (the so-called 'Blackburn Convention') that:

> The party does not seek to abolish private ownership even of any of the instruments of production where such instrument is utilised by its owner in a socially useful manner and without exploitation.[39]

Presumably utility here was seen within the old utilitarian calculus.

Conclusion

By the time of the First World War the basic ideological framework of Australian politics had been set. Around a utilitarian core one could clearly see populist and social liberal orientations. By that time conservatism, in its original Burkean sense, was long since dead and *laissez faire* liberalism, though frequently invoked, was never a serious contender for dominance in one of the more state interventionist of capitalist states. The First World War, moreover, saw a quite marked growth of socialist thought. Australia had apparently come of age. Or had it? As the next chapter will note, people were to remark at several times in the following decades that Australia was coming of age and the debates outlined in this chapter were reiterated time and again.

TWO
POLITICAL IDEOLOGIES IN AUSTRALIA
1918 TO THE PRESENT

THE FIRST WORLD War and its immediate aftermath was to be traumatic for many of the combatants. At an ideological level it shattered the universalistic beliefs of many social liberals and led to a much less sanguine view of human nature. In Australia the creation of the heroic ANZAC myth occurred at a time of utter disillusionment with national leaders. One side of politics was branded as unpatriotic and even pro-German whilst the other was revealed as cynically manipulating war hysteria for its own selfish ends. At a time when mainstream social liberals were seen as woolly-minded idealists and socialist thought was confined to a minority, one would expect the populist mood to have provided fuel for the articulation of new ideologies. This is precisely what happened in a number of countries where a new appeal to the people versus the classes came to create a pseudo-community based on supposedly traditional values, and which eventually allied with domestically-oriented sections of 'the classes' to deliver both material and psychological goods.

Australia, however, did not pursue the fascist path. Fascism's only manifestation was the appearance of some extreme right-wing elements in organisations like the New Guard. One explanation might be that there were few traditional values which could be pressed into service, though the 'traditional' values of most fascist countries were, in fact, hastily constructed packages which did not, in fact, draw upon any rich tradition. Indeed, a pseudo-community could have been created out of the Australian bush myth. Another explanation might be that Australia was not obsessed with national betrayal. But then neither was Italy. A further explanation might be sought in class structure. Fascism, it is said, depends upon a disaffected petty-bourgeoisie which lost its savings in times of depression. There was in fact such a petty-bourgeoisie in Australia;

it was, of course, less hurt than that in Germany though probably not much less hurt than that in Italy.

The best answer to the above question is to be found in the orientation of the Australian labour movement. If one excludes those countries to which something called 'fascism' was imported and those old-style autocratic regimes which were wrongly called fascist by their opponents in order to discredit them, one finds that fascism is a response to a highly developed socialist movement. Fascism was stronger in Britain than in Australia because the British socialist movement was stronger, though in both countries it was pretty weak. Secondly, fascist leadership grows out of a section of the labour movement and is successful in so far as it may break down working class solidarity and replace it with a new synthetic form of community which appeals to the people rather than the working class. Amongst the English and the Scots in Australia there was not much working class solidarity anyway (due to past patterns of upward mobility). Amongst the Irish, moreover, who were immensely influential in the labour movement, as the conscription debates showed, and who were the primary bearers of the populist vision, there was already a long-standing sense of community which cut across class lines (pre-capitalist and, therefore, non-socialist collectivism). Significantly nationalists in Ireland, who might have been predisposed to use a fascist appeal against the Ulster Establishment, rarely did so. And in Australia, despite the fact that the New Guard opener of the Sydney Harbour Bridge was an Irishman, fascism's appeal to the Irish was very slight.

Left-wing populism in the 1920s and 1930s

Though Irish ethnicity was probably a positive barrier to fascism, there is no doubt that the Irish continued to be a major source of the left-wing populist appeal. Indeed, as Dixson shows, the populist phenomenon of Lang Labor in New South Wales (the bitter enemy of the New Guard) can be understood partly in terms of the psychology of Irish collectivism.[1] In Tasmania, where there were few Irish, Dixson argues, the phenomenon of Langism would be unthinkable. In the thinking of Lang Labor, the whole populist ideology was once again rehearsed. Since Lang appeared to start out with an appeal to the Trades Hall Reds (who were clearly socialist) he was seen as a socialist himself. In fact, Lang's orientation was always to the people rather than the working class in opposition to the scoundrels outside and inside the labour movement. Lang, although not particularly hostile to the monarchy and the British connection, came gradually to see New South Wales as the victim of the conspiratorial machinations of British bankers who had suborned the spineless State premiers of his day. In the end he came to see himself as the initiator of the act of redemption. Lang was 'greater than Lenin'.

Lang's appeal was charismatic (a common feature of populist movements, though rare in Australia) but it was not fascist. There could be no attempt to replace existing communitarian spirit, nor did his movement seek an accommodation with one of the 'classes'. Yet in one respect Lang did evoke similarities with the fascist leaders. The most successful of those leaders were caricatures of the hopes and fears of the underdog which, in polite bourgeois society, had been suppressed. So, in Dixson's words, was Lang:

> Lang seemed to align himself with the underdog, though one major dynamic in his makeup is an unconscious desire to regain that status from which, as a boy of seven, he imagined his father was toppled, by bankers, other malevolent plutocrats and dishonest managers. Lang revered the practical and claimed to despise book writers and men of theory—while envying them profoundly. He so suspected and disliked authority that we remember him as a rebel and like Australia's bushranger folk-hero, Ned Kelly, was in social situations often a lout: for example, one can meet him as a young alderman, behatted, pipe in mouth, feet on table, at a municipal council meeting. Yet making the 'match' with strands of our ethos even closer, endearing him even more to us, is the fact that while he flouted public authority on occasions, he was deeply authoritarian. Add to this his suspicion of foreigners, contempt for blacks...yellows...Jews and Lang's charisma begins to seem a bit more understandable. We scarcely need more and yet there is more. With his Scots father (a 'fanatical convert' so he told me, from the Presbyterian to the Catholic Church) and Irish mother, he drew upon Scots and Irish identity components in forging his style of masculinity (the process if partly unconscious), and these constitute the very essence of Australia's chief male ideal which, in many ways, like Lang himself, has tended to be authoritarian, unimaginative but often bluntly honest, and emotionally fairly bleak. Finally, so congenial to us is his massive physical stature that we have affectionately dubbed him 'the big fella'.[2]

Without wishing to discuss the psychological points raised in the above quote, one can think of few better descriptions of the populist image.

The reception of Leninism[3]

The claim that Lang was greater than Lenin was, of course, pure rhetoric. Lenin had, after all, devoted much attention to the national and colonial question and clearly saw the need to reconcile a Marxist position with a left-wing populist appeal. By the time of Lang Labor, however, Lenin was dead and Stalin offered advice to Marxists which was quite counter-productive. Stalin never understood anyone else's national traditions nor their populist manifestations.

The Leninist strategy, which developed out of his theses on the national and colonial questions, called for a united front of workers and peasants led by a discrete Communist Party to oppose imperialism and its agents. In Australia, where there were no peasants, this simply meant that the newly formed Communist Party of Australia (which had a confused birth after sections of the VSP had formed their own Communist Party and the ASP had already achieved Comintern accreditation) would seek leadership over all sections of the labour movement. This was to be achieved through membership of the ALP because that was the party which had already established firm links with the rank and file of organised labour. So much for the theory! In practice the early CPA tended to behave in much the same way as earlier socialist parties in Australia, revealing the influence of the old populist appeal to the people as opposed to the classes, rather than the Leninist appeal to a united front of the people organised and controlled by a Communist Party which articulated the long-term interests of the proletariat. But that was probably inevitable in the early 1920s when the CPA only numbered a few hundred people and when the ALP harboured paranoid fears of infiltration and betrayal. Despite its modest and confused aims, the CPA was easily expelled from the ALP and portrayed by populists (of whom Lang was the most prominent) as another alien force which threatened the long-term goals of 'the common man'.

One is not at all sure just what a successful policy for the CPA should have been in the face of left-wing populist pressure and the boom of the 1920s. When the boom collapsed at the end of that decade, there was scope for CPA expansion, though the CPA and socialism in general were no match for the left-wing populist appeal. There was more political mileage to be gained in a simple theory of bankers' conspiracy (a common populist and Langite theme) than in a Marxist study of the contradictions between domestic and international capital. Once left-wing populists had located alien bankers as the enemy, the xenophobic message could be extended to include agents of another foreign power. Then the attack on Communists could be extended to the socialisation units within the ALP [4], and indeed to any kind of socialist outside the populist control of Jack Lang.

But before one portrays the CPA as the passive victim of the masters of the left-wing populist appeal, one can not deny that the theoretical vision of social democracy, passed down from the Comintern after 1928, did a great deal to alienate working class support. In 1928, Stalin decided that a serious world depression was imminent and that Communist Parties should be ready to meet it. Although Stalin's motives may have had more to do with getting rid of his 'rightist' opponents in the Soviet Union, such as Bukharin who argued that capitalism had stabilised, his diagnosis was undoubtedly correct. From a correct diagnosis, however, Stalin then went on to argue that the impending crisis demanded an end to the united front and a full scale assault on social democratic parties *at all levels* (and not just on labour leaders who certainly in Australia were open to very serious criticism from any socialist perspective). It was argued that the strength and non-socialist nature of social democratic and labour parties in capitalist countries was such that, in the early stages of the impending crisis, they would be permitted by capitalists to form governments to shore up the tottering system. As the crisis deepened, however, workers would lose faith in those parties' ability to remedy the situation. Faced with increased worker opposition, the capitalists would turn to fascism and would recruit a significant portion of social democratic and labour party membership to that cause. To forestall such a situation there was a need immediately to denounce such parties as 'social fascist'.

In the early 1930s the new Comintern line was propagated in Australia by the CPA, which was reorganised on orthodox democratic centralist lines. The CPA sought unsuccessfully to mobilise workers within industrial cells to denounce the ALP and, more successfully, to spread its message through a number of front organisations. In general, though, the strategy did more harm than good to the socialist cause. By attacking rank and file unionists and left-wing ALP leaders, who had previously been sympathetic to communism, the CPA alienated large numbers of potential recruits, who were disillusioned with ALP incompetence, opportunism and the 'treachery' of ALP leaders who had gravitated to the United Australia Party. Indeed, it was not until after the rise of Hitler and another switch in Comintern strategy that the CPA was able once again to make headway in propagating its socialist message.

The debasement of 'politics'

The moderate appeal of socialism in the 1920s and the much greater appeal of left-wing populism in the 1930s were largely attributable to economic causes, though their specific manifestation can only be understood in the context of the collapse of the new social liberal vision and disillusionment with politics. For the social liberal, politics should be an ennobling occupation. It was by participating in politics that the individual citizen could develop his or her personality and so partake in the good life. By the end of the First World War, politics had become a pejorative term, defined narrowly as party or sectional politics. Though the ALP had the opportunity after the conscription split to develop a new set of principles, it ultimately failed to find a substitute for the left-wing version of the social liberalism of the early Commonwealth. For their part, the Nationalists seemed to operate from day to day with little concern with principles. Initially they were symbolised by Billy Hughes, who seems to have gone down in history not as a great war leader but as an opportunist who appealed to the baser instincts of the electorate and who survived by balancing economic interests.

Conclusions about Hughes, however, should not be taken as indicating a total absence of principles in the politics of the right. The right-wing populist temper of the 1890s, it will be remembered, was concerned with articulating considerations of virtue, and some of that thinking survived into the post-war era. By that time, however, the strategy adopted by rural organisations had moved a long way from the populist temper which had manifested itself in farmers' parties in some other countries. The various organisations and parties which came together as the Country Party had long since discarded any notions of a single act of redemption, preferring an electoral alliance with anti-Labor forces. Yet the early founders of the Country Party had maintained the old populist concern for the purity of the rural dweller and refused to assimilate with the Nationalists. After all, the Nationalists were tainted with the disease of 'politics' (in its new conceptualisation), and the leadership of the Country Party was to be very influential in disposing of the Nationalists' arch 'politician', Billy Hughes. Here surely one sees the continuance of the old right-wing populist view that politics was an urban product which had to be transcended. Such was the thinking of the 'true-blues' and other ex-servicemen who rallied to what seemed to be the least 'political' of parties.

Another feature of the old right-wing populist view which survived in the early Country Party was the theoretical rejection of utilitarian prescriptions for a regulator state. Such a state, it will be remembered, was to operate for the greatest good of the greatest number. This inevitably meant urban bias. What was preferred was a state which operated in the interests of what was felt to be the most basic and most productive sector of society. It was obvious, however, in the climate of post-war construction, that the Country Party ideals could not be realised in the foreseeable future. The most that could be hoped for was a deal with the Nationalists whereby concessions were granted to rural interests in return for qualified support for a protectionist policy which transferred income from primary producers to manufacturers and from country to city. The price was the maintainence of a share in state power out of all proportion to the Country Party's electoral strength. By entering into such a deal, the Country Party was, of course, entering the murky area of politics which it professed to despise. And when one basic compromise was reached, so might others. Thus the Country Party, which resisted control by the regulator state, came to support an arbitration system because it institutionalised and, therefore, mitigated class struggle, even though it initially promised a rise in labour costs at the expense of rural employers.

A major reason why right-wing populism was transformed into an interest group orientation was that rural populist organisations based on agriculture were being transformed into alliances of farmers and graziers. The pastoral interests always had a very strong British component which did not fit in with what is normally considered to be a major element of the old populist appeal. The hegemonic domination of the large grazier, over first the large farmer and then the small cocky, produced an orientation which was populist in its hostility to a state under the control of the wrong interests but anti-populist in its desire to see the continued influence of overseas interests in the running of that state. This characteristic of the Country Party, established at its formation, has remained important to this day.

In the 1920s and 1930s the British economic connection was of crucial importance in any understanding of the contradictory mix of political ideologies which characterised that period. On the left, as noted earlier, hostility to socialism and the British connection was to produce the Lang variety of left-wing populism. On the right, hostility to what was felt to be socialism, a distrust of liberal views of the regulator state and an affirmation of the British connection all helped to produce the orientation of the Country Party. As for the Nationalists, the role of the British connection was to produce a utilitarianism in form but not in content.

One of the major motivations, it seems, behind the support of the Country Party leader Page for Bruce as Prime Minister was that Bruce professed to despise 'politicians' and was more interested in replacing the capricious 'politics' of Billy Hughes by sound administration.[5] The price exacted from the Country Party for a 'non-political' Prime Minister was a concession to an ideology of developmentalism which drew on utilitarian principles. In practice, however, the ideology of developmentalism was always modified by the influence of foreign interests. Thus, though manufacturing made great strides during the boom of the 1920s, manufacturing industry was always relatively starved of capital with a disproportionate share of investment going into primary industries which provided raw materials for British industry. The result was far from the greatest good of the greatest number. At the same time the boom was financed by heavy borrowing from British sources which initially hid the harmful effects of the British connection. It was only when foreign capital dried up that the problem was fully revealed.

Though the basic principle of the utilitarian view was not being achieved, arguments deriving from utilitarianism were clearly pressed into the service of policy towards labour. The utilitarian calculus held that the greatest good of the greatest number would be achieved at the point where capital and labour were fully employed. Manifestly, however, the high rate of unemployment which existed in the 1920s, long before the Great Depression, revealed that such was not the case. The regulator state, therefore, should take action to reduce wages to overcome what modern economists would call the 'real wage overhang'.[6] This was in accordance with utilitarian theory which held that notions such as 'the just wage', or 'social justice' in general, were what Bentham called 'fictions'. One knew, moreover, that a reduction in wages would achieve the greatest good for the greatest number because Say's Law maintained that less-restricted market forces would allow the price mechanism to ensure that capital and labour were optimally employed. There was a need, therefore, to move more in the direction of *laissez-faire* capitalism. But this was not the *laissez-faire* of the pre-utilitarian classical liberals, which sought to restrict the power of the central government. In fact, more power had to be given to the Commonwealth Government over industrial matters so that the sources of inflation outside the scope of the present Commonwealth powers could be controlled. Utilitarian theory, it seemed, required one regulator state and could not cope with seven. The Commonwealth Government never won the powers it sought. Instead the defeat of the referendum on industrial powers in 1926 was followed by the adoption of *ad hoc* measures, supported by some powerful voices (such as the economist Shann)[7] who went beyond the utilitarian view back to good old liberal *laissez faire*:

> So far from being a barbarous rule, as Mr. Justice Higgins once called it, the higgling of the market is a sanction of economic wisdom more prompt, delicate and potent in its operation than any rewards or penalties that are within the slow reach of an over-burdened judge or commission.[8]

Such was the climate inherited by the Scullin Labor Government, which had to deal with the full fury of a world-wide depression without any theory of its own as to the causes or the remedies. By that time there were Keynesian and underconsumptionist economists available to give advice. Indeed, R.F. Irvine's eloquent attacks on Say's Law preceded the more famous work by J.M. Keynes; but people such as Irvine had only a temporary influence on a temporary Treasurer (Theodore)[9]. In general, both Federal and State Governments looked to Britain and the disaffected looked to Lang.

Hancock's Australia: nostalgia for social liberalism

Keynesianism was to develop into a kind of social liberalism. But it was not until the Second World War that this became apparent. In the 1930s, the little that was known of Keynes in Australia was his economic analysis, and that knowledge was confined to a few. More influential by far in the Australia of the 1930s was the revived and modified version of social liberalism which was exemplified in Hancock's classic work, *Australia*.[10] Reflecting the organicism of the late nineteenth century social liberals, Hancock's Australia is an individual writ large. In the 1890s, when the bush myth was established, that individual was still in its adolescence, and the fact that the myth was still powerful in 1930 reflected that maturity had still to be arrived at. Maturity, as Hancock saw it, would come when the original ideals of the common good, proclaimed during the heyday of the social liberals, started to be realised. But Hancock was not so optimistic as the followers of social liberals such as T.H. Green had been three decades before. A man who had considered the Italian progression from Mazzini to Mussolini[11] could not but comment that the release of civilising potential, caused by the break with the old world tyrannies, might become corrupted by a new democratic ethos. Such a view was perhaps nearer to that of J.S. Mill's comments about the 'most numerous classes'[12] than the idealism of T.H. Green. It drew explicitly on the fears of Alexis de Tocqueville's discussion of *Democracy in America*.[13] This ethos already took the form of a suspicion of merit and the desire to cut down the tall poppies. There was always the danger of mediocrity and the dullness of the utilitarian state seen as 'a vast public utility, the duty of which is to provide the greatest happiness for the greatest number'.[14] Though Hancock's perspective on that state was Greenian—the state should provide the opportunity for the realisation of the common good by the participation of its citizens in politics in the old laudable sense of the word—he nonetheless observed that the historical role of the state in Australia was such that its citizens set too great a store on the capacity of political activity:

> Australian idealism has put too many of its eggs into the political basket. When some of the eggs go bad their unpleasant odour penetrates into every corner of the national life and infects it with a faint disgust.[15]

Such a view is much less than the social liberal vision of previous decades. Hancock, moreover, despite all his criticism of the pervasive utilitarianism, accepted elements of utilitarianism in his appeal for better economic management:

> The end of the State is ethical—let us say 'the good life'; the end of the railways is economic—let us say 'efficient service at cost price'. The economic end of the railways is a means to the ethical end of the State. If this distinction is blurred, the railways become the prey of selfish interests snatching for advantages in the name of Justice; and the state perpetually vexed and tormented with problems of mere living is not free to take thought of the good life.[16]

If only one could make the distinction between politics and economics that simply! Hancock's views on law were also far from clear. He felt that the excessive legalism, resulting from the way the Constitution had been interpreted, could militate against the 'common good'.[17] Yet one is never quite sure how he would go about retrieving that old social liberal ideal. Perhaps most important of all was the contradiction between the observation that many of Australia's ills were the consequences of separation from Britain and the belief that the mature state, which could realise the Greenian ideal, could only be achieved by a truly independent people. In Rowse's view, Hancock's *Australia* was an endorsement of the subordination of Australian to British capital—the most salient feature of the contemporary economic crisis.[18] One could put it more modestly. The contradiction in Hancock's *Australia* between a desire for maturity and subordination to Britain was a social liberal version of the same contradiction between utilitarian developmentalism and British investment which was described earlier as a major characteristic of the Bruce-Page Government. The fall of that government, Rowse believes, reflected a distrust of utilitarianism and the continued salience of the Deakinite social liberal vision. The popularity of Hancock's *Australia* might be cited as evidence in support of that continued salience. But what Hancock offered was a pale version of the original social liberal vision.

The ideological rag-bag of the 1930s

The original flowering of social liberal thought in Australia had occurred in the optimistic days of the early Commonwealth. The climate in Australia which greeted Hancock's *Australia* could not have been more different. What hope for the social liberal vision was there in a country enduring the Great Depression? What hope was there in a 'working man's paradise' which found itself without machinery to relieve mass destitution and with an unemployment insurance scheme in only one State? The emergency measures to deal with that quarter of the work force which was unemployed were to deprive a significant section of the citizenry of the self-respect necessary for any participation in politics in its better sense. When most people thought of politics, it was in the pejorative sense. They thought of the faction fighting of the Scullin Government, the disintegration of the ALP following the defections which formed the Lyons Government and the charges launched against Theodore, the one leader who had listened to advice for dealing with the depression consistent with social liberalism. For the right, Lang Labor revealed all that was worst in politics whilst, for his supporters, Lang's populist appeal transcended politics. This was not the climate in which to realise the social liberal vision!

Recovery from the depression, it seemed, required a retreat from politics in favour of 'sound administration' (interpreted in terms of the Premiers' Plan and its later modifications which ensured a modest reduction of interest payments to British bondholders). As far as the Commonwealth Government was concerned difficult issues were shelved, as is exemplified by the fact that the 1931 Statute of Westminster specifying Australia's autonomy was not ratified in Australia for over a decade. As the 'mean decade' wore on, few new ideas penetrated federal politics, though a few panaceas were offered by new parties contesting federal elections. For example, the Douglas Credit Party promised to abolish poverty by state use and distribution of credit to equalise production and consumption. But developments like these were few and far between and it was at State level that most new political initiatives were felt. There, left-wing populism was now joined by a partial revival of right-wing populism which had some impact on the movement to create new states and in the Western Australian referendum which voted for secession. It was influential also in the Catholic Action organisation which opposed what Belloc termed the 'servile state', claiming it enslaved the individual and brought about the decline of the family, the destruction of the agricultural economy and rural life in general. For the adherents to Catholic

Action, virtue resided in the communion of the faithful and evil originated from oppressive (urban) capitalism and (urban) communism. The aim was to create a co-operative commonwealth based on the co-operative ownership of property. Neither capitalism nor communism allowed the worker to become an independent property owner—the only guarantee of democratic freedom.[19]

It was at State level also that one could see the inappropriateness of the classical *laissez faire* liberalism advocated by some leading economists. As the States recovered from the depression after 1933, significant moves were made to develop manufacturing industries, often initiated by the State and usually with a great deal of State aid. The idea of pockets of capitalism growing up under the aegis of the state has been referred to as 'marsupial capitalism'. It occurred in all the Eastern States but was most remarkable in South Australia which was transformed in a short space of time from a mainly farming to a manufacturing State. There, a cherry farming premier, who maintained his power by an electoral system which would have delighted the rural populists of the right, took the lead in promoting the most urban of industries, justifying them in terms of what had become a most unrural philosophy—utilitarianism. In Victoria the same thing occurred in even more bizarre circumstances. There the lead was taken by a Country Party government with Labor support. If ideologies were ever closely correlated with party labels, they were now clearly far apart. Even the Communist Party, having abandoned its criticism of 'social fascists' and embraced the united front in 1935, became an Australian party par excellence, claiming John Dunmore Lang, Parkes and Wentworth, as its progenitors.

The ideology of reconstruction

The retreat to considerations of 'sound administration' in the early days of recovery after the depression could not proceed in a political vacuum for long. Sound administration, after all, does not mean very much except in relation to social goals. In Australia the initial moves taken to deal with the depression had been *ad hoc* and piecemeal, whilst it was quite obvious that the countries which were recovering the most quickly from the effects of the depression were those which had developed a holist approach to social change. Pre-eminent here was Germany and, however much one might despise Hitler's holist approach, it appeared to be efficient. In various European countries at that time it was felt that the menace of Nazi holism could only be dealt with by articulating a new and different holism to revivify the demoralised European societies. In the period prior to the outbreak of war, there were constant demands for the reconstruction of capitalist economies and for countering 'totalitarian' planning by planning for democracy.

The high point of thinking about what became known as 'the Age of Reconstruction' was not to occur until the latter part of the Second World War when it found eloquent spokesmen in Karl Mannheim, Peter Drucker and William Beveridge. But the origins of the new mood in Britain could be found in the earlier writings of Harold Laski and, of course, J.M. Keynes. The influence of such thinkers on Australia was by no means inconsiderable and one of the functions of the Australian Institute of Political Science (founded 1932) was to provide a forum for their ideas.[20] The new ideology, received in Australia at that time, had essentially three components—these were (following Rowse) social liberalism, managerialism and psychologism.

The social liberalism of the late 1930s and early 1940s owed very much to the work of Laski; and W.G.K. Duncan, the first director of the AIPS, clearly saw that Laski was in the tradition of T.H. Green. The aim was still the ethical state in which individuals developed their potentialities (positive freedom); but what was essential in the new climate was for liberals to face up to the problem of power and particularly class power. Such a doctrine sounds quite socialist until one considers that the enemy was not so much the capitalist class but the rentier section of it. Rentiers were, after all, the arch enemies of Keynes and were seen to be standing in the way of the fiscal controls necessary to stimulate effective demand. Such a message had great poignancy for Australia after the loans crisis of the early 1930s. A tremendous amount of support had accrued to left-wing populists in their denunciation of finance capital in general and banking in particular. Now that populist appeal was augmented by social liberals who saw finance capitalists standing in the way of the common good. Bearing in mind the imperial nature of banking control in Australia, it was inevitable that the new hostility to finance capital would generate a new form of nationalism which would take liberal thought much further than the ideals of Hancock who still maintained allegiance to the imperial connection.

For Hancock the civilising potential of the Old World could offset the deleterious effects of anti-meritocratic democracy. In the new climate, it was felt that it was precisely because of the Old World connection that Australia still maintained a relation of psychological dependency upon 'the old country'. For the American C. Hartley Grattan, writing in 1942, Australia needed to develop a greater degree of independence by shifting away from a unilateral reliance on the United Kingdom. Australia should be open to influence and capital from a variety of sources of which the United States was very important.[21] He felt, however, that there was a danger of the recrudescence of economic nationalism after the Second World War.[22] In fact, what Grattan hoped for came to pass. One of the consequences of the war was the development of a less British-oriented foreign policy and the determination to create a more independent nation in which to realise the social liberal ideal of the common good. In Hancockian terms, this process was to see Australia's coming of age.

This chapter will argue that the above vision was illusory. The reconstructionist version of social liberalism was not to solve the ills of Australian society which late 1930s social liberals had diagnosed as provincialism, dullness, commercialism and anti-intellectualism; and the United States connection was not to be wholly beneficial. In the war years and the immediate aftermath, however, the social liberal vision did seem to offer a blueprint for the future. The war did provide that *sine qua non* of the social liberal project—a common objective and a sense of unity in which the legitimate search for profits could be distinguished from illegitimate profiteering. As the social liberals saw it, the new society could be ushered in, if only the wartime spirit could be carried over into peacetime and if the international peace could promise industrial peace.

The war not only provided a sense of purpose but also provided the mechanisms necessary to pursue the second element in the ideology of reconstruction—managerialism. The perceived need for the resolute imposition of controls to fight the war was to discredit the United Australia Party, which was seen as a sectional party representing urban businessmen. The Labor Government, which took office at the height of the international crisis, rapidly used its emergency powers to establish planning bodies headed by Keynesians and other managerialists. It brought about unified income tax collection and established the framework for the managerial state. The state was to establish the boundaries in which business operated and would intervene in economic life in the interests of what its leaders considered to be the common good. For a time it seemed that they were supported by all groups in society, receiving even the support of the Communist Party rapidly recovering from its short period of ineffectual 'illegality'.

Yet there were two sides to managerialism and these were perceived most clearly by its arch exponent Karl Mannheim. Paraphrasing Rousseau, Mannheim asked 'who plans the planners?' An obvious left-wing critique was that what was being created was a 'corporate state'. Though Hancock did not have that in mind when he spoke of the 'trajectory of decay' from Mazzini to Mussolini, one might well ponder on his words in the new situation. Indeed, only two years before Karl Mannheim wrote his classic work on managerialism, the ex-Trotskyist James Burnham had taken the intellectual world by storm by declaring that, though Marx was right in seeing capitalism in the process of self-destruction, he was wrong in his belief that the proletariat would come to power. Proletarian power was not growing in the womb of capitalist society. Instead there had appeared a new managerial class, the advent of which would usher in a period of despotism similar to that which characterised the transition from feudalism to capitalism. For Burnham, Soviet Marxism, Nazi ideology and Roosevelt's New Deal were all manifestations of such a development.[23] Could one blame people for feeling that the reconstructionist ideology was achieving the same sort of thing in Australia?

An obvious right-wing diagnosis was that mechanisms were being created for the achievement of what was seen as a bureaucratic 'state socialist' system. Such a belief informed the organisers of a new Liberal Party in 1944 under the leadership of Robert Menzies. Back in 1935, Menzies had campaigned for his first federal seat with the words:

> The nationalisation of banking would mean the first big step in the nationalisation of the whole financial and economic structure. Lenin had stated that it was the first step towards communism. Nationalisation appeared to be the one thing aimed at by both Federal and Lang Labor parties.[24]

The difference between the reconstructionist Labor Government of 1941–49 and the old Lang Labor Party reflected the difference between a social liberal vision and a left-wing populist one. Nevertheless, both left-wing populists and social liberals were united in their detestation of finance capital—the one because it was a parasitical expression of the interests of 'the classes' as opposed to the 'people', the other because it was that and much more. For the social liberals it stood in the way of the managerialist road to the common good. For a time, both left-wing populists and social liberals could be united in their pursuit of greater control over banking and eventually nationalisation. Yet one can understand how an opponent of both left-wing populism and social liberalism would not understand the distinction between them. Chifley's desire to nationalise the banks was in the interests of developing a capitalism consistent with social liberal beliefs. Menzies, however, saw this partly as a return to the dangerous populism of Lang and also as the first step in the development of state socialism or communism. He could not see that a distinction could be made between finance and other capital.

Opposition from the right was to lead in 1944 to the defeat of the Powers Referendum which the Labor Government felt was necessary to achieve the new social liberal and managerialist vision; though perhaps the government itself contributed to its defeat by asking for too much at one go. It led later to the defeat of Chifley's attempt to nationalise the banks. The Labor Government, thereby, was deprived of key mechanisms necessary to achieve its social liberal goals. Under such circumstances the various components of the social liberal ideology began to change. Keynesianism started out as a support for left-wing social liberals. By the end of the Labor Government, it had been turned into a vehicle of the right (called by neo-Keynesians 'bastard Keynesianism'). From a stress on augmenting the income of a fully-employed work force, it concentrated more and more on ways to augment gross national product.[25] By the early 1950s, interest rate manipulation was geared simply to increasing production and not necessarily to higher mass consumption.

The transformation of Keynesianism was not to be fully evident until after the accession to power of the long Liberal Government (1949–72). Yet even during the Chifley Government it was clear that the social liberal vision was receding. Indirect taxes were high and weighed heavily on the poor (they were in fact higher than during the 1960s). The proportion of GNP controlled by the state was only marginally higher in 1949 than in 1941 (15% compared with almost 13%).[26] The Labor Government had failed to get control over the economic levers necessary for exercising decisive control, and yet still retained controls which lost it electoral appeal (petrol rationing for example). By 1949, moreover, industrial relations had deteriorated alarmingly and resulted in the use of troops by a Labor Government to break a strike. Where indeed was the common purpose and consensus at the core of the social liberal vision?

The deteriorating industrial relations during the Chifley Government were due primarily to basic economic causes. They revealed, however, a fundamental miscalculation on the part of the social liberals of that time. This leads to the third element of the reconstructionist ideology—its psychologism.[27] The flowering of social liberalism in the early twentieth century saw the development of a rationalist sociology which was to provide an understanding of the way to approach the common good. At the core of that sociology were rational individuals perceiving and developing their latent capacities. As in utilitarianism, individuals pursued their own self-interest though, unlike in utilitarianism, they did so in the knowledge of their part in an organic whole. That knowledge helped people to realise that which was distinctly human (positive liberty), yet recognised constraints imposed by consideration of the liberties of others (negative liberty). By the late 1930s, such a rationalistic view was in decline. It had to be when whole nations seemed to be caught up in all the elemental irrationalities of a 'people's community'— Nazi style—and its equivalents. One did not explain Hitler's Germany according to a rational calculus but by psychology—the study of what was often quite irrational.

The irrational was, of course, the starting point of Sigmund Freud, though Freudian thought was probably not very significant in the Age of Reconstruction. More important by far was that kind of behavioural psychology which served the ends of the social liberal and managerial vision. In serving the interests of propaganda (defined by some in those days in a positive sense) this psychology informed the thinking of those who, in Australia, wished to formulate a social contract with the workers; such was not the social contract of the old classical liberals but one which made use of what was known about work satisfaction. This approach pressed into service the work of the distinguished South Australian, Elton Mayo, who in the United States had done so much to inspire the 'human relations' school of management. Indeed, a major criticism of ideas of industrial democracy at that time was that it was no more than a means of psychological control. For its proponents, however, it was a way of reaching the social liberal common good.

Perhaps the most important thing to remember about the 'common good' was that it was *common*. There should be no separate development or racial segregation. Thus, in the early 1940s, policies towards the Aborigines changed to those of assimilation to the dominant culture, and the 'New Australians' who came in ever increasing numbers after the war were expected to share in the common consensus. Such an expectation demanded that controls be imposed on the raw material out of which the common good should be forged. The White Australia Policy, which developed out of earlier populist sentiments, was revived and pressed into the service of social liberalism: racism remained as prevalent as ever.

In the early days of the Commonwealth, racism and social liberalism co-existed as strange bedfellows. In the post-war years the hatred of Japanese could still provide a rather curious kind of ideological cement necessary for the social liberal consensus. Such hatred was irrational, since at that time Japan no longer posed any threat. One wonders, however, about the extent to which it was based on wartime memories. Significantly, German migrants were welcomed more than Southern Europeans and, despite their sufferings, Jews were despised more than ever (a fact which is not adequately explained by the activities of the Stern Gang).[28] Unfortunately, despite its promise, psychology can tell one little about the social manifestation of racism in those years. Nor can one be happy with explanations which centre on a dominant class which wished to keep the workers divided. One might guess that, once again, the failure to find real consensus in the social liberal vision was compensated for by an *ersatz* consensus based on the old populist notions of purity. Significantly, in this regard, the Communists after 1949 could be portrayed as agents of the Chinese.

The 'end of ideology' and the market model

By 1949, it was clear that not very much was left of the optimism or social liberal consensus which had developed in the war years. A series of strikes had demonstrated that new psychological methods of management were either ineffective or had simply not been tried. In any case, forces were at work which were to destroy any notion of consensus. Despite the fact that the Communist Party's strength declined rapidly after 1945, it was portrayed as more subversive than ever, especially in 1948 after it moved in line with the Cominform to a more militant position. It was opposed most vigorously by the Catholic Social Studies Movement which, continuing the tradition started by Catholic Action, sought the total transformation of Australian society according to Catholic right-wing populist principles.[29] Those principles were to result in the establishment of one or two bush communities at that time, but the real appeal of the Movement was simply its anti-communism. It supported and supplemented the 'industrial groups' which sought to remove Communists from leading position in the trade unions. Such developments were eventually to result in the ALP split in the mid-1950s. The Democratic Labor Party, which emerged from that split, enjoyed considerable Catholic support but never became anything like a European Catholic party. Kept alive simply by anti-communism and a wowserist notion of virtue, the DLP never developed a distinctive ideology. But, by the 1950s, explicit ideologies were out of fashion (including the social liberalism of H.V. Evatt). The 'end of ideology' was at hand.

It is now commonplace that 'the end of ideology' thesis, promoted in Australia by the Menzies Government in the 'Long Boom', was one of the most effective ideologies ever devised. According to that thesis, ideology was no longer defined as a set of beliefs in which the citizen finds identity as a political actor but as a pattern of behaviour appropriate to an immature or unstable society. Communism, therefore, was seen as an ideology whilst Australian liberalism was not. To achieve this switch, liberalism had to be recast as a set of norms which sustained the political status quo. Thus, classical liberalism, utilitarian liberalism and social liberalism could continually be ransacked for appropriate statements of principle to justify current policies.[30] The early Menzies Government, for example, borrowed ideas about *laissez faire* from classical liberalism at the same time as it used contradictory ideas deriving from social liberalism ('national development') to preserve much of the structure of managerial control built up over previous years. Eclectic borrowing was the order of the day and woe betide any Liberal Prime Minister, such as Gorton, who attempted to take liberal philosophy seriously.[31]

Lest the contradictions between different types of liberalism result in social cleavage, it was necessary for the role of citizen to be redefined. The social liberal believed that a citizen was someone who engaged in politics to develop his or her potentiality to participate in the common good. Some political scientists at the time saw such a view as a recipe for instability, and thus the role of citizen was redefined not as the producer but the consumer of politics. The classic statement in this regard had been made in 1943 by Joseph Schumpeter. For Schumpeter, democracy was 'that institutional arrangement for arriving at political decisions in which individuals acquire the power to decide by means of a competitive struggle for the people's vote'.[32] Schumpeter offered a market model in which elites (which may be self-selected) offer a commodity to be consumed by people who employ the vote as a form of currency. Chapter 3 will return to Schumpeter's elitism. All one need note here is that, for followers of Schumpeter, liberalism was merely a set of norms which sustained that democratic model consistent with basic human rights. The best safeguard of those rights was the availability of alternative commodities.

The above thinking was far from social liberalism. It was based upon the notion of a free market which operated neither in the economy nor in politics (in both fields monopolistic and oligopolistic tendencies were pervasive). It operated with a static view of human nature (the political consumer) which had nothing to say about developing human potentialities. There was no room in the model for participatory notions of democracy since the focus was on the national level whereas most people developed their capacities at the non-national level and in institutions which were now defined as 'non-political'. It ignored, moreover, the contradiction between what appeared to be a democratic political system and the authoritarian structures of everyday life.[33]

Despite criticisms, the above model was the view of liberal democracy which informed Australian politics for a generation.

Indeed, Australian politics became quite notorious as consisting of a sequence of elections in which political parties crudely displayed shopping lists of commodities in return for the popular 'mandate'. As salespeople the Liberal Country Party Coalition proved to be much more astute than its opponents and, when in 1961 the Coalition almost faced defeat, the Menzies Government had no compunction about adopting its opponents' policies as a much more attractive package. The marketing of politics, moreover, was even cruder than the marketing of commodities in the real economy; there, at least, norms about fair trading applied. In politics, a large amount of energy was expended on demonstrating that the opposition's products would poison the consumer (for example a vote for Labor would reduce Australians to Chinese 'coolies').

The acceptance by Australian citizens of their role as consumers depended upon the achievement of self-definition outside conflict situations (that is outside politics). To be respectable was to be 'middle class'. This did not refer to what is normally meant by social theorists as class (Marx's relation to the means of production or Weber's groups of those in receipt of similar life-chances). It referred to a set of attitudes which distanced its adherent from conflict-oriented working class values or the conflict-oriented values of business competition.[34] Such attitudes were not antagonistic to either trade unions or business—instead they were simply uninterested. To be respectable, moreover, was to subscribe to suburban values to the point where one could sympathise with Edna Everidge and yet still laugh at her absurdity. Participation in the Establishment (not the dominant class) was fraught with perils for the common respectable person.

If the common man wished to participate in social life there were a myriad of groups which could be joined. Typically, citizens shared their loyalties amongst several groups. Such a situation prevented any overriding allegiance to any particular group and any unbalanced concentration of power in any part of society. As for the most important groups in society (no longer seen as classes or fractions of classes) they would tend to reach a state of 'equilibriated pluralism'. The common good, therefore, was achieved essentially outside the political life of the state.

But how was one to ensure that the state was acting in the interests of the community between elections? Such, it seemed, was a question as illegitimate as asking how one knew whether a football umpire made correct decisions or that a judge was just. A professional public service could be expected to operate on utilitarian principles and an independent judiciary to preserve the traditional social contract. But, of course, people were never that naive. It was manifestly obvious that equilibrium between groups was not being achieved (whether one believed that the villain was the unions or big business). The arbitration system continually changed its terms of reference and did not seem neutral. The neutrality of the bureaucracy, moreover, could not be assumed. But so long as the 'Long Boom' increased income and opportunities for education and welfare, the poor remained hidden and an idealised view of the Americanised future flooded the media, the dissident voices would not be heard by the majority.

Dissident voices

Yet the dissident voices, both on the right and the left, became progressively louder. Some complained that the government had initiated a general retreat from policy. It neither advocated *laissez faire* nor intervened rationally in the economy; government intervention was *ad hoc* and incoherent.[35] Others, whilst celebrating suburbia, poured scorn on a hidebound Establishment which seemed out of touch with the lives of most Australians.[36] Still others followed Marcuse in seeing 'the end of ideology' as justifying a new and comfortable form of 'totalitarianism'.[37] By the 1960s, the importation of American developmental values, culture and capital was paralleled by the importation of American forms of radical protest.[38] But these thrived only because of very significant domestic concern about the extent of dependency on the United States, the degree to which such dependency made Australia vulnerable to nuclear attack, the fact that the infrastructure necessary to attract transnational firms was provided by the taxpayer and the government's failure to levy royalties on mineral development. To what extent was Australia becoming the foreigners' quarry? The final, and most important, concern was Australia's participation in the disastrous war in Vietnam—electorally popular at first, but then seen increasingly to affect not just national prestige but also suburban families.

Despite the dissidence an effective socialist challenge to the Liberal Government failed to appear. The chastened Communist Party devoted its energy to a specifically Australian road to socialism, identifying itself again with a tradition which extended from the Eureka Stockade through to the legend of the 1890s and which was couched in the old populist terms of 'the people' versus 'the classes'.[39] When the split occurred in the International Communist Movement in 1963, the nationalist appeal would seem to have put the CPA on the side of the Chinese. In practice, however, it decided the Chinese Communist Party was too intransigent[40] and remained in uneasy harness with the Russians until the Czechoslovak crisis destroyed any illusions about the Soviet Union. The pro-Chinese Communist Party of Australia (Marxist-Leninist), which resulted from the 1963 split, was eventually to become even more nationalist than the old party, appealing to all the old left-wing populist norms (except the racist) though maintaining a tiny Leninist core. In the early 1970s, one suspects that it could not decide who was the more important, Mao Zedong or Ned Kelly. The CPA (ML) strategy was to unite the 'people' in opposition to imperialism. This necessitated differentiating between national capitalists and comprador capitalists—a singularly difficult task and one which could not be expected to win support. At the same time it warned against Soviet 'social imperialist' subversion of Australia—incredible now but even more absurd in the late 1960s and early 1970s.

After Czechoslovakia, pro-Soviet elements in the Communist Party left to form the Socialist Party of Australia which remained small though influential in a few unions. What remained of the CPA, now free of what it felt to be intransigents, was left to work out a strategy, which for all its appeal to the working class and the works of Marx, was probably more social liberal in effect than some groups in the ALP. The themes of moral progress and self-development by worker involvement in management would have gone down well with the old social liberals. Indeed, one gets the same impression also concerning many Trotskyist groups. But perhaps that was the only alternative!

The return to social liberalism

The self image of the CPA, in the 1970s, was set largely by its view of the ALP—dominated by 'trendies' and opportunists out of touch with the working class. Outside party circles, on the left, attempts were made to categorise the ideology of the ALP—the most famous consisting of arguments about 'technocratic labourism'.[41] This view held that the ideology which informed the Dunstan Government of South Australia and the Federal Labor Government of 1972–75 was one which attempted to make capitalism more efficient by methods of planning derived from the OECD and practised by the Social Democratic Government of Sweden. Indeed, for a time, people referred to South Australia as 'the Sweden of the Southern Hemisphere'. The aim, it was said, was to produce a collaborationist labour force and to integrate the trade union movement more effectively into a modern mixed economy. According to some versions of the diagnosis, technocratic labourism implied an abandonment of more socialist ideals which had informed the ALP in the past. It was pointed out, however, that the policies of the 1970s could not have involved the abandonment of socialist ideals, since such ideals had never informed the majority of the ALP.[42] The technocratic labourist diagnosis, moreover, might tell us something about the functions of the Labor Party, but was only one aspect of its total ideology (its self image and its image of the world). In fact this aspect was very old and was no more than the managerialist stand which had existed throughout the party's history. That stand always co-existed with a social liberal view and the 1970s were no exception.

In the case of the Dunstan Government, more clearly than in the short-lived Federal Labor Government, the major elements of the social liberal thesis emerged. The Dunstan vision of 1970 was quite clear:

> Labor comes to these elections with the most comprehensive plans for change and growth any state has seen since federation...new ideas in development, new approaches in education, new planning for the environment, new freedom for the individual, and new real, strong, economic and legal protection for everyone...With Labor, South Australia will become the technological, the design, the social reform and the artistic centre of Australia. It will be the state with the most highly developed and diversified economy...a standard of social advancement, that the whole of Australia would envy.[43]

For half a decade, at least, the above vision held. Social liberal ideas about the self-developing individual remained at the centre of a whole series of social reforms which came even to embrace policies on industrial democracy. That those reforms were seen as helping to promote a more streamlined capitalist mixed economy there can be no doubt; but, then, they never pretended to be anything else. Significantly many of them were subsequently adopted by some of the less hidebound Liberal governments in other States (Victoria for example) which saw no inconsistency between them and the traditional Liberal Party doctrine. The social liberal vision had, after all, once been influential in both of the major parties.

The recession of the 1970s

As long as a managerialist notion of efficiency could be combined with the social liberal view of the developing individual, the policies of Labor governments enjoyed a wide spectrum of support. It was when the Federal Labor Government began to falter, and incoherently to flirt with a type of Keynesian economics in a situation which Keynes had never envisaged, that its opponents branded it as 'socialist'. Ironically this reached its height after that government had stifled socialists within its own ranks and had even silenced economic nationalists like Rex Connor. As in the Great Depression of the 1930s, the 1970s recession was inimical to social liberal thought. It was just too expensive, it seemed, to provide the conditions for the self-developing individual; and such attempts could be lumped together as 'socialist', meaning no more than simply big government.

If the depression of the 1930s is any guide, two sorts of ideological responses should have grown out of the slump of the 1970s. First one would have expected the restatement of classical *laissez faire* ideologies and for these to have been embraced by the Liberal Party in power. This indeed came to pass and was supplemented by the strident tones of the American 'New Right'. The claim of Ayn Rand that 'capitalism is the only system geared to the life of a rational being and the only moral politico-economic system in history'[44] was greeted enthusiastically in some Liberal Party circles. Secondly, because of the traditionally crucial role of the state in promoting economic development, one would have expected those ideologies to have only a small effect on Liberal Party policies. This again seems to have been the case; and it must be borne in mind that the Fraser Government was, at that time, the highest spending and highest taxing government in Australia's history. The effect of traditional liberal ideology and the new moralising was not to damage the idea of the utilitarian regulator role of the state; but was to ensure that the direction of state spending was away from welfare and other concerns of the social liberals. The Liberal Government was still 'statist' in Ayn Rand's terms.

A second expectation, based on the experience of the 1930s, would be for a loss of confidence in the Labor Party as to the effectiveness of the social liberal vision and in those who promoted it. There was some evidence of this amongst trade unions dissatisfied with 'middle class' labour leaders who came to define 'progressive' in terms of moral issues rather than in terms of more egalitarian economic policies. Indeed, one characteristic of Australian Labor has been the latent hostility between a non-union leadership which considers the trade unions to be reactionary (because they do not share the moralism of the social liberals now interpreted as a form of moral libertarianism) and unionists who still cling to the populist view of the state as something to be conquered and pressed into their own service. And yet, unlike the 1930s, unions were not mobilised behind a left-wing populist banner. Perhaps this was because the recession was not sufficiently acute, or because the blue-collar sector was relatively much smaller. Or perhaps it was the case that populist ideology in Australia was now seen as being the preserve of the right.

The revival of right-populism

This chapter has argued that right-wing populism has been present in Australian politics since the nineteenth century. The institutional forms created by such populism tended to be assimilated into a dominant political structure legitimised by utilitarian values. Such was the fate of right-wing populist groups which dissolved into the Country Party or of Catholic Action which was assimilated into the Democratic Labor Party. Yet such assimilation appears to have been only partially effective. One can not foresee any recrudescence of Catholic populism in the near future, but one can not fail to observe the continued manifestations of populism in what is now the National Party in Queensland.[45] There the regulator state has been accused of acting against the interests of the most productive sectors of society (the primary sector), and social liberalism is once again equated with socialism. At first sight, the ideology of the Queensland National Party seems like a form of classical liberalism. There is an affirmation of small government. There is a call for equal rights for unequal people (an effective device to counter Aboriginal land rights which have been described as violating equality of rights for all Queenslanders). Great stress also is laid on the regulating role of the market. Yet surely this is a form of populism rather than classical liberalism. Virtue is seen as residing in one section of society (the primary producer). There is a conspiratorial view of politics which sees the Commonwealth in the hands of cunning parasites, and that view has given rise to a local nationalism. The state, therefore, is not a device to preserve the common good but an instrument to be seized by the virtuous. There is, moreover, the old mixture of moralism and racism which makes talk of equal rights somewhat hollow. What is absent, however, from the original right-wing populist vision is the old economic nationalism and the demand for autarchy. On the contrary, the National Party in Queensland has done more than any other party to secure the participation of transnational capital in Australian development. This is legitimised by particularising the threat to virtue. The enemy is in Canberra not in New York or London, so big business and the Queen can be pressed into the service of populism.

Queensland populism is very different in one crucial respect from the old left-wing populism of Jack Lang. The contradictions of Langite populism were somehow crystallised in the personality of

Jack Lang. The odd mixture of the noble and the grotesque appealed to a frightened electorate with contradictory aspirations and emotional responses to the depression. Queensland populism, on the other hand, has flowered in a State which is one of the least depressed in Australia. What is appealed to is not a frightened and self-doubting electorate but one that feels great pride in its State's achievements and feels protective of its native sons and daughters. This pride is, of course, based on some real achievements but has also been very carefully fostered by some of the most skilful public relations experts in Australia.[46] Perhaps the most able of those experts, has also been responsible for creating the image of Sir Joh Bjelke-Petersen. And so a rather pedestrian peanut farmer has been remodelled as the new populist hero; the noble and the grotesque are largely the products of the image-maker and are modelled on a shrewd analysis of mass psyche. Indeed, the image is so effective that it thrives upon those Labor campaigners who come to Queensland to criticise it.

European and Australian experience of the 1920s and 1930s would seem to suggest that socialist influence is best countered by a populist appeal. Could the converse be true? Alas the recent Australian evidence does not suggest any conclusion. In the heyday of left-wing populism in New South Wales, the orthodox ALP was demoralised, ineffective and not a little corrupt. The Queensland Labor Party has recently shown itself to be in a similar situation. A new leadership is trying to rescue it; but if that leadership tries to propel it along social liberal lines, one can only foresee success if the economy continues to improve. Social liberalism does not thrive in a general recession, and even less in a State economy which contains pockets which are positively thriving and whose beneficiaries are unwilling to share their good fortune.

Conclusion

This chapter has argued that the three most significant strands in Australia political ideology have been utilitarianism, social liberalism and populism (of the left and right). The crucial role of the state in the economy has always made classical liberal ideas fairly ineffective, though they do achieve prominance at times of depression and clearly have some effect on state budgeting. Burkean and other forms of conservatism became of little importance after the early nineteenth century. A few Burkean arguments crop up from time to time, but the few consistently Burkean politicians (such as Jim Killen) always seemed slightly ridiculous. Socialism also has been relatively uninfluential in Australia. This may have been because the working class was suburbanised at a very early stage (before manufacturing capital became dominant) or because upward mobility for the working class was quite visible whilst downward mobility remained hidden. A further set of explanations centre on the leadership of the labour movement and the continued split between dull machine people and morally progressive intellectuals. The former are usually rather inert and only become militant when depressed economic conditions give rise to left-wing populism. The latter, it seems, only come into their own when the economy is experiencing a boom—that is when conditions are ripe for social liberalism.

In the recent economic recession it became fashionable once again for scholars to relate cycles of boom and depression to the fortunes of political parties. Such is seen in the recent work of Catley and MacFarlane who, following Kalecki, lay down the economic conditions under which a Labor government might be expected to win office.[47] When one considers politics at both the Commonwealth and State levels one can not altogether be convinced that the correlation between Labor fortunes and boom or depression conditions is all that neat. The analysis presented by Catley and MacFarlane has, however, suggested a correlation between ideological salience and various points of the business cycle—at least with regard to the three main ideological strands in Australian political life. Utilitarian liberalism has for long provided the ideological norm in which Australian politics operates. That norm, however, has been severely modified by social liberalism under two conditions. First social liberalism becomes salient during the optimism at the onset of a boom. This was the case after the depression of the 1890s, and during the Age of Reconstruction. Secondly, there tends to be a revival of social liberalism at the end of a boom when people are tired of the uninspiring banalities of utilitarianism. Such was the environment of the late 1920s which found echoes in Hancock's *Australia*, during the first part of 'the Dunstan Decade' and the period of the Whitlam Government. Though most social liberal thinking may be found in the ALP, that party has by no means a monopoly of social liberal thought. Henry Mayer demonstrated that conclusion long ago when he qualified the idea of the ALP as 'the party of initiative'.[48]

Finally one comes to the case of populism. Both in its right and left-wing forms this seems to occur as a response to depression or recession. Such was the case in the 1890s and 1930s. Which form it takes depends on whether its origin is amongst workers (rural or urban) or farmers and miners. The right-wing variety, moreover, may emerge under slightly different circumstances—as the response to pockets of development in an otherwise depressed economy. Such seems to have been the case in Queensland in recent years. The result could be secession (in Callaghan's words 'nothing secedes like success')[49] though one doubts it. The preceding analysis would suggest that if the recession recurs, the Hawke Government could pursue a populist path. The 1983 election did suggest something of a 'Hawke is greater than Lenin' flavour. Yet the politics of reconciliation have all the hallmarks of social liberalism. Which will win out in the short run depends on the world economy. If there are no goods to deliver one might expect the manufacture of symbolic goods of a populist nature. Modest economic improvement, of which there are signs in 1984, could see a sustained revival of social liberalism which certainly would be more in line with the predilections of the present leaders of the ALP. As for the long-term one hesitates to predict. Who knows, one might see a polarisation between a right-wing populist Northern Australia and a left-wing populist and depressed Southern Australia; or, more cataclysmically, one might see the collapse of the suburban dream along with the economic system which sustains it. It might even result in *socialisme avec doctrines*. But if one looks at the present Labor Government, that seems a very distinct prospect.

PART TWO
POWER

THREE
INEQUALITY AND POWER[1]

Inequality

AUSTRALIA HAS OFTEN been portrayed as a society with a high degree of equality. This seems to be supported when one looks at its relatively low *Gini* co-efficient of income inequality, calculated by Broom and Jones in the early 1970s at 0.34.[2] But one has to look further than income. When one considers wealth, a different picture emerges. Shareholding is fairly concentrated. Various studies of the 1950s, 1960s and 1970s show that some 5% of shareholders in the largest companies control over 55% of all shares.[3] Wealth in general is highly concentrated, though estimates of this concentration vary. Broom and Jones, in the early 1970s, estimated that the top 0.5% of the population controlled some 10% of the country's wealth and Groenewegen estimated, in the mid-1960s, that the top 11% owned some 40% with the bottom 15% owning less than 5%. Figures provided by Raskall, from the early 1970s, are even more startling: the top 1% of the adult population owned 22% of personal wealth, the top 5% owned 46% and the top 10% owned almost 60%; half of all Australians owned less than 8% of the total and the top 5% owned more than the bottom 90% put together. Raskall shows a *Gini* co-efficient of concentration of 0.702 which provides a picture very different from that of income.[4] There is also substantial agreement that the distribution of wealth has not changed very much since 1945. Indeed, Podder and Kakwani show that if one looks at the distribution of wealth since *1915*, the situation is only dramatically different with regard to the top 1%. In 1915 the top 1% owned 30% compared with 22% in 1970; but the remaining 19% of the top quintile has retained about 50%.[5]

Society is much better off than it was in 1915, but the relative resources which may be called upon by the rich have not altered very much. Moreover, the abolition of death duties and the absence of wealth taxes or capital gains legislation makes Australia somewhat anachronistic by international comparison. Australia also differs from comparable capitalist countries in the concentration of ownership amongst boards of directors. McMichael's study, based on interviews of 409 board chairmen in the mid-1970s, showed that 40% of the boards had more than 50% of the shareholders' voting power directly under the boards' control.[6]

In Australia, research into this latter problem is complicated by the dominant role played in sectors of the economy by transnational corporations with controlling boards located overseas; this problem is highlighted in the work of scholars such as Wheelwright.[7] The extent of foreign ownership in Australia is, indeed, very marked. Foreign ownership includes, for example, over 80% of the assets of the motor vehicle industry and assets producing over 50% of sales and over 40% of employment in mining.[8] A significant number of Australian financial institutions are owned by overseas companies and much of the future direction of mineral exploration is in the hands of foreign companies. There is also a large agricultural sector in foreign hands. The degree of overseas ownership resulted in a situation where, in 1977–78, profits and dividends paid overseas amounted to $1.5 billion, over one-third of total after-tax company income.[9]

Power as individual capacity and the current sociological mood

What do the above figures tell us about power? Taking power in the sense of coercion, the figures reveal a potential for the exercise of power; but one may not read off power relations directly from them. One has to examine the institutional framework within which power is exercised. If, however, one takes power in a different sense—not power over someone but power to realise individual interests, then something may be said immediately: the distribution of wealth in Australia is not conducive to social liberal aims, much less socialist ones.

Most social liberals and socialists, it will be remembered, take as their starting point the real objective interest of ordinary citizens to control their own lives and realise their capacities (positive freedom). To achieve that, government should intervene in the economy to provide genuine equality of opportunity. This equality of opportunity is not just equality of opportunity in Crosland's classic social democratic sense, of providing a more equal start in the race of life,[10] but, in Tawney's sense, of making the race less arduous.[11] Yet the rhetoric of all major parties has more in common with the sentiments of Crosland than Tawney.

The social liberal and the socialist visions are blunted also by the fusion of ethnic and gender differences with the economic. Whilst social liberals celebrate land rights, they often ignore the plight of the urban Aborigine. While they welcome the growing political activity of 'ethnic' groups, they often give little attention to the social forces which maintain an 'ethnic underclass' which is unemployed, semi-employed or located at the bottom end of endangered manufacturing industries; nor do they give sufficient attention to the apalling condition of women in that 'underclass'.

Whilst many social liberals might be found in university departments of sociology, they are rarely willing to analyse power as individual capacity. There are a number of reasons for this. First is the influence of Weber's famous definition of power:

> Power is the probability that one actor within a social relationship will be in a position to carry out his own will despite resistance regardless of the basis on which this probability rests.[12]

Secondly, the social liberal conception of power as individual capacity involves an element of teleology—now very unfashionable in sociology. The social liberal and socialist projects demand that one apply an external standard in evaluating social life—a procedure which is at odds with the current practice of showing how everything is socially constructed. It involves also an *essentialism*—another unfashionable word. Following Foucault, many sociologists declare that what is required is an ascending, non-essentialist explanation of power as conflict and not a descending, essentialist explanation of power as capacity.[13] What can they mean?

It is easy to see what such advocates are against. They do not like explanations of power which start from some essence which is taken to be fundamental (for example, the sovereign individual, the capital relation, the gender relation etc). They do not like discussions of power which are couched in terms of relations which 'descend' from the global to the minutiae of everyday life. Finally they dislike using the word power unless there is observable conflict. That some descending, essentialist explanations are crude and that some explanations which talk about individual capacity are unduly metaphysical there can be no doubt. But what would the alternative look like? One suspects that power would become such a slippery concept that it would not be worth the effort of explaining it. All one would have is a map of changing contingent relationships. One waits, with baited breath, for some theoretical 'breakthrough' which finally comes to the conclusion that 'social facts' are really coincidences.[14]

This chapter will be traditional. It will start out with a discussion of pluralism which derives from a utilitarian view. This is a description rather than an explanation (descending or ascending), but it is essentialist in that its all-important essence is the interest-maximising group. The chapter will examine the claim that group competition diffuses power in the coercive sense. It will do this from the perspective of explanations which are quite clearly descending and essentialist (Marxism, Weberianism and Feminism). If coercive power is not being diffused, what are the implications for power as individual capacity? The chapter will then look at an alternative description which, focussing on the concentration of power, talks about elites, and will consider the arguments that Australia is developing in a corporatist direction—an approach which posits the state as the all-important essense. Perhaps, at some stage in the future, this chapter will be seen as redundant in the face of a coherent non-essentialist ascending explanation. But one doubts it!

Pluralism

The origins of pluralism are pre-utilitarian. They lay in the aristocratic liberalism of the early American Republic. The American Constitution was such that interests were divided so that government might select all that was best in *the public interest*. Society consisted of private groups each pursuing its own ends. Harmony, however, was achieved not just by some Smithian 'hidden hand' but by the actions of wise government. The point about the public interest was that it was *public*. It accorded a status to the public sphere not matched in contemporary Australia. Nor could it be when one considers that what passed for a public sphere in New South Wales at that time was British, self-seeking, autocratic and corrupt. The status of the public sphere was never to be very high in Australia. For Hugh Emy:

> Australia is unusual because it has not fully developed the distinction which 'open' societies usually make between the public and private spheres. Political actors have not made a complete distinction between the purposes and values of the public order, the political realm itself and those of the individual's private sphere. People do not ascribe a separate sense of worth to the public order or idealise democratic politics; instead they have adopted a view of political authority which is both pragmatic and disdainful.[15]

Though Feminists would have every right to challenge Emy for underestimating the importance of the public-private distinction in securing male dominance, he is right if one considers the term public in the way public interest theorists used it in the early United States. Classical pluralism was not, and is not, a major feature of

Australian life, despite the wishes of many social liberals to make it so.

A second version of pluralism sees state policy simply as the outcome of competing group claims. The utilitarian principle of the greatest good of the greatest number of individuals has changed to the greatest good of the greatest number of groups which have the muscle to influence government policy. The public interest is collapsed into the private interest. This view, celebrated in the United States at the beginning of this century, was later criticised in that country as a degenerate form of pluralism. In Australia it has always been the dominant form. It holds that the successful exercise of power occurs when a combination of pressure groups sways the decisions of government in the direction of their perceived interests. According to this view even government itself might be seen as just another group.

A third version of pluralism, which also derives from utilitarianism, sees the government not just as another group but as a regulator. More properly regulation, or policing the rules of group competition, is the business not of the government but of those arms of the public power known collectively as 'the state'. Earlier chapters have referred to this 'regulator state'.

There is a lot of truth in the second and third versions of pluralism as applied to Australia. Problems occur, however, once one begins to define a pressure group. Conventionally:

> A pressure group can be defined as a group of persons, or a formal association or institution, that communicates demands to public authorities and that seeks to influence the content of public policy and how policy is administered.[16]

Such is a narrow definition. Clearly it can not include those Australian accounts which see the public service as a group fragmented into sub-groups and the Federal Cabinet as another.[17] It is a definition which excludes government organs. It excludes also major political parties (though not single-issue parties such as the Marijuana Party) since pressure groups seek merely to influence policy and not to aggregate demands and take office. But how fruitful is it to make a distinction between groups outside the public sector and those within it, and how might one make the distinction between parties and the groups upon which they depend for their very existence?

To exclude the public sector, it may be argued, ignores the point, made earlier, that the distinction between public and private sectors in Australia is not sharply drawn. Various branches of the public service, not to mention 'quangos' (quasi non-government organisations), are closely associated with private groups with which they have to deal. They often apply pressure in decision-making which is often as organised and as potent as those of groups in the private sector. Secondly, though it makes good sense to distinguish the primary goals of major political parties from pressure groups with a much narrower interest, the fact that political parties aggregate group demands in different ways and with different biases does suggest that the distinction between group and party is not all that clear-cut. Socialists, who regret that the ALP is a catch-all party which all too frequently represents little but its own desire to be in office, have to admit that union influence, from time to time, gives it something of a group flavour. Chapter 4 will return to this discussion of the nature of Australian political parties.

If, however, one falls back on to a broader definition where groups are everywhere, then one is confronted by the question raised by Talcott Parsons in his criticism of utilitarianism (but sidestepped by the followers of Foucault who seek 'ascending' explanations). How is social order possible? One may not posit a state structure which gives order to the anarchic competition of civil society because that state structure is subject to the same kind of competition. One must, perforce, seek a wider view of the structure of power outside the operation of groups.

A second objection to pluralist accounts is that they operate with only a 'one-dimensional' view of power. This, according to Lukes:

> involves a focus on *behaviour* in the making of *decisions* on issues over which there is observable *conflict* of (subjective) *interests* seen as express policy preferences revealed by political participation.[18]

Power in society is simply an extension of power among individuals. In Dahl's words, 'A has power over B to the extent that he can get B to do something that B would not otherwise do'.[19] It ignores the way decisions are prevented from being taken ('nondecision-making') and the conflict of real (as opposed to perceived) interests outside the context of decision-making (which Lukes calls 'two-dimensional' and 'three-dimensional' power). It has nothing, moreover, to say about the development of individual capacities.

When one considers pluralism and social order one has a political parallel to a problem which Adam Smith clearly realised. The higgling of the market (advocated in *The Wealth of Nations*) offered no solution as to how economic *order* was possible. That was why he first had to address that question in *The Theory of Moral Sentiments*. Smith was concerned to show how the values which sustained certain economic arrangements came about. His intention was to put forward a programme to change people's values, not to celebrate what existed. Many modern pluralists, however, are not concerned with the problem of social order. That is just assumed or explained away. Talking of Australia, Wolfsohn observed:

> The political system...is...almost universally accepted as a fairly efficient umbrella whose defects can be remedied by political and administrative action.[20]

One doubts the empirical claim. But even if it be granted as true, what is this political system which is accepted and how is its acceptance maintained? On what does the legitimation of power rest? It is no use saying that society is held together by rules. Those rules are defined as norms governing effective competition; therefore effective competition binds society together. Where do the rules come from?

One answer to the question as to where the rules come from might be that they may be derived from Australian democratic tradition. In the utilitarian account, Australian democracy rests upon a negative conception of freedom (freedom from interference) and thus upon the dispersal of power. In pluralism the successful exercise of power occurs when a shifting combination of groups sways the decisions of government in the direction of its perceived interests. Because of the need for combination, however, these groups tend to compromise one with another, thus dispersing power. Because the nature of decisions change and because individual citizens might be members of different pressure groups, power is further dispersed. Thus, for Wolfsohn, in his famous nine-point pluralist manifesto:

> Power itself as a physical phenonemon has evaporated by being diffused over a wide range of public and private organizations run by skilled experts of one kind or another.[21]

This dispersal of power is legitimised by considerations of negative freedom and utilitarian democracy which, in turn, give rise to rules which facilitate practices which further disperse power.

Even if it be granted that one is here only talking about 'one-dimensional' (decision-making) power, the view is still very questionable. Pluralists might be right in saying that pluralism is felt to be legitimate because it is believed to diffuse power. But has a diffusion of power really taken place even in the one-dimensional sense? Mainstream sociology would deny that it has. To illustrate that point let us examine the question from the perspectives of important strands of thought in contemporary sociology—Weberian, Marxist and Feminist.

Weberians and the pluralist thesis that group competition diffuses power

Weber did not just talk about groups. For Weber, power in society was expressed in three ways—class, status and party. An economic class was simply an aggregate of persons in similar market situations enjoying similar life-chances. A status group was a self-conscious community with some form of closure, and a party was an association with office-holders and a platform. Contrary to the views of some of his interpreters, Weber did not see these dimensions of power as unconnected or contingently connected.[22] In times of relative stability (as in contemporary Australia) market monopolies tend to develop. The resulting economic classes seek legitimation of their position by drawing upon respected cultural symbols and acceptable patterns of consumption. An ideology of status honour is developed which becomes embodied in institutions, and these institutions, in turn, reinforce the ideology of status honour. Dominant economic classes transform themselves into status groups through the ideology of status honour and that status honour, in turn, conditions the way the market operates to produce economic classes. In this way economic classes, in combination, change into social classes (large status groups which condition the market and the formation of economic classes). Thus, the efficacy of parties or groups is conditioned by ideologies of status honour and the institutions which create and reinforce them. Group competition will only diffuse power if it weakens status groups. For Weberians, a more normal occurrence in times of stability is for group competition actually to concentrate power. This is because being open to competition in a late capitalist society is often itself seen to be one of the symbols of status honour. If a status group wants to accrue power, there is nothing so good as being open to competition in a situation where one can not lose.

To exemplify the Weberian approach in the contemporary situation, consider the Australian medical profession. The idea of medical doctors simply as one group among many trying to influence government health policy is insufficient from a Weberian perspective. Medical doctors might be seen as an economic class which managed to achieve a degree of monopoly pricing. The transition of this class into a status group was easily effected by the achievement of a certain degree of closure, by pressing into service highly respected technological and humanitarian cultural symbols and by adopting consumption patterns envied by the bulk of the population. The status honour achieved was embodied in medical institutions which themselves reinforced that status honour. The medical market and the place of doctors on the wider labour market was, in turn, conditioned by that status honour. When it was simply an economic class, the life-chances of doctors were determined by the market. When it became a status group, the profession itself came to create the conditions for attaining its own life-chances. As such, it forged a commonality of interest with other market-conditioning status groups and became identified with dominant social classes. In its battle with chiropractors it could not lose. The outcome of that battle was enhanced legitimacy for a medical profession which tolerated competition (really never any match for it) and which made every use of the opportunity to involve 'science' to discredit its opponents. Even the power of government itself could only slightly dent its position. It could be that the status honour accruing to doctors might change. The crudity of its party, the AMA, has not helped its image, and the existence of other parties in the profession might lead to a redefinition of its status honour; but there are few signs as yet.

Clearly, for most Weberians, the status groups in modern society which are the most likely to prevail and concentrate power are those which can draw on the symbols of science and organisational efficiency. This is a consequence of the rationalisation of the world—that essence which provides the basis for this 'descending' explanation.[23]

For Weber, the rational concentration of power as domination undermines power as individual capacity in three areas. First there is capitalism:

> The private enterprise system transforms into objects of 'labour market transactions' even those personal and authoritarian-hierarchical relations which actually exist in the capitalistic enterprise. While the authoritarian relationships are thus drained of all normal sentimental content, authoritarian constraint not only continues, but at least under certain circumstances, even increases. The more comprehensive the realm of structures whose existence depends in a specific way on 'discipline'—that of capitalist commercial establishments—the more relentlessly can authoritarian constraint be exercised within them, and the smaller will be the circle of those in whose hands the power to use this type of constraint is concentrated and who also hold the power to have such authority guaranteed to them by the legal order.[24]

The comfortable personal authoritarianism of the family firm is dying. It is replaced by an impersonal authoritarianism where the rule of masters appears to be the rule of technological imperatives. In Australia, such a development is facilitated by the nation's long tradition of liberal utilitarianism and the rejection of personal domination. This tradition, one suspects, hinders the reception of Japanese management techniques which aim to give capitalism a human face by retaining pseudo-kinship networks and an ideology of pseudo-community.

Secondly, there is bureaucracy, which alienates the citizen from the means of administration as effectively as the worker is alienated from the means of production. Once again such alienation derives strength from tradition. One recalls Encel's remarks that the Australian tradition of egalitarianism, rather than challenging it, actually renders more powerful, impersonal bureaucratic authoritarianism.[25] Chapter 5 will return to his discussion.

Thirdly, individual capacity is undermined by the increased dominance of instrumental-rationality. This form of rationality produces utility-maximising individuals who calculate actions without reference to ultimate values. Such individuals may be free in some negative sense but they are not free to develop their capacities in any positive sense. In Weber's discussion of personality, there was clearly a notion of positive freedom,[26] though it was different in many respects from that of the old social liberals and their teleological views on human reason. Weber, after all, never budged from the position that an individual's choice of ultimate values was based on an non-rational decision.

Weber believed that the development of a 'modern' society, such as one sees in Australia, concentrates power and undermines individual human capacity. Yet his was not a crudely 'descending' account as some of the critics of that way of thinking maintain. The development of modern rationality, in demystifying the world, also deprived it of meaning. Once it was seen that ultimate values might not be derived from science, one might expect more and more acute clashes between individuals and groups with different value orientations. This value conflict, he felt, would not be managed, balanced and transformed through the mechanisms of representative government as pluralists believed.[27] Value conflicts would become more acute and could threaten social order. They might undermine the legitimacy of the institutions of representative government—'institutions that in the long run can only function to *mediate* conflict, as they are supposed to do, in the pluralist world-view, to the extent that they are not the *objects* of conflict'.[28]

Weber, one might say, wrote in a more turbulent day in a more turbulent continent than Australia. One is not so sure. Writing of our own day, Habermas notes the contradiction between the need for discipline and the commitment to representative government.[29] The legitimation crisis today may be seen, in Weberian terms, as one where greater rationality is no longer adequately served by institutions appropriate to the liberal state. Preceding chapters, however, have shown that such a view has been around for a long time. There were always people who saw representative institutions not as regulators but as the objects of conflict. Is the situation any worse now? If one looks at the matter with the time-span typical of most politicians, one has to conclude that, as a regulator of group conflict, the institutions of state are doing better in 1984 than they did in 1982. In the long-term, though, one suspects that the 'rational' restructuring of Australia's uncompetitive industry will occur in a climate of heightened value conflict, in which the legitimacy of liberal institutions will come under strain. Contrary to the pluralist thesis, acute group conflict might be the consequence of power concentrated to pursue rational economic objectives. Weber would surely have said: I told you so.

Marxism and the pluralist thesis that group competition diffuses power

Weber's argument, outlined above, was that competition between groups did not inevitably lead to a diffusion of power. On the contrary, under some circumstances heightened group competition, centering on different values, might be seen as *consequences* of already concentrated power. Marx, too, would deny the pluralist thesis. For Marx, the logic of market competition under capitalism led to a concentration of power in the hands of corporations that were best able to survive the periodic cycles of boom and depression endemic in the mode of production.

Marx's starting point was production. In capitalism the (dare one use the word) essential cleavage was between those who purchased labour power (alienated labour in the form of a commodity) for the realisation of profits and those who sold it. The basic power relation in society was a property relation. Capitalism was simply a system of power organised as property. For Weber, the market determined the formation of (economic) classes. For Marx, the mode of production determined both the formation of classes and the structure of the market. Classes, therefore, were not categories thrown up by the market. They were aggregates of people (with the capacity to become self-conscious groups) defined in terms of ownership (real or *de facto*) of the means of production. Classes both shaped the market and were shaped by it. Classes, moreover, were different aspects of a changing totality. Class analysis took as its starting point the total power structure; thus one could not conceive a class except in relation to at least one other class. Connell and Irving (though professing 'socialism' rather than Marxism) offer a classic formulation of this 'descending' explanation:

> There is a pattern of constraint and control at the top of the power structure, as there is at the bottom. If the two can be brought into relationship, or a common rationale can be found, a very powerful piece of social analysis will have been achieved. It is precisely this that class analysis attempts to do. Class analysis is based on the idea that the activities of the rulers, and especially the constraints on what they do and what they think, the boundaries in which they move, are shaped by certain highly general features of social relationships which also shape the everyday life of the quietest of their subjects. Mrs. Jones of Sunshine is linked to the Prime Minister, and to the Chairman of General Motors, by chains of circumstance that may be invisible to all three but are so tough and resistant that they need a massive convulsion of society to break.[30]

Class analysis for a Marxist (or a Connell-type socialist), therefore, demands that an analysis of group competition should be seen in the context of a total picture of power, determined by an essential capital relation. That relation also determines, or at least conditions, the role of the state which (in the pluralist scenario) groups seek to influence.

There are many Marxist views of the state[31] but none of them can conceive of group competition as diffusing power at the highest levels. The first, or 'instrumentalist' view, takes its inspiration from Marx's statement in the *Communist Manifesto* to the effect that the state executive is a 'committee for managing the common affairs of the bourgeoisie'. This view is theoretically very crude but is implicit in some writing on Australia. Here the state executive is so staffed that its decisions will always favour big business in opposition to any other interests. By definition, the personnel of state will act in the interests of concentrating power. According to the state-monopoly-capital ('stamocap') version of this, monopoly interests are so fused with the state[32] that the state becomes not just the executive committee of the bourgeoisie but the executive committee of only the monopoly fraction of it. Government, therefore, might be expected to discriminate against small business and against competitive rather than monopolistic or oligopolistic sectors of the economy. Some support for this position might be found in the way some Australian State governments favour transnational corporations in infrastructural development often to the detriment of smaller Australian businesses. Yet the picture is too crude. Bulbeck's study of Australian tariff policies, for example, shows that governments have been caught in the bind of desiring, on the one hand, to expand the economy and increase revenue and, on the other, to maintain electoral support by not exacerbating unemployment in manufacturing industries in the competitive sector.[33] The result has not been unambiguous support for the monopoly or oligopolistic sectors.

A second set of theories posits some 'relative autonomy' between the state and capital. They maintain that it does not matter much who staffs the executive arms of government. In fact, some go so far as to say that one of the characteristics of liberal bourgeois states, such as Australia, is that they are never staffed to any appreciable extent by capitalists. Nor would one expect governments always to support any dominant fraction of capital. What is important about capitalist states is the way they function to maintain the capitalist mode of production as a whole. This might be achieved for example by separating economic, political and ideological structures,[34] by adopting a state form which ensures the fulfilment of functions favourable to capital,[35] by providing conditions where considerations of 'business confidence' may skew state actions in a certain direction,[36] or by moderating class antagonism enough to secure continued accumulation, but not to the point where organised labour constitutes a drag on that accumulation. Many and varied objections have been raised about such theories, questioning their level of abstraction, their expansion of the state to engulf large parts of civil society and their willingness to ascribe to the state, as 'ideal total capitalist', a fictitious personality with a knowledge it can not possess. Indeed, many economists on the right have remarked, that if the state is an ideal total capitalist it is a pretty useless one. How is it possible to see tariff policy as aiding capital as a whole, except in the trivial sense of preventing disruption that ultimately might paralyse the capitalist economy? Whatever the objections, the point is that, however much the state might favour certain fractions of capital from time to time or might make concessions to the voters or organised labour, it is rooted in a mode of production which Marx felt ultimately must concentrate power. The Friedmanite notion that capitalist competition diffuses power and, if left to itself, produces greater equality is dismissed by all Marxists as an ideological rationalisation of the interests of those who actually promote greater concentration.

It is not too difficult to see how the various brands of Marxist views listed above might be applied to Australia. The defeat of bank nationalisation has been seen from an instrumentalist view whereby the bourgeois personnel of state ensured that only the representation of certain groups would be considered legitimate. Adherents to the relative autonomy viewpoint might point to the actions of the present Labor Government (which does not contain many businessmen) in securing business confidence. They might look to the actions of the High Court in preventing certain government actions in terms of the effect of a social formation which separates the political from the economic and the ideological. All such examples suggest mechanisms which concentrate rather than diffuse power.

For a Marxist, to concentrate power at one level means to diffuse it at another. In so far as the power of big business is concentrated, the power of small business is diffused. As one class acquires power, other classes are demobilised. This is not very different from C. Wright Mills' observation that diffusion of power occurs only at middle levels of society, and diffusion at that level might facilitate concentration at higher levels.[37]

How then do Marxists see social order as being possible? Many of the old instrumentalists used to talk simply about coercion. That is inadequate! In recent years there has been a revival of Gramsci's concept of 'hegemony', and Connell and Irving have been its most famous Australian exponents. For them, hegemony is:

> a situation where the subordinate class lives its daily life in social forms created by, or consistent with the interests of, the dominant class; and through this daily life acquires beliefs, motives and ways of thinking that serve to perpetuate the power of the dominant class.[38]

The second part of the definition is the part which has gripped the popular imagination. The pattern of group formation is structured by an information system skewed towards the interests of a dominant class. Chapter 1 raised some doubts about its validity and suggested an alternative way of looking at things. Here the question will be explored further.

The analysis of media reveals a frightening degree of concentration. In the late 1960s, Australia had the second highest degree of daily press concentration in the Western industrialised world (after Ireland); it now probably has the highest. Four newspaper groups own 87% of the metropolitan press, 82% of the Sunday press, 54% of the regional press, 52% of the suburban press and 89% of the Australian large magazine market. They share in 47% of all metropolitan television stations and 36.7% of metropolitan radio stations.[39] This potential for control led Colin Bednall to remark to the Senate Standing Committee on Education, Science and the Arts in 1973:

> You could not imagine a worse situation in any country...where four telephone calls enable anybody in power, or trying to get

into power, whether it is politics or the commercial field, to muster up pretty well the entire media of the country.[40]

The argument is about potential. One needs to go further and enquire into political content. The few studies here confirm what is intuitively obvious—that the dominant ideology celebrating property and deprecating trade union militancy overwhelms any alternative presentation. But one needs to go even further and engage in the extremely difficult task of evaluating the *effect* of that dominant ideology. In Britain the dominant ideology thesis has been challenged most eloquently by Abercrombie, Hill and Turner,[41] and a specific research project has been tailored to a Melbourne sample by Chris Chamberlain.[42]

Chamberlain distinguishes between two kinds of hegemonic approach. The first of these maintains that subordinate classes accept the abstract premises of dominant class ideology and apply them to their concrete life situations (exemplified in the work of Playford, McQueen, Theophanous, Windschuttle, Williams, Connell and Irving)[43] whilst the second, which he calls the quasi-hegemonic approach, maintains that subordinate classes merely accept dominant class ideology at the abstract level but not with regard to items in their direct experience (exemplified in the work of Wild and Kriegler).[44] Thus, according to this second approach, a worker might condemn strike action in general whilst supporting the strike action of his or her own union. For both of these approaches Chamberlain finds only a little support. In general, his sample shows that most people have a very clear idea about the class divisions in Australian society and very few at the bottom end of the scale swallow the myth of Australia as a classless society and the anti-unionist propaganda provided by an oligopolistic media. There is, in short, a high correlation between people's values and their structural location. The implication of Chamberlain's findings deserve to be underlined. Working people do not form groups or support groups which act in their long-term interests not because they do not know what those interests are but for other reasons. Could these include the fear of chaos ensuing from class-based opposition—the fear that they might finish up as worse off than they are now? Secondly, it is not just politicians who treat ordinary people as stupid but also many academics on the left who continue to assume that ordinary people swallow any nonsense that is dished up for them.

Chamberlain's findings are not inconsistent with the first part of the above definition of hegemony. One might quite easily live one's life in social forms consistent with the interests of a dominant class whilst totally rejecting the values of that class. Such considerations, in recent years, have changed fundamentally Marxist views on education. A few years ago, Bowles and Gintis argued that one should understand the school system as reproducing and, therefore, preparing material for the monotonous discipline of factory life. Children were 'socialised'.[45] Nowadays the focus is on the reproduction of cultural symbols.[46] Children reject at an early age the values transmitted to them. Delinquency is often a form of class protest. It is identity-reinforcing activity but not purposive struggle. In adult life, group formation and even modest pressure group activity can serve the same ends. But purposive action, which might threaten house and garden and other identity-reinforcing aspects of life, is too risky. Subordinate classes may be kept quiet without the need for any dominant ideology at all. Perhaps Abercrombie, Hill and Turner are right; a dominant ideology only usually convinces the dominant class.

For many contemporary Australian Marxists, then, group competition at the bottom of the pile probably does diffuse power. But that is not what the advocates of pluralism mean when they put forward its ideological defence. Indeed, what is diffused at the bottom of the pile is, more often than not, power as individual capacity—that kind of power which social liberals and socialists seek to maximise.

Feminism and the pluralist thesis that group competition diffuses power

Theories of hegemony argue that ordinary people live their lives in conditions shaped by the capital relation. They also, surely, live their lives in conditions shaped by other relations which some take to be just as essential. One of these is the gender relation which is clearly also a relation of power. It was argued earlier that the dominant ideology thesis, which sees the ideas of society as everywhere those of the dominant class, is empirically questionable. One suspects the same to be true concerning gender relations. One would like to see research conducted along the lines of Chamberlain, showing the degree to which women accept a male-dominated ideology which accords them subordinate status. Using Wertheim's method outlined in Chapter I, it is arguable that a counterpoint relationship between ideas of autonomy and subordination, effectiveness and dependence is a more useful way of looking at the situation. One is just as unwilling to accept the attribution of stupidity to women as one is to workers.

That the normal family system which exists in Australia supports patriarchy is undeniable. What is contestable, however, is that participating in life outside the family is on its own any more liberating. A lot of work has been done showing patriarchy in the work-place and the concentration of women in subordinate work-roles. This often reduces women to a position more subordinate than they experience in the family. The same goes for participating in group activity.

It is well known among political activists in Australia that the inclusion of women in groups dominated by men, initially at any rate, consigns women to a service role within the group. Group effectiveness and group discipline in conditions of acute competition, it is felt, must not be undermined by the instability caused by any rapid change in customary gender roles. The situation is ironical. The kind of woman who wishes to participate in group activity is more likely to be the one who has not been cowed by domesticity and who has a partner not hostile to her participation. Nevertheless, the nature of her involvement is such that she is likely to find herself in a situation more subordinate than she experiences in the family. In this respect, group competition, in the pluralist scenario, may exacerbate gender power differentials. Within large groups and political parties, the situation is clearly changing, presumably because those groups can afford to tolerate a greater degree of initial instability. One wonders, however, as to the extent things are changing in the small pressure group.

Participation by women in groups which aim to improve the position of women and which consist entirely of women, on the other hand, may be expected, in the long-run, to diffuse power between the sexes. In the short-run, however, defensive identity-reinforcing actions taken by men could actually exacerbate power differentials. In both of the above manifestations of pluralist competition, the diffusion of this particular form of power is problematical.

The elite structure

Group competition, outside the purview of democratically-elected bodies, some of its critics argue, has created an alternative political system which is the antithesis of democracy

> A sort of subterranean political system has developed where industry pressure groups maintain steady liaison with Commonwealth officials and Ministers in furthering their own interests. The result is that great decisions are being taken, affecting the direction of the whole economy and the profitability of individual companies, spasmodically and to a large extent beyond the knowledge of the mass of the people and beyond the reach of public criticism.[47]

This sort of pluralism is the enemy of democracy. It is felt to be particularly dangerous because it diverts attention away from what is, in reality, a very elitist form of rule. Some people argue, therefore, that a more realistic analysis should locate elites and the bases of their power.[48]

What, then, may be said about the elite structure? Classifying elites in terms of the degree of integration and patterns of recruitment, Giddens identifies four elite types—a uniform elite (with a high degree of integration and a restricted pattern of recruitment), an established elite (with a low level of integration and a relatively closed pattern of recruitment), a solidary elite (with a high level of integration and an open pattern of recruitment) and an abstract elite (with low integration and open recruitment).[49]

Table 3.1 Elite Typology

	High degree of integration	Low degree of integration
Closed recruitment	Uniform elite	Established elite
Open recruitment	Solidary elite	Abstract elite

Clearly, in Australia, different types of elite might be classified under any one of the above categories. To the extent, however, that there might be a super-elite, which occupies a number of key positions in dominant social institutions, Wild believes one should speak of the *established* rather than any of the other patterns.[50] There is an Establishment, with a relatively closed pattern of recruitment but with a much lower degree of integration than the picture of the American power elite given by C. Wright Mills.[51]

But what does it mean to say that this super-elite is more or less integrated? In Australian sociology, methodological individualism is clearly pervasive and characterises the network studies undertaken in the volume *Elites in Australia* by Higley and others. That book suggests, but does not prove, a far greater degree of interpersonal integration amongst members of the Australian elite than the comparable American one. Though here, once again, the picture falls far short of that presented by Wright Mills.[52] This methodological individualist position is pervasive even amongst writers who claim, or who are claimed, to be Marxist. Indeed, many 'Marxist' writers, claiming to be talking about a 'ruling class', are in fact engaged in elite study of a methodological individualist kind. Campbell, for example, analyses the interpersonal and inter-familial connections of 60 rich families who are said to own Australia.[53] Playford, whilst attacking Campbell's simplicity, likewise is concerned (in the manner of Miliband)[54] to show the interlocking directorates and personal affiliations of individuals.[55] Though what he refers to as 'the ruling class' is divided on many issues, it derives a common view on the rightness of the social and economic order through its common background and education. All that is particularly Marxist in this approach is the view that political power stems from ownership of the means of production. There is a crucial difference, however, between a common view on the rightness of the social and economic order and a common consensus in maintaining the rules of elite competition whilst excluding outsiders. The latter is presumably what Encel means in his picture of various elites united by 'a governing consensus'.[56] It is spelt out in more detail by Higley and others, who claim:

> To conclude that the Australian elite is...more disunified than the Russian or Chilean would be a serious error. The situational and structural constraints under which a consensual unified elite operates are very different from those of the other two types of elites. Mutual trust and tolerance (the 'norm of restrained partisanship') characterize consensual unified elites. 'Leaders see one another as legitimate contestants in a mutually beneficial game, rather than as belligerents in a ruleless war.'[57] Because of this, members of a consensual unified elite can hold and express sharply differing opinions about current issues without endangering themselves or the political system they help to operate.[58]

The descriptive value of the elite model, based upon individuals and their interconnections, is apparently quite great. On closer examination, however, one must demonstrate rather than assume that common background leads to common action.[59] One must advance reasons why certain elites form part of the 'established' super elite and not others (trade unions for example, which clearly do not fall into the established pattern). One must demarcate boundaries between elite and non-elite according to some non-arbitrary criteria. The division between elite and 'mass' is clearly unsatisfactory when the 'mass' is defined in terms of the elite.[60] The argument is circular! One must also show the conditions under which elites cohere to form a super-elite and under which they engage in competition. Finally, one has to demonstrate in what sense elites actually exercise power.

Australian elite studies handle the above questions inadequately, yet for all their shortcomings, they show a picture of democracy far from the social liberal ideal. As the Higley study puts it:

> The data do not square with optimistic notions about how policies should be formed in a democratic society. They presume that the

public, or at least a large part of it, can be informed about most issues and disposed to participate in deciding them. Those who are elected or appointed to specific governing tasks need have no special influence and should remain essentially interchangeable with those they govern. They should produce decisions that would be supported by a majority of the public if there were time for the public to consult fully on them. Contrary to these notions, however, the data trace a system of participation in policy-making that is elitist in character and in which the public are regarded by those who participate as inattentive to issues and without a majority opinion on most of them.[61]

The conclusion of Higley and others, coupled with the view that Australian elites 'exhibit much greater cohesion and integration than is compatible with the standards of representative democracy',[62] causes no surprise; though it does contradict much of the electoral rhetoric with which the Australian voter is assailed. But does the conclusion disqualify Australia as a democracy? It does not, it would appear, if one changes the definition of that term. Chapter 2 noted that, some four decades ago, Schumpeter, in his classic work *Capitalism, Socialism and Democracy*, created a 'market model' of democracy which portrayed various self-appointed elites engaged in competition one with another to maximise their share of the popular vote.[63] The elites acted out of consideration for some utilitarian calculus, and people voted for them for similar reasons. This view, which contradicted the beliefs of both socialists and social liberals, was later blown up into a fully-fledged theory of 'democratic elitism.'[64] All democracy was, it appeared, was a system whereby elites became periodically accountable to the electorate. Even if it be granted that such indeed was democracy, one can not but observe that most elites in Australia are not accountable to the electorate as a whole and many of them are not accountable to anyone at all.

Corporatism

Elite theory, on its own, is no more capable of providing an answer to the question of how social order is possible than pluralist theories. Yet, as has been noted, it does seem much more attractive to some Weberian and Marxist sociologists. After all, it may be seen to be a consequence of the concentration of power in society and might be bent into a descending explanation. As has been described, for Weber, complex modern societies were characterised by a process of rationalisation. The ensuing process of bureaucratisation of the state, private business and even organised labour suggested the formation of elites. In that the process of bureaucratisation was similar, one would expect elites at the top of the hierarchy to fuse. It is this way of thinking which has led to a renewal of discussions in recent years concerning corporatism. In the classic words of Phillipe Schmitter, this was:

> a system of interest representation in which the constituent units are organised into a limited number of singular compulsory, non-competitive, hierarchically ordered and functionally differentiated categories, recognised or licensed (if not created) by the state and granted a deliberate representational monopoly within their respective categories in exchange for observing certain controls on their selection of leaders and articulation of demands and supports.[65]

Corporatism is a magic word which superficially unites many diverse schools of thought. Liberals, noting that pluralist group competition has not resulted in a diffusion of power, talk about the transition from pluralism to corporatism. This may take two forms. First, competition between interest groups might eliminate competitors so that one group has a monopoly of representation to government of a particular sector of economy or society; this is called societal corporatism. Alternatively, the government might intervene to select a group with which it will deal or even set one up itself; this is called statist corporatism. In so far as corporatism exists in Australia, Loveday observes, the societal type dominates. It is characterised by the following:

> Groups cease to be in conflict or confrontation with government, but come to co-operate with it—which is not to say that conflict is the basic or normal pluralistic relationship. They are given official recognition in negotiations and official places on a variety of boards and committees. They have an official place close to government and each comes to depend on the other. They are expected from time to time to carry out tasks for government but above all they are expected to be answerable for their members—to ensure that members don't break agreements they have made, on their members' behalf, with government. Dissentient interest group voices, especially those which are unwelcome to government, are not given recognition and are kept in a position of relative powerlessness.[66]

Liberals see this process as government incorporating various groups and welding them into subordinate positions in the elite hierarchy. Weberians see this as an example of the developing rationality of the administrative system—which, one will recall, is one answer as to how social order might be possible.

Yet corporatist theory may also seem plausible to some people in the Marxist tradition. They might see the situation not as government doing the incorporating but big business. For some of those of the state derivation school (purveyors of the ultimate essentialist, descending explanation) there is a logic to the late capitalist state which requires corporatism to ensure that the state performs functions necessary for capital accumulation.[67] Others see corporatism (in Dahrendorf's term) as 'institutionalising class struggle'. Still others see corporatism as a response to 'fiscal crisis', 'legitimation crises', 'motivation crises', 'crises of crisis management' and the like.[68]

Consideration of the arguments in Chapters 1 and 2, as well as those of Loveday, suggests that in Australia corporatism is not a new thing. Earlier chapters pointed out that Australia always lacked a coherent and strong *laissez faire* tradition. Right from the start the state played a major role in promoting industry—a process referred to as 'marsupial capitalism'. With the development of the arbitration system, moreover, there was clearly also a form of 'marsupial unionism'. Indeed, as Rawson suggests, this dependence of unions upon the state has served to legitimate the (usually successful) attempts by Liberal governments to control and alter the way unions run their own affairs.[69] A decade and a half ago McFarlane observed that:

> Australia's hydra-headed system of planning, the network of government regulatory agencies linked with trade union bureaucracy, evolves into an (admittedly mild and diluted) form of corporate economy.[70]

It is difficult to tell whether the new interest in corporatism in Australia reflects an actual real trend, the reception (belated as usual) of a body of European literature on the subject or simply its affirmation by the current Prime Minister, Bob Hawke, in his desire for consensus. Here Hawke is in a very long tradition of social liberal thought which, at the end of the nineteenth century, welded Hegel's favourable view of the corporate state into a particular brand of liberalism.[71]

This social liberal affirmation of corporatism has found recent theoretical expression in Australia. Dow, Clegg and Boreham, for example, argue that corporatist strategies are necessary to achieve the class representation of labour in a crisis-prone economy. They welcome the establishment of EPAC and other tripartite bodies which bring government, labour and capital together:

> Corporatism, then, to the extent that it means the involvement of business and unions in the making of economic policy represents an expansion, not a diminution, of democratic control of the

economy. It represents an affirmation of the central significance of class politics in contemporary circumstances.[72]

Democracy, here, simply means the incorporation of organisations claiming to represent class interests into the organisations of state. It is not a conception of democracy usually discussed in democratic theory. This is not representative democracy in the parliamentary sense celebrated by John Stuart Mill. Nor is it participatory democracy, also stressed by Mill, and developed by social liberals. The old social liberal position stressed not only corporatist strategies but also the fostering of democratic bodies at grass-roots level in which people could develop their potentialities as citizens. To advocate the former without the latter is to advocate working class power without the development of the capacities of working class people to enjoy it—a recipe for elitism.

The advocacy of corporatism might be a recipe for elitism. Yet, in so far as it exists, corporatism is itself a consequence of elitism. But how far is Australia really developing in the corporatist direction noted by so many scholars in Europe? Loveday concludes that there is insufficient evidence to say that Australia is any more corporatist today than it was in the past. The literature he surveys is not that which supports corporatism but that which is critical of it. It dislikes the concentration of power, regrets the integration of elites by government and uses bogey words like the 'state' to imply a monster of great power. Australia, he feels, does not have a monstrous state. The formal bureaucracy is divided against itself; there are relatively independent statutory authorities not easily coerced; the federal system divides power and the High Court imposes very real constraints on the actions of government. On the other side, interest groups are fragmented. Some are even based overseas and do not lend themselves to government control. The pluralist model may be found wanting but the opposite picture is equally deficient.[73]

Strangely enough, one could think of Marxist arguments which would support Loveday's picture. Precisely because the state is fragmented, a reforming government is not powerful enough to do very much. In the absence of a one-party government, big business, particularly foreign business, is probably better served without a corporate state. The above quote from Dow, Clegg and Boreham is, therefore, just wishful thinking.

Those liberals who fear the growth of corporatism consider the government to be the prime mover in elite integration. Some Marxists would consider the prime mover to be business organisations. Still others see governments bowing down before organised professional elites. Governments, after all, are often not competent enough, nor have they the time, to sort through the technical complexity of proposed legislation, sifted, polished and made abstruse by the legal and other professions.

The growth of professional power might provide the basis for what Alvin Gouldner has called a 'new class' of intellectuals.[74] But one is sceptical! Even Gouldner's new class was fatally flawed by the division between its technocratic and humanistic wings. Perhaps instead one should consider David Apter:

> Since an industrial society is based on high information, the type of political system best able to facilitate information formation would appear to be a reconciliation system. But this type is the very one that because of excessive instrumentalism is always in danger of losing its legitimacy...the fundamental predicament of highly industrial societies is that high degrees of embourgeoisement produce radicalisation.[75]

Apter's view is shared by David Kemp in his study of Australian political attitudes and voting behaviour.[76] Kemp argues further (following Kristol) that one also sees evidence of a cleavage between professional groups and business. This form of 'legitimation crisis' throws doubt on the realisation of any corporatist state. Indeed, if one combines this view of 'legitimation crisis' with one which comes from the other end of the political spectrum (that of Habermas discussed earlier) one becomes even more sceptical.

Who dominates when?

This chapter has argued that Australia is not an equal society and that group competition does not diffuse power; but then neither is the concentration of power such that one may talk of a power elite in the sense used by Wright Mills. One is also a little sceptical about arguments concerning a corporate state.

The argument has not been that it is wrong to talk about group competition or elite structure; it is that in any general account of Australian society one has to have some answer as to how social order is possible. Descriptive accounts which talk about groups or elites on their own will, by themselves, offer no answer to that question. Nor, one suspects, would any 'ascending' explanation which starts from the minutiae of everyday life. Proponents of such an approach have to demonstrate how society is not just an accident. To believe that is to announce the death of macro-sociology.

At the level of society as a whole, one has to talk about essences. One needs a plausible explanation of how patterns of domination and subordination in society as a whole are produced and reproduced over time. As long as one believes it legitimate to ask questions at that level of generality, one needs something like class theory. Significantly, those sociologists, who reject 'essentialism' as defined above, can no longer ask that question.

When one considers the question of how patterns of domination and subordination are reproduced in society as a whole, the starting point can not be groups or elites. That is because those subjects of power are not defined in relation to other subjects in a total network of relations. One must, perforce, turn to an account of class be it Weberian, Marxist or some other theory which posits connections between those who rule and those who are ruled.

This chapter has suggested ways that Weberians and Marxists might tackle the question. Increasingly both have borrowed each others' categories. Significantly, many Marxists talk about the integration of the interests of capital not through consciousness of capital's overall interests (a very debatable notion), nor by interpersonal connections (the cleavages are often as sharp as the commonalities), but through the mechanisms of a rationalised state[77]. For many Marxists, a dominant class dominates only in the sense that its collective behaviour determines the constraints within which the institutions of state may act. This is power in Lukes' third dimension.

Let us illustrate the problem. It is in the interests of capital to create a favourable investment climate and to maintain business confidence. Such is also in the interests of government, since economic improvement generates support. In so far as the various groups and elites can prevail upon government, and the institutions of state outside government, to discipline organised labour, those elites and groups constitute a dominant class. The question is basically how patterns of domination and subordination in society are maintained. The previous Liberal National Party Government was found wanting in this regard. The present government is more amenable. One may not, however, explain the election of that government in terms of dominant class activity. Obviously it was elected because of subordinate class perceptions of economic mismanagement (amongst other things).

To start by talking of a dominant class is only useful when one is confronted by questions of a high order of generality—which consider the integration of society as a whole. When one talks of specific investment decisions and the like, then it makes sense to talk about elites and groups. To be sure, the actions of those elites and groups are constrained by class relations, but usually only vaguely. The descending explanation, attacked by the followers of

Foucault, is often a straw person. Few analysts believe in a rigid class determination of all group conflict or the rigid functionalist explanations of some stamocap theorists. The degree to which class antagonism between capital and labour influences group competition is an empirical question which may not be solved beforehand by theory. There is not some inexorable logic involved in 'descending' analyses. But the point needs to be underlined. Just as one should not collapse group competition into class analysis, one should not treat class analysis merely as another form of group conflict. One's approach depends upon the order of generality of the question one wishes to pose.

The model of power one uses, therefore, depends on the questions one wants to ask and on one's level of analysis. When the interests of one class as a whole are seen in relation to the interests of another class, then it makes sense to talk in terms of a dominant class. When one's focus is the internal politics of the state apparatus, then it makes sense to talk of elites because there one may usually draw a line between elite and subaltern power. When one is tracing through concrete decision-making, it might be useful to talk in terms of a plurality of groups. It should be possible to weld all this together into a composite picture integrating it with questions of gender and ethnicity, though such has not been achieved. Encel's early attempt sought to use a post-Weberian distinction between class, status and power to achieve synthesis.[78] The result was an impressive collection of data which could be used either to support a view of the power structure of Australia as one of discrete elites or conversely one which supported a rather diffuse notion of rule by a dominant class. In the end one is left with the question: when and how does the dominant class dominate? Wild's more theoretically self-conscious attempt uses the more orthodox Weberian categories of class, status and party coupled with Giddens' attempt to combine Marx and Weber. Following Giddens, Wild distinguishes between four types of power structure: *autocratic* where the limits of power are not restricted and power is in the hands of a relatively small group; *oligarchic* where the limits of power are relatively restricted but power still rests with a relatively small group; *hegemonic* (in a sense different from that used above) where the limits of power exercised by elites are not restricted but where power is constrained from below; and *democratic* where the power of elites is limited and tied to power from below. Using this schema, Wild believes Australia belongs to the hegemonic type.[79] As a general description such seems to be the case. Yet much depends upon the type of power one is talking about. When it comes to dominant class power over the share of the economic cake, it could be argued that the oligarchic description fits the bill. When one is talking about the operation of pressure groups for the attainment of a particular decision, the democratic label sometimes fits. And when it comes to a major constitutional crisis, as in 1975, then what else may one describe the situation as being other than autocratic. Amongst Marxists, the old instrumentalist view has been criticised and structuralism seems to have passed Australia by (at least it did not give rise to much empirical work). The focus of hegemony by socialists such as Connell is, moreover, quite stimulating but one must question a view which sees a 'ruling class' ruling once in a generation (when, for example, it mobilised over bank nationalistion). This chapter has argued that, as the determinant of 'business confidence', the dominant class dominates most of the itme. Elites in various sectors exercise power most of the time, and a plurality of pressure groups act upon government at various levels—again most of the time.

An example and a conclusion

A number of different approaches to power in Australia have validity at different levels of analysis. One should not collapse a manifestation of the exercise of power into an explanatory framework appropriate to a different level. Group theory will give a very misleading picture of the overall dynamics of the capitalist system. For its part, class theory cannot do much more than provide a framework for the analysis of particular decisions. Elite theory might tell us much about those who control certain institutions but not much about the relationship of those institutions to society as a whole and to the catch-all category known as 'the mass' (or 'non-elite'). Moreover, to reduce patriarchy and ethnicity to class and vice versa is a recipe for disaster.

To illustrate the problem, consider how certain industries come to be regulated. Classical theories of the public interest would say that a neutral and impartial government selects all that is best in the various advice put to it by interest groups and distills a regulatory policy in the common interest. Hard-nosed pluralists, however (egalitarian-minded or not), might say that the government responds to pressure on the part of that coalition of interest groups which is able to mobilise support sufficient for a governing party to realise that it is in its own interest to yield to that coalition's demand. According to what has been called a 'producer protection model', a government will supply regulation to an industry if that industry is willing to pay for it (in terms of resources or votes). The ability of an industry to secure regulation will depend upon its size, concentration, intensity of employment and geographic location.

The assumption here is that the benefits of regulation are more concentrated than the costs (which are borne by the taxpayer). The regulated industry may deliver the votes because the dispersed taxpayers are not likely to realise the extent to which they are subsidising a particular industry much less mobilise their votes in their own self-interest. It has been pointed out, however, that regulation is often achieved in which the benefits are more dispersed than the costs.[80] This is explained by an entrepreneurial variant of public choice theory which talks about entrepreneurs who derive gains from supplying a public good (as in consumer protection). This last approach has become fashionable in recent years among right-wing economists (promoted by the Centre for Independent Studies in 'New South Wales) who wish to curtail the role of regulatory agencies:

> Explanations of the activities of institutions (governmental and others) are sought in the incentives and constraints confronting their managers, on the assumption that the latter behave as rational utility-maximisers (or economic men).[81]

Since such is believed to be the case, efficiency is best served by widespread deregulation—a familiar plea in times of recession in Australia, as Chapter 2 noted.

A combination of the above two approaches will tell us a lot about how decisions concerning regulation are arrived at (the exercise of power in the first dimension). Problems, however, begin to arise when one considers ideologies and structures within which the exercise of power is to take place. What motivates behaviour are often not real costs and benefits but perceived or imagined long and short-term costs and benefits about which expert opinion is divided. Should, for example, the mining industry be regulated in such a way as to prohibit the extraction of uranium? Calculation of the costs and benefits in that case is something of a lottery, and the adversary nature of political campaigning is constrained by a press which is not exactly neutral. The question of uranium mining involves power in the first dimension. Many environmental non-decisions, however, are a different matter. They have been kept off the political agenda by elites or indeed have not yet reached the status of a conscious non-decision. Criticising Marxists, Conybeare observes that obviously the contention that all regulation favours monopoly capital is inconsistent with almost any observable data.[82] But who but a bovine fundamentalist believer in stamocap could claim that it did? All a sophisticated Marxist would claim is that the politics of regulation, non-regulation and deregulation should be seen in a context where monopoly capital to a greater or lesser extent sets the limits of political action. One has only to look at the automobile industry to see that the nature of government regulation has been tightly circumscribed by the interests of overseas boards of directors. Similarly, the regulation of agriculture is not explained well by the capacity of rural interests to obtain benefits in return for the vote. 'Protection all round' was the result of a deal between two elites, or if one likes two fractions of capital.

Structural factors are also of vital importance in evaluating the implementation of government regulation. Bureaucratic routines may facilitate or impede that process, perhaps to the point where regulation 'may be little more than a negotiated cluster of routine patterns of behaviour bearing little resemblance to the original regulatory goals'.[83] These bureaucratic structural constraints may be the result simply of flows of information within the bureaucracy or the result of the power of a bureaucratic elite. Chapter 5 will return to this problem in a discussion of the role of the public service. It might also be the case, as Offe argues, that crisis management demands regulation which generates new crises and new regulation. In short, regulation generates its own structural constraints.[84]

Considerations of gender and ethnicity pose limits on regulation which are just as important. These, one may predict, will become more apparent as the present Labor Government attempts to promote the goal of equal opportunity and respect for women. One can, for example, imagine the furore which might be caused by attempts to regulate further the entertainment industry. Any policy geared to affirmative action for women will initially probably lose votes rather than win them. If the government pursues action along this line, one suspects that explanations of its motivation might only be in terms of the old-fashioned idea of the public interest. To sustain that motivation, however, the government will have to break with its own tradition of concern more with short-term party advantage; at this point one can have only a modicum of hope.

There are, therefore, many different approaches to power, depending upon the level of generality at which problems become salient. Such acknowledgement, however, should not lead one to rest content with the post-Weberian distinction between class, status and power and to argue that each dimension is incommensurable. This chapter has maintained that Weber himself did not do that. For Weber, class, status and party were all dimensions of power. For Marx, capitalism was simply a system of power organised as property. In both traditions there is a need to relate types of power and different levels of analysis to an overall framework. Such is an immensely difficult task which may not be sidestepped by a concentration simply on the immediately testable and mathematically elegant.

PART THREE
INSTITUTIONS

FOUR
PARLIAMENT, PARTY AND POLITICAL PRACTICE

The decline of parliament

THE INSTITUTION OF parliament, it seems, is everywhere in decline. The only matter of controversy amongst historians and political scientists is when that decline began. At the end of the eighteenth century the pioneer anarchist Godwin observed that parliaments were alienated from the citizens and inevitably brought out the worst features of national leaders; parliaments were divided into factions and were characterised by a competition for esteem which did not contribute to the welfare of individual citizens; parliamentary debates, moreover, were dominated by orators who took advantage of transitory prejudices and were distorted by having to be terminated by a vote; truth could never be decided by numbers and the constant threat of the vote prevented the best decision being made.[1] In the early twentieth century Sidney and Beatrice Webb observed:

> (Parliamentary institutions) have no regard for knowledge. If they are now so rapidly losing public respect, and the support of popular consent, it is because members of Parliament and Cabinet Ministers show themselves not only so ignorant of their job, but are also so complacently unaware that they have anything to learn, and therefore quite unconscious of the need for making the electorate any better educated than they are themselves.[2]

Parliament, apparently, has been declining for a long time. Clearly, in Bagehot's terms, parliament no longer belongs to the 'efficient' part of the constitution. Nor, as Crisp insists, has it shifted to the 'dignified' part along with the Crown and its representatives.[3] In truth, after 1975, there does not seem to be much left of the dignified part of the constitution. Perhaps one should invent a new category—the moribund. This word is better than 'redundant' because there ought to be a place for parliament in modern societies, be they capitalist or socialist. Both Marxists and liberals would agree that, even though the proceedings of parliaments are dominated by executives and constrained by organised interests, they do provide a channel whereby the public might be kept aware of the actions of those executives. People might disagree as to the extent to which parliament has the potential to serve as a mechanism for making executives responsible to the people or the extent to which members of parliament may actually represent those who authorised their membership, but few would argue that the attempt should not be made. The attempt is worthwhile, but one has serious doubts about the possibility of meaningful change within the confines of the existing Constitution. Before discussing reform, however, let us unpack the myths which legitimise the Australian Parliament.

The methods of ideal-type construction

Conventional wisdom holds that Australia has a Westminster system of government. What does that mean? There seem to be two ways into making sense of the claim. First, one might identify some essence of the British system and examine whether it also may be identified in Australia. Alternatively, one might construct an ideal-type out of the various elements claimed for the British system and chart reality against it. The first approach leads to triviality. The essential feature of the British system, it would seem, is that the executive is drawn from parliament and is responsible to the people through parliament. Such a claim is useful only in the trivial sense of comparing a British-type parliamentary system and an American-type presidential system. On close examination, however, the claim is misleading. The executive in both Britain and Australia is drawn from parliament in the sense that it must consist of members of parliament, but it is not chosen by parliament, is rarely responsible to parliament and, in so far as it is responsible to the people it is through the mechanism of political parties. As such, it may be more accurately described as responsive rather than responsible.

Though courses in civics might wish to dwell upon the essence of the system, it is more common among political scientists to construct ideal-types of government and measure reality against them. Two methods of ideal-type construction are commonly employed. The first of these is exemplified by Parker who identifies 'central axioms' of the 'Westminster syndrome'. These axioms are 'precepts' which constitute an 'abstract model of a set of institutions and of relationships between them'. They consist of:

1 'Responsible ministers' in parliament

2 A partnership of elected ministers and appointed officials (the latter not necessarily permanent)
3 A relationship between ministers and officials; both are engaged in 'policy' and 'administration' but the minister should be able to have the last word at any level, and officials should be loyal to the current minister
4 Accountability which runs from official to minister, to cabinet to parliament, to voters. This is to enable demands of interests pressing on one part of the administration to be measured against competing demands in 'the public interest'.

Parker holds that:

> The Westminster syndrome was emulated in Australia, and is still recognisable here; and that we can avoid confusion if we keep the term 'Westminster' for these central axioms of British origin, and separately identify supplementary Australian precepts.[4]

There is no doubt that the precepts of the 'Westminster syndrome' were initially adopted as the axioms of the parliamentary systems of the colonies. They exist today largely as *ideological symbols*. Thompson's comment is pithy:

> So far from being an adequate analytical model, or even a useful shorthand phrase, involving the 'Westminster system' in Australia has become a political reflex used to justify certain approaches to political issues.[5]

Though elements of responsible government exist in Australia, ministerial responsibility is not a defining characteristic of the Australian system. It is invoked as a justification for the executive to get rid of ministers who might cause embarrassment or for oppositions who wish to challenge the high-handed actions of the executive. Secondly, the relationship between elected ministers and officials seems more to bear out the conclusions of Max Weber on bureaucracy, or for that matter the theme of the popular British television programme *Yes Minister*, than the venerated precepts. But one should not underestimate the ideological strength of the precepts. Both utilitarian and social liberals might derive strength from the appeal to 'the public interest'. Let us, however, distinguish the ideological rationale from the actual practice of politics.

One should go further than just questioning the basic precepts of the Westminster syndrome. An approach which identifies Australian government as a deviant descendant of a British grandparent is itself inadequate. To what extent are Parker's 'supplementary precepts' not supplementary at all but really basic? After all, the grandparents of the current federal system were not exclusively British. This consideration leads to a second method of ideal-type construction—the so-called 'Washminster mutation' constructed out of two ideal-types—one British and one American.[6] Historiography demands a close examination of the forced marriage of the British system of 'responsible government' and the incompatible American federal system. Many of the resulting strains were indeed predicted by the founding fathers and a wealth of historical and legal writing has dwelt upon them.[7] Such an exercise, however, should not detract from an examination of what has emerged as peculiarly Australian.

This chapter will examine four areas in which the Washminster mutation has replaced the Westminster system—the sovereignty of parliament, responsible government, representative government and bicameralism. It will note, however, that there have emerged basic elements of government which are uniquely Australian. These are products of the contradictions between elements of the original models, but perhaps not inevitable ones.

Parliamentary sovereignty

As has been noted, it is a commonplace amongst those who see Australia as manifesting a 'Washminster mutation' that the Australian Constitution was a deliberate combination of two sets of precepts which were, and are, inherently incompatible. In Britain, it is argued, parliament is legally sovereign in that it can amend, or even abolish, the constitution by simple legislative process. Its authority to do this stems from its responsibility to the electorate. In the United States, on the other hand, the sovereignty of Congress is limited by a written constitution which safeguards rights and interests against the possible tyranny of the majority. Australia, it is said, adopted the principle of responsible government from Britain but sacrificed the sovereignty of parliament in favour of the American principle of safeguarding interests. The result was theoretical confusion and practical inertia. There is a lot of truth in the above description, but it is much too crude.

To bring out the subtlety of the contradictions, let us start with a controversial observation. The American Constitution is older than the British Constitution. In essence the American Constitution was based upon the principle that individuals had fundamental rights with which the state could not interfere, and that democracy took as its starting point regional interests as well as individual citizens. In affirming these principles the American Constitution owed much to Locke and the theories of classical liberalism. The British Constitution was based on a much later set of principles and merely appeared older because it was unwritten and sanctified by historical myth. The British Constitution, which emerged in the nineteenth century, owed something to classical liberalism but derived much more from a combination of utilitarian liberalism and modern Burkean conservatism. As James put it:

> If it was Bentham's rather than Burke's conception of parliamentary sovereignty which became integrated into the standard nineteenth century interpretation of the British constitution, Burke's celebration of convention triumphed decisively over Bentham's ambition to suppress the common law and replace it with a fully codified system of statutes. It was in this way that the British were able to reconcile their conviction that their fundamental rights were secure with their assumption that the powers of parliament were unlimited.[8]

The contradiction inherent in the above core of the British Constitution was just as glaring as that between the so-called British Constitution and the American. Bentham could contemplate unlimited parliamentary sovereignty because parliament could pursue legal reform according to a scientific social calculus. Parliament had the power to legislate that black was white, but such would not be rational. Its sovereignty was ultimately limited by reason. Burke, on the other hand, was worried that uprooted rationalists might legislate that black was indeed white. He was concerned to see that the common law rendered such legislation ineffective, and that rationalist pretensions might be countered by an appeal to the Crown (Bagehot's 'magical' part of the Constitution). The Crown, of course, also had unlimited sovereignty but convention had rendered that unlimited sovereignty 'fictional'.

The inconsistency between an unlimited parliament and the persistence of common law and between that parliament and a Crown which also enjoyed unlimited sovereignty was welded together into a powerful legitimising ideology by Bagehot and those who came after him.[9] Perhaps the most eloquent statement of this ideology was made by Dicey who celebrated the unlimited power of parliament mitigated by convention.[10]. What was seldom mentioned, however, was that many of the so-called conventions were, like the English 'gentleman', of recent vintage. The British Constitution has, moreover, conveniently been inventing conventions ever since.

It is a commonplace, in courses on British constitutional law, that everyone starts by learning Dicey and then spends the rest of the time demonstrating how wrong he was. A major problem, it seems, is that no one can agree on what a convention actually is; there is no convention about what constitutes a convention. There is a mass of literature which talks about the differences between a practice, a convention, a tradition, a usage and so on. Such talk has clearly been going on since the time of Edmund Burke who managed to palm the Whig Settlement after 1688 off as the 'British tradition'. If a convention is a time-honoured usage, then one has to specify the length of time necessary for the honour to be bestowed; and if such is the definition how do conventions become established in the first place? One suspects that all that is meant by convention is a 'gentleman's agreement'. In the late nineteenth century there appeared to be sufficient numbers of gentlemen in power to constitute a quorum. There are now ladies and a whole lot of people who are not considered, should not be considered, do not consider themselves and do not want to be considered as gentlemen. Parliament is not like the Atheneum Club. One should surely not continue to refer to a definition of conventions which stemmed from the period of that club's heyday—the heyday of Empire.

One of the distinguishing features of the dominant ideology of late nineteenth century Britain was that the conduct of gentlemen should not be bound by written rules, whereas the relationship between interests should be governed by contract. Thus the Australian Constitution, which was born at that time, is more like a contract than a blueprint specifying how the government of Australia should act. The proverbial Martian political scientist, who knew nothing except its provisions, could get the impression that:

> the executive government is carried out by the Governor General personally, advised by a Federal Executive Council comprising ministers and others holding office at the Governor General's pleasure (SS, 61, 62, 64) (though without a Prime Minister who is nowhere mentioned); that Departments of State are staffed by officers appointed and dismissed by the Governor General in consultation with the Federal Executive Council (S 67); that the ministers put in charge of them need not be Members of Parliament (S 64) (provided they are changed every three months) and that Parliament has no ultimate role or authority in any of these matters.[11]

Such was never the intention, nor has ever been the practice, of government in Australia. The real Australian Constitution, like the British one, is unwritten and consists of a whole series of 'conventions' which range from the simple and uncontested to the mysterious and, at times, highly divisive. Though a body of statute law has developed which also refers to extra-constitutional roles such as that of Prime Minister (for example laws governing the establishment of an Ombudsman and Freedom of Information), the major limitations on the formal roles of parliament in Australia remain unwritten. As the 1983 Adelaide Constitutional Convention noted, a powerful case could be made for actually writing them down. In this day and age it is quite silly to refer to some mysterious historical social contract or to the 'magical' properties of the 'Queen in parliament'.

The exercise of transforming 'conventions' into statutes must alter fundamentally the nature of the written Constitution as a document which protects interests. After all, a major limitation on the powers of parliament should be the protection of rights. In popular usage, the terms rights and interests are often confused. In defining the term right (in a strong sense) Dworkin suggests 'if someone has a right to do something, then it is wrong for the government to deny it even though it would be in the general interest to do so';[12] this is a point which many utilitarians fail to appreciate. Rights, of necessity, impose limitations upon the actions of parliament and, thus, advocates of the nineteenth century 'Westminster myth' did not engage in human rights legislation. They seemed to prefer the old Burkean notion that historically specific rights ought to be safeguarded by time-honoured institutions. Chapter 6 will argue that a case may be made for an entrenched Australian Bill of Rights, but advocates of such a case must be quite clear that such a bill imposes limits on the sovereignty of parliament. This is precisely what the American Bill of Rights does. Two centuries ago such limitations were justified by appeal to a (Lockean) notion of natural law. Nowadays it is unfashionable to talk about 'natural law', it being more common to talk about an evolving set of conventions reflecting the principles upon which the social order is based. This is what Hayek does, though it is difficult to see how his 'higher law' is any different from the old natural law.[13] His Australian disciples, associated with the Centre for Independent Studies in New South Wales,[14] clearly opt for a version of natural law when faced with the contradiction between parliamentary sovereignty and constitutionalism. In Hayek's words:

> Although there is good reason for preferring a limited democractic government to a non-democratic one, I must confess to preferring non-democratic government under the law to unlimited (and therefore lawless) democratic government. Government under the law seems to me to be the higher value, which it was once hoped that democratic watch-dogs would preserve.[15]

Hayek's fears lead him to propose a very limited role for democracy. What passes for majority rule in countries like Australia are merely coalitions of minorities, united to seize control over the sovereign body and direct policy towards the satisfaction of their particular ends. Liberal constitutionalism, in Hayek's view, should prescribe the limits to that kind of democracy. Yet the kind of constitutional limitations on parliament prescribed by Hayek and his Australian disciples promise a society with which many people would be most uneasy. The rights which would be preserved are those which maximise the advantages of the strong in the competitive capitalist market. Other rights, such as the right to work, embodied in the Universal Declaration of Human Rights, would not be included because (in the capitalist system) they impose no corresponding duty on anyone to implement them. But why should there be symmetry between rights and duties? If, moreover, the introduction of such rights leads to changes in the prevailing economic system, then so be it. There is no doubt that human rights legislation will limit the formal powers of parliament, but this does not necessarily mean that democracy itself will be limited. The 'human rights' limitations imposed upon parliament as a sovereign body should not be abstracted from the outdated logic of an earlier capitalist system. On the contrary, they should be geared to developing the potentialities of citizens to act as creative and productive human beings—to an expansion of the capacities (power) of citizens as discussed in the preceding chapter.[16] Limitations on the formal mechanisms of democracy, through human rights legislation, might further institutions in which that potentiality may be fostered. This could then have an effect on the quality of the original representative forms. Democracy, thereby, may only be enhanced.

Understandably, though, the concerns of the founding fathers of the Australian Commonwealth focussed not on rights but interests. Their concern was the sheer mechanics of welding together the interests of separate colonies rather than the fine points of jurisprudence. The result was a federation with divided sovereignty. That federation, like all federations, was in Dicey's words to be weak, conservative (in a behavioural sense), rigid and legalistic.[17] The legalism was enhanced by the provision of a High Court which served as arbiter, and the rigidity was reinforced by a Senate with considerable powers deriving from the myth of its representation of States' rights. Though the unconstrained nature of the British Parliament was a myth, it was doubtless the case that the Australian Constitution imposed *legal* constraints on parliament far in excess of Britain. Furthermore, although the conventions celebrated in Britain were not all that time-honoured, the Australian conventions were always weaker—be they the provisions of the common law or the fictional nature of the 'unlimited' powers of the Crown. 1975 was to testify to that latter point in a very forceful manner. But the fact that the constitutional crisis of 1975 came as such a shock testifies to the force of the British Westminster myth. The powers of the Crown, it seems, are not, as was supposedly the case in the British myth, a matter of 'magic' but have legal constitutional clout.

If one probes the Westminster myth a little more deeply, one finds a whole lot of other problems underlying the 'magic' of the Crown. With qualifications, the executive authority of the Queen may be 'fictional' but the sovereignty of the Crown is invoked to justify many practices which hit at the core of parliamentary sovereignty. After England's constitutional crisis of the seventeenth century, many of the statutory powers of the monarch were removed; but what were not removed were certain monarchical powers embodied in the common law. One of these was the right of the monarch to withhold documentary material from the courts. In modern times, this doctrine of Crown privilege is exercised by an executive (the Cabinet) which can withhold any information it likes from the purview of parliament if the release of that information is not 'in the public interest'. That public interest is, of course, decided by the Crown, or in practice the Cabinet. To challenge the right of the Cabinet in this is an unconstitutional attack on one of the principal sources of sovereignty. To what extent is parliament sovereign if it is limited in its sources of information by another sovereign body? Hugh Emy has documented many contemporary examples in recent Australian history of Crown privilege being abused, and there is no need to repeat them here.[18] Suffice it to say that there is a pressing need to redefine what is meant by the Crown—if indeed such an institution is to be maintained at all. Whatever happens, there will always be a case for some privileged information and thus some limitations on parliamentary sovereignty. It should not, however, be beyond the wit of legislators to limit abuse.

Though the problem of Crown privilege is a problem no less in Britain than in Australia, the separation of power between Crown and parliament in Australia seems to have a peculiarly Australian flavour. The separation is much more marked (and potent) than in England and differs from the situation in the United States where the Constitution was designed to provide an elaborate system of checks and balances. Discussion of federalism in Chapter 6 will look further at the wider context of that separation.

The nature of the Australian party system

It has been argued above that the notion of parliamentary sovereignty enshrined in the Westminster myth was essentially the product of late nineteenth century Britain. It was internally confused and contradicted thinking on federal constitutionalism which derived from an earlier period. The Westminster myth, moreover, was elaborated at a time when modern party systems were only just beginning to form. The development of modern parties was to affect profoundly the way government was seen as responsible to the citizens and the way those citizens were represented. This chapter will go on to argue that in the twentieth century, ideas about responsible government and representation enshrined in the Westminster myth became increasingly divorced from the reality of party politics. But before doing that, it will digress at some length on the nature of the Australian party system.

Political parties may be, and have been, defined in a multitude of ways. Even a cursory examination of the literature will reveal a plethora of definitions, based on a number of different emphases— for example, on purpose, function, or type of organisation. Most common are definitions which centre on winning political power, and exercising it. Most modern parties have the winning of power as one of their explicit aims, but this seeking after power is not a sufficient definition. Many other organisations also seek to obtain and use power, in the public as well as private arenas.

A further problem arises when one asks on behalf of whom power is to be won and exercised. Chapter 2 argued that the correlation between class interests and the self-identification of the purposes of the major parties is now virtually non-existent. It remains true only of a few minor socialist and communist parties. Indeed it is a complaint of the Socialist Left of the ALP (especially in Victoria) that the Labor Party no longer defines its purpose in terms of class interests. Nor, one might add, does any major party nowadays define its purpose even in terms of a sectional or group interest. It has been noted that the DLP never developed into a Catholic party. The Country Party, moreover, in changing its name to the National Party, specifically repudiated the attribution by others of sectional interest. There are a few small parties which do define themselves according to sectional interest. These are seen usually as hardly more than pressure groups. But one should note that the most successful of these pressure group-type parties, the Nuclear Disarmament Party, very clearly defines its interest as national, if not international.

But, one might legitimately ask, of what value is a definition in terms of self-proclaimed purpose? One has to look at functions. As the preceding chapter indicated, this is to plunge into very muddy theoretical waters. Functions only have meaning in terms of a wider whole. How may one conceive the wider whole? One way to define the whole is in terms of political economy. Thus, a utilitarian liberal might argue that political parties perform the function of articulating or aggregating interests on the basis of different conceptions of (and sometimes in direct opposition to) optimal social utility. A social liberal might argue the same way but would replace the notion of optimal social utility by 'the common good'. Some Marxists, on the other hand, argue that political parties perform the function of representing different classes or fractions of capital (for example industrial interests as opposed to mining interests) and of diverting the attention of the voter from considering the interests of capital or the working class as a whole.

An example here would help. As has been noted, the National Party defines its purpose as 'national'. A liberal utilitarian critic, however, might argue that its function is to serve the interests of miners and large farmers against the greatest good of the greatest number. A utilitarian supporter, however, could argue that the function of the National Party is to secure long-term optimal social utility by promoting those parts of the economy which are ultimately the most productive. Thus, a utilitarian social scientist, with pretensions to 'value freedom', could maintain that the functions of the National Party differ from those of other parties due to a different calculation of what Bentham referred to as the time span according to which the effects of certain policies might be felt. A social liberal, however, would probably be less magnanimous. Such a person, it will be remembered, sees the purpose of politics as developing the potentiality of each citizen to realise the common good. Manifestly, a party which serves the interest of a minority is not doing and can never do this even if such a party ultimately provides the greatest material good for the greatest number. A Marxist might be even more critical; the function of the National Party is simply to serve the interests of two fractions of capital (foreign-oriented mining companies and large rural interests) and to obscure the real class struggle, (between capital and labour) by focussing attention on the contradiction between mining plus rural capital on the one hand, and industrial capital on the other. He or she might note, however, that the salience of this contradiction, internal to capital, does allow for a relative degree of autonomy to be exercised by the state. It is probably only the right-wing populist who has no problems in locating the functions of the National Party in the Australian economy. Since, to the right-wing populist, the farming and mining sectors are ultimately the producers of all value and most virtue, it stands to reason that what is good for them is good for Australia, and only a nit-picking academic or a divisive politician would attempt to separate them from other sectors of the economy. This last view is precisely that of the National Party itself.

A definition of the National Party in terms of function in the political economy is much easier to achieve than a similar definition of the ALP, the Liberal Party or the Australian Democrats. Indeed one must be extremely sceptical about attempts to construct such definitions. All that would probably be achieved is the statement that the major political parties function to maintain the capitalist system. Though this would not satisfy red-necked ideologues who are convinced the ALP is a revolutionary party, it is academically so uncontentious as to be trivial.

Rather than focussing on political economy, most mainstream political scientists in Australia offer a functional definition of party in terms of elections. The electoral system is the wider whole against which functions are assessed. Thus, following Sartori:

> A party is any political group identified by an official label that presents at elections, and is capable of placing through elections (free or non-free), candidates for public office.[19]

This definition will, of course, exclude a few groups which identify themselves as political parties (including the CPA [ML] which sees itself as *the* Party). It will tend also to arrange parties according to a hierarchy of electoral importance. Thus, the Liberal Party of Australia and the ALP have clear governing potential—the expectation of winning sufficient seats to form government—and stand at the apex of the hierarchy. But how does one assess the electoral importance of other parties of which the governing potential is not so clear? To illustrate the problem let us compare the National Party, the Australian Democrat Party and the Democratic Labor Party.

The definition from Sartori has implications for party organisation. A party must be organised in such a way so as effectively to contest elections. Thus, organisational considerations would suggest that parties with better national organisation should be considered as playing a more important role in national elections. Such a conclusion is questionable. The National Party lacks an effective national organisation. It is important as an electoral and parliamentary force in only two States, is viable in only four States and does not even exist in Tasmania. Its electoral (rather than rhetorical) appeal is to a particular electorate and it draws most of its support from rural localities. Thus, despite the efforts of Premier Bjelke-Petersen to propel the Queensland party away from its geographic sectionalism, the party elsewhere is still regarded nationally as a 'quasi-party', a 'half-party' or even as the rural wing of the Liberal Party. Such a view would have shocked its populist founders and does annoy their right-wing populist successors in Queensland, but surely it is at least partially justified. From an organisational point of view the National Party is not very significant nationally, but one could argue that electorally at that level it is very significant. Similarly the Democratic

Labor Party, from its foundation in 1955, was confined to Victoria and Queensland, and after 1974 to Victoria. Nevertheless, until the early 1970s, it might be argued that the DLP had an appreciable effect on national elections. The Australian Democrats, on the other hand, have a very effective national organisation and have contested almost all seats in all elections since their formation. But is that party more effective electorally?

To assess the electoral significance of the National Party, the DLP and the Australian Democrats, one has to look further than organisation and consider coalition potential. This is the basis of the National Party's claim to national relevance. The Liberal Party has formed a government following 11 of the 17 general elections between 1946 and 1984 and, in all but two (1975 and 1977), Country Party numbers were necessary to produce a majority in the House of Representatives. In all but two elections, the Country Party was apparently able to determine which major party would form the national government. But did it have any real power behind its demands for concessions in return for support? Not since pre-war days has any section of the Country Party allied itself with Labor (the very temporary alliance in Victoria was atypical). This is because the Country Party, of the five parties, is the most ideologically integrated and at its core are symbols most hostile to the cause of organised labour. Despite all the claims about the opportunist perfidy of various individual leaders of the National Party, it remains more of a party of virtue than either the ALP or the Liberals. People may not like the type of virtue it manifests and may remark on the apparent lack of congruence between its profession of virtue and the personal probity of various leaders. It is virtuous nonetheless! Following various elections, purely instrumental concerns could *in theory* have dictated an alliance with Liberal *or* Labor to form a government. But such alliances would have destroyed the Country Party's electoral credibility which depends on the profession of virtue. In reality the Country Party had no choice. There was never any doubt as to where the Country Party numbers would go. The potential of the Country Party to influence the relationship between other parties by offering support in return for concessions was not a viable option. At a federal level the National Party needs the Liberal Party more than the Liberal Party needs its minority partner. In terms of coalition potential, the National Party must rank fairly low, a point which raises a range of questions as to why the Liberal Party dog, so often, has allowed itself to be wagged by its Country Party tail.

The same kind of argument can be advanced for the DLP. That party was also ideologically relatively well-integrated. Indeed its very *raison d'être* was to keep the ALP, with its alleged 'Communist taint', permanently out of office. Its electoral success was in the Senate from 1955–74. It never came near to success in the House of Representatives nor in the States (apart from an 'election by accident' of one member to the New South Wales House of Assembly in 1974 when the Liberal Minister of Health forgot to nominate). At no time, however, could there have been any possibility of DLP senators trading support for the ALP in return for concessions. The DLP had no coalition potential. When the Whitlam Government was elected in 1972 and the Party had manifestly failed in its primary objective, it began to fall to pieces.

What the DLP claimed to be able to do was to influence the results of elections, even to decide who governed, by means of its preferences. It was able to threaten the Liberal Country Party Coalition, several times by arguing that unless certain actions were taken (such as the removal of Gordon Freeth from the portfolio of Defence following his statement that Russian fishing boats in the Indian Ocean were not a threat to Australia's security) or certain policies were emphasised, preferences would not be directed to the Coalition. While the DLP voters did follow the 'how to vote' card almost to a person, the threat of 'blackmail' was an empty one; if the Coalition had called the bluff of the DLP, then it could *not* have given its preferences to Labor. In real terms the DLP, like the National Party, was able to appear to be powerful, and exercise power, only because the Liberal Party allowed it to do so!

The Australian Democrats present a very different picture, which allows two quite different assessments of their advent into the party system. Like the British Social Democrats, the Australian Democrats are almost totally lacking in any explicit ideological integration, and express only one 'total-commitment' policy—anti-uranium. They also lack the traditional patron-client type of integration characteristic of ALP 'machines' or Liberal Party 'old boy' networks. Though there is a national organisation, it can not be compared with the quasi 'democratic centralism' of the ALP. What seems to hold the party together is a simple populist distaste for politics (in the old pejorative sense noted in Chapter 2) and a populist appeal to the common sense virtue of the suburban voter without any of the other elements of the traditional populist mood (whether left or right). At first sight it would seem that the appeal of *idéologie sans doctrines* (to coin a phrase) would be only short-lived. But one can not be so sure. What may be said, however, is that the Democrats are coming to play a quite significant electoral role precisely because they are not ideologically constrained.

Formed in 1977, the Australian Democrat Party has contested four national elections and the stability of its electoral support is obviously still to be tested. In 1977, the Democrats won 9.4% of the votes for the House of Representatives and 11.1% for the Senate; in 1980, 6.6% and 9.3%; and in 1983, 5.0% and 9.6% respectively. In 1983, the Democrats held one seat in the Tasmanian lower house, two seats in the ACT Assembly, and two seats and the balance of power in the South Australian Legislative Council. Most important, following the 1984 national elections, the party holds seven seats and the balance of power in the Senate. All of its seats have been won under a system of proportional representation.

What then is the nature of the electoral role of the Australian Democrats? One can not speak of coalition potential since the party explicitly rejects any suggestion of coalition with any other party. The Democrats have also explicitly rejected the use of preferences as a means of political pressure, although this has been a matter of debate especially in the Victorian branch. A party needs to achieve two things to utilise preferences as a 'blackmail' potential. It must win a sufficient proportion of first preference votes to affect results in marginal seats—to have the numerical potential to decide which major party will win. The second condition is a guarantee that a substantial majority of second preferences goes to the party of its choice. Given the first condition, the Democrats have explicitly stated that they would not attempt to achieve the second. In national and state contests, the Democrats issue a 'double sided' 'how to vote' card, indicating a second preference for the ALP on one side and for non-Labor on the other, leaving the choices of preference allocation to the individual voter. Such a move is probably quite shrewd when one considers that the Democrats draw support from many people not previously associated with any political party and whose party identification is weak. Any attempt to direct preferences would probably alienate potential supporters. As it is, the above exercise of 'anti-political' politics reinforces the ideological commitment to *idéologie sans doctrines*. The electoral role of the Democrats, therefore, is to make political capital out of anti-politics. It tries to alter the direction of party competition through its electoral strength and to erode the support of other parties. At a national level its members in the Senate have repudiated a claim to 'coalition potential' but not to the exercise of a balance of power, though typically this has been referred to as 'the balance of reason'; how ideologically anti-ideological can one get? When all is said and done, though, an important element of the old idea of 'coalition potential' is retained—support in return for concessions. On this score the Australian Democrat Party looks like being much more effective than the National Party or the DLP. A new element is present in Australian politics, and the party system against which any functional definition of party must be made itself requires reformulation.

Before the advent of the Democrats one could define the Australian party system simply as an electoral maximising system, a network of interaction in which political groups identified by official labels competed with each other for votes in order to maximise their governing potential. If one takes the Democrats at face value, then the party system which may be emerging is a network in which some parties compete for votes to maximise their governing potential, whilst at least one other competes for votes, not to maximise its own governing potential, but in order to steer policy-makers in a particular direction. Here is the paradox for the Democrats; if they begin to specify their preferred direction of policy, they lose their appeal as the party of *idéologie sans doctrines*. How long, one might ask, will voters continue to take the Democrats on trust? Is the firm Democrat policy on uranium the first chink in its electoral armour?

To assess the role of the Democrats to some degree requires a crystal ball. For example, the decline in its electoral support since 1977 looks very much like the slow but steady decline of the DLP. But there are significant differences. One reason for the decline of the DLP was that it took sides in the party system, had a negative *raison d'être* from its beginning and did not look like capturing the Catholic vote. It was wiped out in the 1974 double dissolution—squeezed out by a governing party concentration. The Australian Democrats not only survived the 1983 double dissolution, but increased their control of the Senate to a complete balance of power, and hence achieved a springboard for publicity—a factor which is invaluable for a minor party.

But another assessment is possible. It can be argued that the advent of the Democrats came at a time when the centripetal drive of the Australian party system had been reversed—at least for the Liberal Party. As Malcolm Fraser took the rhetoric (if not the practice) of the Liberals to the right, then a 'partial vacuum' was left at the centre. The Democrats emerged within this space, and have been able to win support only so long as the space exists. Hence, if its leadership draws the Liberal Party back to the moderate (pragmatic) centre or towards more social liberal policies, the Democrats would be in danger of being squeezed out.

In 1984, however, the dynamics of the party system offered increasing potential for the Democrats. The National Labor Conference saw the combination of Hawke pragmatism and the new Centre-Left faction elevate electoral realism as the battle pennant of the party. At the same time, the Liberal Party continued to flounder in search of an identity, and showed unequivocal signs of moving to the right. The party took up issues of immigration (the 'Asianisation of Australia') and opposition to Aboriginal land rights, and leader Andrew Peacock gave the impression that he saw the way back to government through a greater emphasis on classical rather than social liberal policies; he was careful, however, to modify this emphasis prior to the 1984 election.

The discussion so far has considered two conceptions of the wider whole against which party functions may be defined, the political economy and the electoral system. A more comprehensive approach, which embraces the above two, is to define party in terms of the structure of social conflict (whether of political economic origin or not). Thus, for Lowi, 'party in a democracy institutionalizes, channels and socialises conflict over the control of the regime'.[20] A political party, therefore, is an institution concerned with legitimate social control. As MacPherson sees it, the modern party system has assuaged the fears of John Stuart Mill about the power of 'the most numerous classes'.[21] Here one is led to the question; control in the interest of whom? This chapter, however, is not the place to repeat the analysis in Chapter 3 of the relative claims of those who believe that Australia is dominated by a ruling class, an Establishment, a power elite or is simple 'pluralist'. The more modest aim is simply to show that Australian political parties generally seek to control conflict *to serve their own interests*. In this they are like most political parties in most countries. What is distinctive about the Australian situation is the intensity and dominance of political parties in almost all political processes. Secondly, there are few Western polities in which parties are so blatantly self-serving and so seemingly contemptuous of the intelligence of those upon whose votes they depend. Thirdly, it will be argued, this contempt is facilitated by an unwillingness on the part of any significant section of their leadership to propose legal constraints on party activity.

Unlike America, where parties in national and state politics are surrounded, defined and, to varying degrees, controlled by laws, Australian parties conduct their activities almost outside the legal system. Until 1977 the very existence of political parties was not even recognised in the Constitution.

The above will be demonstrated by an analysis of two functions which supposedly legitimise the way conflict over the regime is controlled. These functions, which parties are supposed to exercise, are first to ensure that government is *responsible* to those who elected it and second to facilitate the *representation* of citizens in the government of the country.

Responsible government

Celebrating the Westminster ideology in 1867, Bagehot identified cabinet government as a 'buckle' or a 'hyphen' between the executive and legislative powers.[22] The existence of this buckle is said to be a distinguishing characteristic of the Westminster as opposed to the presidential system. The key convention upon which it rests is the notion of ministerial responsibility to parliament. In Parker's words, 'ministerial responsibility is a core component of the Westminster system'. It is 'essentially an internal relationship between ministers and their fellow members *in parliament*'[23]. At a *technical* level, then, 'ministerial responsibility' means that the government and its members hold office on the basis of a majority in parliament, a majority which can be tested by a vote in the parliament. Parker expands on this *technical* level:

> Ministers must have a seat in parliament. Each has final executive authority over the parts of the administration entrusted to him by the chief minister or by statute—subject always to the restraints of other statutes and common law. The chief minister is chosen and, like all ministers, appointed by the titular chief executive (sovereign or governor)—but that choice must be based on the politician's capacity to muster a majority in the ('popular' house of the) legislature. The chief minister nominates for appointment all other ministers and can effectively recommend their dismissal. The ministry hold office only while they retain majority support in the legislature—in its popular chamber if there are two. 'Support' means willingness to vote for motions favoured by or favourable to the ministers, and against motions adverse to them. Majority support may be eroded by some members changing their attitude to the ministry, or by a change in the membership of parliament of which the most important cause is a parliamentary election. On losing majority support on a significant motion (providing the ministry judges it significant enough), the chief minister either hands in the resignations of his ministry or recommends a dissolution and general election (which the chief executive may refuse if he can install an alternative leader able to muster a legislative majority among the current membership). The chief minister can recommend a general election at any time within the maximum term of the legislature (or its popular house) whether he has lost the majority or not—and if he has a majority his advice is likely in most circumstances to be accepted.[24]

These technical rules are unarguable, as is Parker's conclusion that:

> There is no doubt that, so far as they go, the Westminster rules in this technical sense were adopted in every detail, were practised and are practised in every parliamentary government in Australia.[25]

But the point is that the above rules are simply *technical*. They mean little unless one considers that the Australian polity is one based upon *party* government which need not necessarily be responsible. Party government subjugates parliament and government to party. It severely qualifies much of the Westminster myth if not the reality of the British prototype. Despite the fact that throughout the nineteenth century many British writers (including Bagehot) found the doctrine of ministerial responsibility wanting and despite the fact that a majority of Australia's founding fathers explicitly avoided including clauses about responsibility into the Constitution,[26] the key elements of the Westminster doctrine of responsibility were celebrated throughout the twentieth century. Government was to be responsible to parliament and individual members of government (the ministers) were individually responsible to parliament. Furthermore, parliament collectively and its members individually were responsible to the electorate.

Neither of the first two senses of responsible government, cabinet or ministerial, applies in Australia. Cabinet is not responsible to parliament. It responds to the caucus, to the party and, in periodic elections, to the people. In the sense of holding government responsible for its actions, parliament in Australia is impotent. It is the party, not parliament, which decides on the role, actions and policies of the government. In the same manner, individual ministers are responsible not to parliament but to the party in parliament, and it is up to the party—caucus, Cabinet or leader—to pass judgement and apply sanctions. In Australia, the roles and functions of government and party have become one, with a consequent decline if not disappearance of responsibility in government.

Parties in government have asserted that responsibility has not been eroded but merely transferred to the electorate. This argument, based on a concept of party responsibility, accepts not only as inevitable but regards as of positive value the concentration of party authority over all levels of government and parliament, and holds that the party, and hence the government, is accountable to and responsible to the voters. There is, therefore, a conjunction of party authority, government and party responsibility. Behind such a claim lies a false assumption central to the Westminster myth. It is taken as axiomatic that the electorate is informed, aware, rational, open-minded, discussive, involved, motivated and judgemental. Though most people know that assumption to be false, to question it in practical politics leads to the charge of undemocratic elitism. Political science, therefore, which does not make such an assumption, is not allowed to intrude into the celebration of party-led democracy. But the problem is more serious than that! Party leaders themselves are well-aware that the rational-judgemental electorate is a myth and often employ advertising agencies which operate on very different principles. The result is sheer hypocrisy! The voters, by and large, may not engage in rational calculation of the pros and cons of party policies but, as Chapter 3 underlined, they are not stupid. It is surely apparent to large numbers of people that politicians' appeal to a judgemental electorate is in violent contradiction to parties manipulating the 'political consumer' in the manner of sellers of soap powder. In such a situation why should the electorate be rational and judgemental? To say that government is responsible to the people through the mechanism of the party is like saying that breakfast cereal manufacturers are responsible to the consumers through the mechanism of advertising agencies.

Confronting the above criticisms, party activists often claim that there is not really a contradiction between their belief in a rationally-activist electorate and their treatment of that electorate as passive and rather unintelligent consumers of political packages. The electorate as a whole, they claim, is not unintelligently protean but the swinging voter is. Electoral appeal must be made to the swinging voter; between elections parties may act more responsibly. Elections, however, occur not every three years but seemingly, in one place or another, every year. Parties are thus geared to permanent electoral politics and a permanent campaign dictated by the perceived orientation of people they despise.

Take, for example, the debates in late 1982 about a wages pause. Whatever the rights and wrongs of the issue, there was a considerable body of opinion in the ALP which was aware of the arguments that such a policy might be expected to widen the gap between those high wage earners in receipt of fringe benefits and those who were not, and that the policy might lead to a further weakening of effective demand and more unemployment. It was felt, however, that marginal voters might be impressed by 'public-service bashing' and Labor activists were urged to moderate their criticisms. Meanwhile trade unions did not feel so constrained. This produced the appearance of schizophrenia in the union activist who was also an ALP activist and as such did not enhance public confidence. In situations like that, why should voters not remain cynically responsive rather than become rational activists? The root of the problem is the same as that diagnosed in Britain by the Webbs over sixty years ago—the total inability of any major party either to educate the public or to ascertain whether the swinging vote might actually be a rational response to the venality of leaders.

In sum, therefore, governments and oppositions are not responsible to the electorate through the medium of party. Rather governments and oppositions are responsive to what the party believes to be the characteristics of the swinging voter, or worse, are cynical manipulators of consumer demand. That they have increasingly come to perform the latter role has much to do with the part the media plays in political communication. Until its recent abolition, political commentators were constantly critical of legislation demanding radio and television black-out before elections. One astute critic remarked, however, that a case might be made for such a black-out on the grounds that, at least in part of the media prior to elections, there was some relief from an advertising campaign which insulted people's intelligence.[27] Though not wishing to support that argument, the point is well taken.

A media black-out ought to have been done away with because surely any information is better than none; but how is the information to be provided which might make a government more responsible to the people? Long ago, broadcasting parliament, advocated by Scullin and implemented by the Chifley Government, was aimed to short-circuit the misleading rubbish which passed for political information. Recently the televising of parliament was advocated by the then Speaker, Sir Billy Snedden.[28] Sir Billy was apparently reasonably satisfied with the relatively-long experience with radio-broadcasting. Broadcasting was apparently necessary because 'it is unreal to think that people read the whole of *Hansard* each day'[29]—a classic understatement if there ever was one. He claimed, moreover, that broadcasts of parliament were listened to by a surprisingly large audience. Original fears that the broadcasting of parliament would lead to grandstanding and the further moulding of parliament into the desired party image, he maintained, were grossly exaggerated. If the televising of parliament comes, he felt, the viewer-citizens will not mistake grandstanding for statesmanship any more than they mistake pretty faces for true acting talent.

Now moves are being made to televise parliament, one must be somewhat less sanguine than Sir Billy. One wonders what a large listening audience means and whether broadcasting of parliament is often any more than sonic wallpaper. And just what message is derived from listening to a parliamentary debate? Is the citizen conscious of the subtlety of debate or just responsive to the constant reiteration of party rhetoric? Could the citizen just be tired of what often appears to be procedural mumbo-jumbo, interspersed with questions and statements to the advantage of party, but actually outside the purview and control of the national parliament? Should, for example, the Senate be used to raise questions about the alleged broken electoral promises of a *State* government?

Perhaps the most one may hope for, in the present circumstances, is that the televising of parliament might help to expose the irrelevance of parliament in making a government responsible to the people. It might reinforce the view that the party is the mechanism which connects government and citizen and that connection is not primarily one of responsibility. At worst it might reinforce the understandable apathy of the electorate. The televising of the Vietnam War had two effects. Amongst some people, it reduced a human tragedy to the level of another *Gunsmoke*. Amongst others, it produced real concern because real people were being killed. The latter view was eventually to be the most important; but it was so because the Vietnam War *was* important in ordinary people's lives. One wonders whether the televising of parliament will have the same effect. Parliament is not important in ordinary people's lives. It might be argued that the *absence* of parliamentary checks might be, but that is a message which television is unlikely to convey. What is needed are parties versed in 'two-step' theories of communication which demand that media messages be reinforced by personal communication. It needs parties committed to public education. But where are they?

This chapter has argued that political parties have inhibited the responsibility of government to citizens. A different kind of political party is required—one committed more to the values of popular participation. Such a party need not be weaker than existing parties. Indeed in some respects it must be stronger. This is particularly the case in the relationship between party, government and bureaucracy as has been argued by Richard Rose in Britain.[30] Though an independent and neutral civil service could not be claimed to have developed in Britain until the 1920s,[31] the idea of a public service which simply executes the details of an Act of Parliament had been enshrined as part of the earlier Westminster myth. But in Australia, as elsewhere, in recent years the public service has increasingly taken, or been given, a legislative role in the political process. As the occurrence of delegated legislation burgeoned, so the power of the public service to make laws rather than simply to administer them also developed, to the point where parliament could no longer keep a check on the process. The style and procedures of parliament today do not allow for reasoned consideration of regulations. Hence, so long as party controls government, and so long as it is party policy which directs government activities, then there should be some means whereby party policy will be reflected in delegated legislation. As it was, the Whitlam administration of the early 1970s suspected the legislative activities of its public servants who followed policies and procedures worked out in the preceding 23 years of Liberal Country Party government.

In case the above might be seen to contradict the earlier argument about parties, let us restate the argument. Since government is not responsible to the people through parliament, it may be made more responsible through newly constructed parties which must both respond to and educate people in political participation. If this is achieved, a strengthened role for political parties might be envisaged in acting as a check on legislation delegated to the public service. Parliament could then become the arena in which that function is assessed. The best mechanism whereby this could be achieved is an extension of the system of review committees.

The development of a committee style of legislative procedure in the Senate owed much to Labor Senator Lionel Murphy, who became opposition leader in the Senate in 1967 and who was determined that the Senate should be more important and should be seen to be more important. Both houses individually, and jointly on occasions, had utilised a series of committees of inquiry into specific matters since Federation; these were select committees appointed on an *ad hoc* basis for specific purposes. In combination with Clerk of the Senate, Odgers, a proposal was eventually made and accepted by the Senate for a new series of *standing* (permanent) committees with wide and significant terms of reference.

The need for such committees was obvious. The volume and complexity of legislation coming into parliament is increasing all the time. No member of parliament can claim to be an expert on all but a few topics. Yet the current system in the House of Representatives requires debate and legislative activity to be undertaken by all members. Clearly all should have an equal right to participate in debates but it is bizarre to assume that all are experts. A meeting of a full house, moreover, does not lend itself to an investigatory and scrutinising role. This is especially the case when the government uses late night sittings, conducts legislation by exhaustion or uses the guillotine. Such was clearly recognised by the official handbook of the House of Representatives:

> The principal purpose of parliamentary committees is to perform functions for which the houses themselves are not well fitted to perform, that is, finding out the facts of a case, examining witnesses, sifting evidence, and drawing up reasoned conclusions.[32]

The establishment of committees did much to revitalise the Senate as a house of review and to provide Senators with a potential for great political and legislative authority. The Senate now has a number of permanent committees which carry out important activities in audit areas. They undertake investigations and analyses of government financial proposals and scrutinise the details of supply and budget bills. They enquire, moreover, into public accounts and delegated legislation.

Such a system clearly has a great potential to revive the institution of parliament and to restore some elements of the notion that parliament performs a function in making government responsible to the people. It can, moreover, make the government more accountable in a way that the opposition is unable to do in the environment of party discipline in both houses. Nevertheless, the further development of the committee system has been insufficiently encouraged by either major party in government and the introduction of such committees into the House of Representatives has been lukewarm at best. Commenting on the failure of the House of Representatives to follow the example of the Senate in establishing a committee system, one member noted:

> Governments do not want them. The aim of a government is always to have its legislation passed with a minimum of questioning and bother, and committees would undoubtedly cause both.[33]

What exists at the moment is a hodge-podge of committees with overlapping functions, and attempts to rationalise the structure and make committee surveillance more efficient have been resisted. Committees have been hampered by executive control of information, executive control of the staff available, and executive control of travel funds necessary to gain information. The executive, moreover, has been unwilling to submit proposed legislation for scrutiny, and has been tardy in accepting (or even noticing) advice. There is no way committees may force governments to take note of their reports. Perhaps it is precisely *because* the committee system has such potential to restore parliamentary responsibility that it has been resisted by all governments.

This is a point of which the media seem blissfully unaware. The media, after all, are geared to sensation and conflict; and conflict typically manifests itself in the chambers and not in the committees. By focussing on sensational chamber confrontation, therefore, the media fail to contribute to processes which might make parliament more responsible. Indeed, because of their focus, the media abets executive irresponsibility. It should be stressed, however, that though committees might weaken party control over parliament, they do provide a means whereby party control over the public service might be enhanced. Above all they provide a means whereby members of parliament might learn a little about the mechanisms of bureaucracy; they offset the undemocratic nature of bureaucratic rule, fears about which have beset social scientists at least since Max Weber. Though the provision of official information might be restricted, there is much information outside the public service which is of better quality and which is capable of producing a much wider range of policy alternatives than seems to exist at present.[34]

Though party fears about a loss of control constitute a major factor in inhibiting the role of the committee system, one must also lay blame on the stubborn and persistent belief in that crucial element of the Westminster myth—the neutrality of the public service. The persistence of that myth no doubt explains why the use of party appointees is not more widespread at senior levels in the public service. If the role of the public service is to offer options which are at least somewhat near the objectives and overall programmes of the governing party, then party personnel should be located amongst the advisory personnel. Such a process has occurred in some of the appointments of departmental heads in the past decade. It could be formalised by means of contract appointments for the term of a party in government. Such is a matter under serious consideration by the Hawke Government. A quasi-presidential cabinet system would allow policy-making to be openly a matter of party, but might retain the principle of lower-level administration by a career bureaucracy. By such changes, the Australian political system could give formal recognition to the importance of the public service in government and to the role of the party in policy-making and administration in the public service. By such changes, public servants 'might improve their ability to meet existing role expectations', and, by establishing this ability and awareness, increase their 'political contribution to government'.[35] Central to the argument here, moreover, is that an open denial of the 'neutral' role of the public service in policy-making would remove the ideological blinkers imposed by the Westminster myth upon those committees charged with scrutinising the activities of the public service.

The argument should once again be underlined. There is no neutrality in policy-making; and for that reason policy-makers must be responsible to the people by some mechanism or other. This applies to the public service and, as noted earlier, also to that part of the Constitution which Bagehot considered to be simply 'magical'. In so far as the Governor General has potential policy-making power over a wide range of areas, he must be made responsible by constitutional *legislation* rather than the mere recording of conventions. The Westminster myth must not stand in the way of action on that score.

Representative government

Government, it has been argued, is responsible to the people only in the limited sense of through political parties. Policy-makers of the public service, moreover, are responsible to no-one and may only be made responsible to the people through party appointees scrutinised by parliament. Likewise the 'magical' part of the Australian Constitution masks the responsibility of the chief executive to no-one—unless one resurrects a Burkean social-contract between the living, the dead and the yet to be born, which in Australia (let alone England) seems antediluvian. Much of government, then, is irresponsible. But is it representative?

To begin to answer that question, one has to look at the representative function of members of parliament from whom government is drawn. What exactly do members of parliament represent? Conventionally three models are put forward.

The first of these is the trustee model deriving from Edmund Burke's arguments with his constituents at Bristol. Trustees are authorised by a particular constituency but do not represent the actual constituents. Trustees represent the historical continuity of the social whole; this is, in fact, like the claim for the Governor General—Burke's mystical covenant between the living, the dead and the yet to be born. Authorised because of their character, trustees may listen to the arguments of parties, pressure groups and their own constituents, but in the final analysis will carry out the trust in terms of an independent judgement of the historically determined national good. The task of the constituents is merely to evaluate the performance of that role.

The second model is that of the delegate who is mandated by constituents and is bound by the majority will of the constituents. Delegates are required to subordinate their own views, their own consciences and the will of the party which helped them get elected to that concern. The delegate differs from the third type—the partisan who, though listening to the arguments from pressure groups and constituents and expressing his or her views within the party room, is bound by the party line. As will be clear from the above discussion of responsibility, parliamentary representation in Australia is of the partisan type.

A minimum requirement for political parties to promote the representation of the will of individual citizens, one might suppose, would be a set of norms, conventions or laws independent of party control. In Australia, on the contrary, the content and the processes of political representation have not only been decided on by the political parties themselves but have been formulated in such a way as to serve the interest of those parties. Parties in Australia dominate totally the components of political representation, electoral choice, the competition for office or power, the recruitment for leadership, the mobilisation of opinion and the redress of political grievances.

The machinery by which parliaments are elected, including electoral boundaries and the voting systems adopted, were almost entirely the result of parties in power stacking the game in their own interests. It was perhaps the case that the motivation of various parties in the past stemmed from ideological preferences. Thus, a weighting in favour of rural areas might be justified on the classical liberal grounds of productivity or the populist claim to virtue. Similarly, the demand for proportional representation might be advanced on utilitarian principles. Nevertheless, when all is said and done, political parties have consistently advocated the electoral system which would maximise their own electoral advantage. Though there is legislation governing the procedure of elections, that legislation has nothing to say about matters such as misleading political advertising. Such was the opinion of the High Court which was asked to comment on the matter in 1980. In response, the Liberal Government noted that 'nothing can be done, nothing should be done, nothing will be done'.

The Hawke Government's 1983 Bill, incorporating major changes to the Electoral Act, included the first ever mention of this area with the clause:

> 161(1) A person shall not, during the relevant period in relation to an election under this Act, print, publish, or distribute or cause, permit or authorize to be printed, published or distributed, any matter or thing *that is likely to mislead or deceive an elector* in relation to the casting of his vote (emphasis added).

The penalty was set at $1000 or six months' imprisonment for an individual, or $5000 for a 'body corporate'. Any such proposal was a welcome innovation, despite the problems for the legal system; what, for example, is 'deception', and how could it be proved? But such questions could be answered by case law.

This clause, and any reference to misleading electoral advertisements, was removed from the Act in the last days of the pre-election parliament. In October 1984, the Labor, Liberal and National Parties in the Senate combined to delete S161 from the Act. The Australian Democrats voted for its retention, arguing that to delete it provided a 'license to lie'. The other parties argued that the clause was insufficient, both in definition and in penalty, and promised a new 'electoral consumer protection' Act after the election.

The field, therefore, remains open, untrammelled by any legal restraints, for any party in any election to use almost any method of propaganda it wishes, regardless of truth. As Chapter 2 observed, such a situation stands in striking contrast to the commercial sphere which is bound by principles of 'fair trading', trade practices and consumer protection acts. The implications for representation are quite profound. A political party may distort any inputs it gets from citizens at any level and can make fraudulent claims about the interests it articulates. In short, it can lie through its teeth. Can there be adequate representation without moderately reliable information?

Given the lack of any external control over the relationship between political parties and the system of representation, how do individual parties see that relationship? Part I of this book argued that the influence of Burkean conservatism on Australian political ideology was very slight. But that is not to say that Burke has not been pressed into the service of the Liberal Party. In its propaganda, that party claims that its members in parliament are trustees of the national good rather than the representatives of sectional interests; as such they are 'the only truly national party'. The Liberal members of parliament are not 'delegates' bound by any 'pledge'. They are supposed to be Burkean representatives who were chosen because of their qualities rather than their effectiveness as channels of communication between leaders and led. One wonders, however, whether Burke, who was often a powerful dissenter on conservative principles, would recognise the virtual absence of dissent amongst Liberal members in debate. Of course, it might be argued that the proper place for members' dissent is in the party room rather than on the floor of the House; but that is not a Burkean principle; it is more like a species of 'democratic centralism' which allows for a wide-spread canvassing of opinions before a decision is made but absolute conformity to the party line before battle is joined. In this respect, the ALP is not more Leninist than the Liberal Party; it is simply more explicit in its party rules and, in adopting a collectivist rather than an individualist conception of representation, a little more honest.

The fault of democratic centralism, it may be argued, lies not in the requirement for discipline in debates over vital issues but in that most issues become seen as vital issues. Thus moral issues, over which a free vote might be exercised, are frequently less the result of a commitment to freedom of moral conscience than a confession of failure of party whips to get the numbers, or the reluctance of a party to reveal its policy cleavages. Discipline surely may only be a means to an end. When it becomes an end in itself, a party becomes no more than a secular church. It is not always clear, in the Australian context, whether the exercise of discipline is not in the interests of subordinating the membership to the leadership, choking off challenges to that leadership and programming time in such a way as to preclude the articulation of subversive thoughts, rather than in the interest of carrying through vital issues deriving from a coherent vision of a better life. One may only reiterate: Liberal and National Party members are neither trustees, nor delegates from their electorates. Like Labor members, first and foremost they are partisans. Clark ignores the odd non-Labor rebel but he is close to the mark:

> No member of Parliament, or Parliamentary candidate, of any Party, is allowed to dissent in the slightest degree from the decisions or actions of his Party leaders, whatever he believes to be his duties towards his constituents, the needs of the country as he understands them, or the voice of his own conscience. If by any public word or action, or even by any implication or inaction, he expresses the slightest disagreement, the whole weight of the party machine is turned against him.[36]

Some one-party states do somewhat better than that! Or do they do better than that because they are one-party states and do not have to keep close ranks in face of constant threat from an organised opponent? One is not totally convinced by Crisp's point that the dangers of excessive discipline are mitigated by a free electoral system in which several parties compete.[37]

The above discussion dealt only with parliamentary behaviour or the behaviour of candidates for office. In mitigation, it might be argued that the extensive constituency work undertaken by members reveals a very real and valuable role for the representation of citizen grievances. This can not be denied, though the nature of that representation is usually confined only to individual *grievances* and generally affects the operations of the bureaucracy rather than the legislative process. The observations made earlier about representation are not refuted by the acknowledgement of the value of constituency work. They would, however, be severely modified if it could be shown that extensive lobbying by constituents resulted in legislative change. As Chapter 3 argued, it is probably the case that the only really effective lobbying is that undertaken by interest groups with political clout much greater than might be provided by single constituents.

Political parties, therefore, are not effective in representing individual citizens in the legislative process. But do parties effectively represent the views of their own members? Here the evidence is less clear cut. It is often argued that the ALP, in selecting persons for office, gives undue scope for the representation of powerful affiliated unions. In policy matters, however, it has a democratic process of representation. There is some truth in this, at least in a formal sense, at State level, though one must note the effectiveness with which party machines set the agenda for formal discussion and manipulate the parameters according to which pre-conference consensus might be achieved. In the various States there are powerful party oligarchies (and sometimes more than one) integrated according to an elaborate network of patron-client relations.[38] Indeed it is probably fair to say that those relations are more important than the formal structure of organisation. A sociology of Trades Hall bars and ALP restaurant networks has yet to be written. It should provide the basis for comparison with that other 'black box' of political sociology—the politicking of establishment clubs and chambers of commerce.

The existence of powerful patron-client relations in the ALP suggests that the best one could hope for at State level is a form of asymmetrical representation. Perhaps it would be naive to expect any more than that; but surely it is less naive than to claim actual equality of representation for all rank and file members.

The problems of representation of members is compounded by the peculiar federal nature of the ALP. The paradox is striking! A party committed to greater centralisation is organised federally, and one suspects that individual State machines would be loath to surrender power over their clientele. The central structure remains fairly weak and the Federal Executive has rarely had the power or the will to intervene in individual States. On the one hand, this prevents the representative function being totally eclipsed by a central machine. But on the other hand, it prevents the Federal Conference adequately representing anything but State machines. A historian of the party has noted that the Federal Conference was for many years 'all platform' rather than floor.[39] It thus 'lacked the representative vitality of the annual British Labour Party Conference'. It is true that the Australian Federal ALP Conference has greater power over the parliamentary party than its British counterpart (though the British situation is changing). It is, however, clearly less representative of rank and file and the national cleavages in the party.

The Liberal Party shows even less evidence of representing the views of its own members. In fact, the structure of the party specifically denies the membership *any* control over the elected members. Where the Labor Party platform binds parliamentary Labor members (through the pledge), the Liberal Party maintains a strict division between the two. The organisational wing labours long and hard to produce the party platform, replete with principles of liberalism, policy objectives and more-or-less clear statements of intent, but none of these are binding in any way on the parliamentary wing of the Liberal Party. The theory of representation that permeates the party's rhetoric is a combination of individualism and parliamentarianism. The practice, of course, denies both—the Liberal Party is cohesive to the point of being highly disciplined. The more interesting aspect for intra-party relations is how the dues-paying, grass-roots members of the party have also been apparently quite satisfied with the Burkean rationale of their own representatives, the theory and practice of telling Liberal organisation members that their views *may* be listened to, but that there is no guarantee that they will be followed.

The Australian Democrats can claim, at least in their present stage of development, to be based on a social liberal theory of representation. The Democrats conduct 'participatory democracy' in policy-making, pre-selection and all the other components of intra-party organisation through ballots of members via the party's newsletter. Further, they reject any notion of caucus or party control of parliamentarians. Whether such commitment and practice can be maintained in the face of the necessity for organisation, if the party grows, remains to be seen.

Bicameralism

Those who discuss the Washminster mutation, quite naturally, spend most of their time discussing the bicameral system. From the 'Westminster myth' comes a series of arguments justifying the existence of the Senate as a house of review. According to that myth the ideological defence of bicameralism is Burkean. The lower house is chosen to represent the people's immediate interests, whilst the upper house represents institutions which embody a traditional social contract involving the living, the dead and the yet to be born. The upper house, therefore, is required to ensure that legislation is in conformity with a historically-determined public interest. Though this Burkean argument has been celebrated in Australia, it is quite patently silly. If there really existed institutions in society which embodied the historical social contract, then surely that contract was nullified once the upper house was elected by the same people who elected the lower house.

It is probably the case that the Senate has never really acted as a house of review. Towards the end of the First World War a British all-party committee, under the chairmanship of Lord Bryce, suggested the following functions for the reformed British upper house:

1 Comparatively leisurely and thorough examination of Bills dealt with necessarily and hastily by the busier Lower House
2 Initiation and shaping of less controversial Bills in order to economise time when they reach the Lower House
3 Interposition of so much delay (and no more) in the passing of a bill into law as may be needed to enable the opinion of the nation to be adequately expressed upon it
4 Full and free discussion of large and important questions in circumstances which do not involve the fate of the government.[40]

The Senate's performance of the first function has been woefully inadequate. This has often been due to the fact that proposed legislation reaches the Senate too late for any detailed consideration (let alone 'leisurely' consideration). Most amendments made in the Senate have been government amendments made in response to pressures from outside the Senate. It may well be the case that an enhanced Senate committee system (especially the newly established Scrutiny of Bills Committee) might alter the situation, though government opposition towards such activities is quite marked. It will probably be the case that the more significant amendments to proposed legislation will continue to arise after it has been scrutinised by the appropriate party committee. The Senate's record on Bryce's second point has been patchy and, on the third, one wonders just what the mechanisms might be whereby the opinion of the nation might be expressed. In a situation where the 'opinion of the nation' is often manufactured by the media, one does not hold out much hope on that score. And how is one to assess the opinion of the nation? What, after all, were the lessons of 1975 in which the fate of the government *was* involved: popular endorsement of the Senate's actions or a Liberal landslide resulting from popular fears about inflation and unemployment? Finally, on Bryce's fourth point, one can only remark that the Senate debates on major issues, which characterised the early Commonwealth, have become quite rare. Such, no doubt, reflects the frenzied pace in which a growing body of legislation passes through both houses. What suffers, however, is the expressive role of parliament—a necessary feature of the Westminster myth.

Arguments about the review function of the Senate were overshadowed in the deliberations of the founding fathers by consideration of the representation of interests. Rather than dwelling on a Burkean social contract, the concern was with *local* interests. This was the same concern as that of the American founding fathers.

But there were crucial differences between the terms of reference of the Americans and the Australians. Though the American Constitution owed much to Locke, the Lockean argument that the people vested sovereignty in parliament, subject to parliament observing the terms of the social contract, was replaced in the Declaration of Independence by a denial that sovereignty could ever rest with the American equivalent of parliament. Sovereignty rested with the people. In practice, of course, this meant that local government was immensely powerful. Right from the start, American constitutional thought saw Congress as representing *interests*, and the Senate, in reality, as representing the constituent States. Eventually the myth of a sovereign people resulted in a situation (noted in Chapters 2 and 3) where the public interest was seen as a balance of private interests and majority rule simply as rule by a dominant coalition of minorities. The drift to what eventually became known as pluralism was often eloquently resisted; but eventually the purpose of representative government to forge a national interest out of particular interests gave way to the reduction of public authority to the interplay of private interests with a consequent alienation of the citizenry. Both enthusiasts and critics have argued that such was the consequence of the original constitutional vesting of sovereignty in the people; though it is fair to say that many of the founding fathers, whilst describing the role of partial interests, would have been most dismayed to see interest group liberalism elevated from description to ideology and then to virtue.[41].

The American experience really did result in bicameralism acting as a channel for different sorts of interests. This was not to be the case in Australia. The notion of parliamentary sovereignty was retained, and the justification of States' rights in terms of popular sovereignty could not be advanced. At the State level, the State Parliaments were sovereign. One had perforce to fall back on the rather thin Burkean appeal to historical tradition; but it was by no means clear why States rather than any other time-honoured interest should be seen as embodying an historical social contract nor, as has been argued, why Senators from the States should be elected. Indeed there hardly seemed to be any rationale at all for why a States' house should exist merely than the historical fact that, without one, the Commonwealth would never have obtained the necessary agreement to be formed. Without an ideological rationale for the existence of States' rights, pressures towards centralisation could not be resisted by reference to the danger to popular sovereignty; on the contrary some held that the abolition of the States and consequently the Senate would enhance popular sovereignty—a very un-American argument.

It is, of course, debatable whether the Senate ever did represent the interests of the States. Deakin's prophesy of 1897 was soon clearly borne out:

> The contentions in the senate or out of it, and especially any contention between the two houses, will not and cannot arise from questions in regard to which states will be ranked against states... Contests between the two houses will only arise when one party is in possession of a majority in the one chamber and the other of a majority in the other chamber... The men returned as radicals would vote as radicals; the men returned as conservatives would vote as conservatives. The contest will not be, never has been, and cannot be between states and states... It is certain that once this constitution is framed, it will be followed by the creation of two great national parties. Every state, every district and every municipality will sooner or later be divided on the great ground of principle, when principles emerge.[42]

Though one might wish to question Deakin's point that party competition is really based on *principle*, one has to admit that, at least by 1909–10, the Senate was no longer a States' house. One, indeed, can not be certain whether it was before that date, though clearly the job of whips to bring Senators in line was hardly an easy one and some Senators refused to follow party lines or even attend party meetings.

Despite the above, there is no doubt that the appeal to States' rights is still very powerful. Explanations for this have something to do with the geographical isolation of States, the deliberate cultivation of local populism etc. To these considerations Chapter 6 will return. In the meantime all that need be noted is that no effective federalist ideology has emerged to rationalise the various emotional appeals. In view of the fact that the Senate represents party interest just as effectively as the House of Representatives, one can not but be surprised that the ideological rationale has remained so primitive. Clearly the absence of the American tradition of popular sovereignty has made it difficult to incorporate a symbolic role for the Senate in the ideology of pluralism, but why has myth-making not developed along similar lines? Why, in Australia, are legitimising myths so undeveloped?

Though the American ideology of 'we the interests' started off unequivocally as 'we the people', the Australian Constitution implied a qualified 'we the States'. Nevertheless, as against Griffith's demand that the representatives of the States should have the power to veto any legislation,[43] the advocates of responsible government managed to achieve some degree of success. The result was an incoherence which was quite honestly recognised. A government was to govern only so long as it maintained a majority in the lower house; but a government with a majority in the lower house could not govern effectively unless it also controlled the upper house. As has often been remarked, the powers of the Senate were much wider than those required to ensure the federal principle—indeed the only power the Senate did not have was to initiate or amend money bills. In fact, it may be argued that the Senate has *more* power than the lower house and more power than in comparable federations. Whereas the Governor General may dissolve the lower house as he sees fit, he may not dissolve the Senate without satisfying certain conditions for the dissolution of both houses. As was clear in 1975, by refusing supply, the Senate may be in a position to bring about a situation whereby the Governor General dissolves the lower house. This power is absent in the American and Swiss cases which are the classic models whereby both houses enjoy equal power in a (con) federation.[44]

The contradiction between the 'Westminster' principles of responsible government and the constitutional powers of the Senate has been written about at great length, especially since 1975. Central to the discussion here is not the American argument about the conflict between various interests, nor the old British argument about the conflict between current popular will and historical continuity. It is a contradiction between two ways of representing the interests of political parties and sets of party representatives elected at different times. It is difficult to give that contradiction any theoretical rationale.

Until recently, the Senate was not a highly regarded institution in Australia. The policy of the Australian Labor Party has long sought its abolition. Such, however, is regarded as impossible because of constitutional provisions and the fear that its abolition might imply the abolition of federalism itself. In recent years, however, the Senate has grown in prominence following three developments. First the threat (1974) of refusal of supply to the Whitlam Government by the Liberal-National majority in the Senate, and the refusal to pass supply in 1975, which sparked off the constitutional crisis, elevated the Senate to public prominence. This, not unnaturally, produced different reactions in the electorate.

Second, as has been noted, was the loss of control of the Senate by both major parties. The DLP held a numerical balance of power in the Senate from 1967 to 1974, but its numbers, on all substantive matters, came down on the side of the anti-Labor parties. Since 1980, the Australian Democrats have held a balance of power, and they have been less predictable, and less oriented against Labor. The result has been increased media attention devoted to the Senate.

Third—a development which has often escaped public attention—has been the growth of the quite significant committee system referred to earlier. This chapter has registered doubts about the further development of such a system, though clearly such would do much to change the Senate from a house of 'echo' to a house of review.

One might doubt also the success of the allied proposal to exclude ministers from the Senate coupled with an upgrading of the role and salaries of Senate committee chairmen to that of government ministers. Clearly such a policy would enhance the interests of responsible government (at least in a formal sense) and would strengthen the review powers of the Senate. It seems, however, that whereas the ALP might support the restriction of ministers to the House, an enhanced role for Senate committee chairmen would only be acceptable if the powers of the Senate to refuse supply were curtailed.[45]

Considerations such as those above would seem to suggest that the new improved visibility of the Senate has enhanced the legitimacy of the bicameral system. Such observations, however, should be seen in the context of a general cynicism towards the subordination of any notions of checks and balances to the interests of political parties. Doubtless it was to counter that cynicism that the ex-Speaker, Sir Billy Snedden, called for a more independent role for the Speaker.[46] Predictably Sir Billy invoked the Westminster tradition, though it is extremely difficult to consider the role of the Speaker in Britain as 'independent'. The only major difference between the roles of the Speaker in the two countries concerns the British practice whereby the major parties normally (though not invariably) do not oppose the Speaker at elections and that the Speaker remains in office when governments change. Change to such a practice in Australia would be extremely difficult to bring about. First, it must be noted that the British convention does provide a field-day for minor parties which can capitalise on winning votes which might have otherwise have gone to a major party candidate opposing the Speaker. There is every reason to suspect that, in Australia, there would be a greater chance of such minor party candidates actually winning. Secondly, the British practice is facilitated by a process of re-selection much more centralised than in Australia. One wonders to what extent local constituencies in Australia would be content not to be represented effectively so long as their member remains as Speaker. Of course, the cynic could remark that it did not matter very much since local constituents were not effectively represented anyway. But that would gloss over the very real point that, by and large, the processes of pre-selection in Australia do reveal more intra-party democracy than their British counterparts. A final problem concerning a more independent role for the Speaker centers on the lack of an upper house in Australia which may confirm 'life after death'. In Britain, Speakers conventionally retire to the nominated upper house and take on the role of elder statesman. There is no similar role in Australia. As a consequence, several have returned to the normal cut and thrust of partisan politics in the House. Anticipation of such an eventuality cannot be said to contribute to their image of impartiality.

Fixed parliamentary terms

The legitimacy of parliament would probably not be affected very much one way or the other by a more independent Speaker. What could enhance the legitimacy of parliament would be regularity in its terms of office and complementarity between the terms for each house. The electorate, after all, does seem to get very perturbed at a Prime Minister calling elections purely when the time seems appropriate for party advantage. The Hawke Government maintains that there is clearly a need for fixed terms and that terms for the House should be longer than at present. But the promise of a fixed term, which emerged prior to the 1983 election, has disappeared from the agenda of the government. The Constitutional Convention does have the question somewhere in its committee structure, but Liberal and National parties have not supported the proposal.

In the run-up to the 1983 election the ALP promised a referendum to incorporate a fixed, four-year term for the Australian Parliament into the Constitution. Following the election, this had been diluted to a proposal for a referendum to increase the parliamentary term from three to four years, but without a fixed term. In the event, the referendum was abandoned.

The maximum life for a parliament of only three years contributes to the tendency for parliamentarians to be obsessed with short-term electoral advantage and to their unwillingness to consider the long-term future. Perhaps a four-year term for the House might make it formally less responsible, but it might also make its members less protean. As has been pointed out, a four-year term might ensure that only two of the four years would be spent by members preening themselves for the next election campaign.

Fixed parliamentary terms would undoubtedly act as a powerful curb on the 'reserve power' of the Governor General to dismiss a popularly-elected government, but they do not guarantee that the time for elections may not be engineered for party advantage. A recent West German election was, after all, brought about by a Christian-Democrat Chancellor orchestrating a vote of no confidence against his own government. There is, however, a greater chance that the cynical manipulation of transitory electoral prejudices might be lessened. The problem arises, however, when one tries to fit in the proposal for a lengthened fixed term for the House with the provisions governing bicameralism. Should the present constitutional provision be maintained whereby the term for the House is coupled with a term of double that duration for the Senate? Four years for the House might be appealing, but would eight for the Senate be equally appealing. If not, then how could one prevent an even greater mess developing than exists at present concerning the relationship between the terms for each house? A simple proposal for the simultaneous election of both chambers was unsuccessfully put to referendums in 1974, 1977 and 1984. What chance is there for a far more radical proposal which is even more unlikely to obtain consensus within the major parties? One could indeed imagine the self-interested arguments put by opponents of longer terms. An electorate, already doubtful of the probity and altruism of its representatives, is hardly likely to respond positively.

Further, a fixed term entrenched into the Constitution would require that the constitutional power of the Senate be limited. And that is the issue on which Liberal and National Parties will stand firm. A fixed term would necessarily remove the power of an opposition majority in the Senate to refuse a budget and hence force a government to an election. This is unacceptable to the anti-Labor parties.

The Washminster mutation?

Perhaps the key argument that prevents party agreement on fixed terms concerns the powers of the Senate to block supply. A fixed term for the House would only be practicable if no institution outside that House had the power to force it to an early election. At root, then, is the issue with which this section began—the strange bicameral configuration of the Australian Constitution. This is no Washminster mix; in America there are fixed terms and a House which may not be dissolved at the will of other branches of the Constitution; in Britain there are no fixed terms but there is a relatively independent House.

In comparing the American presidential system and the British-type parliamentary system, Blewett has pointed to the existence in the former of a tug of war between separated institutions, of which the executive is one. This leads to inertia but has the advantage of allowing for greater open scrutiny of the executive than exists under the parliamentary system.[47] In Australia the tug of war between separated institutions with equal power likewise leads to inertia but, because the executive is not separate, the cause of open government is not in the least furthered. Australia has inherited the worst features of both systems without the balancing advantages. Blewett goes on to argue that:

> The presidential system provides a more participatory legislative system, legislation being much more open to influence by individual backbenchers, constituents and pressure groups, than does the parliamentary system. *But* the parliamentary system provides far more unity and coherence in policy than does the presidential system where policy tends to be incoherent and diffuse.

In Australia party control inhibits the development of a truly participatory legislative system whilst the peculiar bicameral system prevents coherence in policy-making, or so long as different parties have majorities in the two houses or while the balance of power (or 'reason') is held by a minority party. Again we see the worst features of both systems.

Finally Blewett maintains

> The presidential system, because of the requirement that executive officers cannot be members of the legislature, has a far greater pool of executive talent to draw on than has the parliamentary system. But the parliamentary system gives a greater guarantee that executive officers will have political experience, political authority and will work as a term than does the presidential system.

Prime Minister Hawke, in his Boyer lectures, has called for the appointment of ministers who are not members of parliament (at present they must become members within three months of appointment). Hawke clearly wants to enlarge the scope for expertise. Pending constitutional change in that direction, one can perhaps be content that ministers do have a lot of political experience. Unfortunately the evidence suggests that most of the present ministers have little *parliamentary* experience. Indeed the Prime Minister himself is one of the least experienced. But perhaps he makes up for that by other political qualities.

Conclusion

In summary, Cabinet is not responsible to the parliament. It responds to the caucus, to the party and, in periodic elections, to the people.

In the sense of holding government responsible for its actions, parliament in Australia is impotent. It is the party, not parliament, which decides on the role, actions and policies of the government. In the same manner, individual ministers are responsible not to parliament but to the party in parliament; and it is up to the party—caucus, Cabinet or the leader—to pass judgement and apply sanctions. In Australia, the roles and functions of government and party have become one, with a consequent decline if not disappearance, of responsibility in government.

Parties in government have asserted that responsibility has not been eroded, but merely transferred to the electorate. This argument, based on a concept of *party* responsibility, accepts not only as inevitable but of positive value the concentration of party authority over all levels of government and parliament, and holds that the party, and hence the government, is accountable to and responsible to the voters. That is, there is a conjunction of party authority, government and party responsibility. This chapter has argued that the problem is that this depends, in the final analysis, on an informed, aware, rational, open-minded, discussive, involved, motivated and judgemental electorate. The electorate may not be so described, nor can it be until parties, particularly parties-in-government, deliberately set out to promote, encourage and assist the development of an informed and critical public.

Every text-book on political parties, in one form or another, contains a list of the functions or activities a party performs with regard to the electorate (mobilisation, education, information, socialisation), to policy making (aggregation, expression, communication, formulation), to government (representation, expression, administration, recruitment) and to the polity (participation, integration). How well do the Australian parties carry out these functions, and in whose interests? Are parties really interested in educating the public? Or are they more interested in mobilising and socialising the public to support party interests, party policies and, ultimately, their election to office? To what extent is there a commitment, in practice, to freedom of information? Whom does a party represent in Australia? Do parties encourage participation? Is the Australian party system an instrument of integration?

The problem is that 'parties not only aggregate and select, they eventually deviate and distort'. They not only express and reflect public opinions, but:

> shape, and indeed manipulate, opinion... There is manipulation and manipulation; and as long as parties are parts (in the plural) a party system lends itself to expression from below far more than

to manipulation from above. It may well be that the people have no opinions of their own or that their opinions are largely formed by opinion makers. However, this circumstance only confirms the extent to which a multi-centered, crosscutting manipulative impact differs from a unicentered, self-reinforcing type of manipulation, thereby indicating that real manipulation, or 'repressive manipulation', takes over precisely when party pluralism subsides.[48]

Australia's two major parties reflect the latter interpretation of 'manipulation'. In Australia, the creed of both major parties seems to be that of party above all, and my party above all others. When King wrote that:

> the political party's role in Western industrial society today is more limited than would appear from its position of formal pre-eminence,[49]

he obviously did not take Australia into account. The Australian party system, is, more than ever, the key to understanding the polity. In Australia, the domain of political parties is coterminous with the domain of politics, and almost every function performed in and by the political system is linked in some way to political parties. Writing of America, Janda concluded that 'the decline of parties as organisational forces frustrates, rather than enhances, popular control of government'.[50] The opposite case needs to be put for Australia; the political parties have appropriated the political system to themselves, and to *their* interests. The imperfections evident in the processes of representation, responsibility, and the federal parliamentary system of responsible government are not a result of the structures of politics, but are caused by political parties which have manipulated the structures to their own advantage.

This chapter has not argued for an end to party politics. That would be both naive and futile. Parties exist, and will continue to do so. Further, government by pressure group, by vested interest, or by bureaucracy would even less be an expression of the wants and needs of the society as a whole. The argument disagrees with such thinkers as Burke, Madison, Ostrogorski and Michels who, while occupying different ideological positions and deriving their conclusions from differing sets of premises and evidence, all assert that political parties are inevitably destructive of democracy.

At the other extreme of attitude to party one finds vehement assertions by Neumann, Schattschneider and others that 'democracy is unthinkable, save in terms of party'. Certainly this seems to be the position taken by the conventional wisdom of Australian politics—that the removal of party from the trial of parliamentary government would spell the end of democracy. To Jupp, for example, 'parties are indispensable to modern politics... neither good nor bad but simply necessary',[51] while to Webb:

> In so far as we have political democracy, it has been possible by party government, and it is therefore prudent to assume in the party system some degree of immanent wisdom.[52]

The complaint of this chapter has not been that there are parties and party government. It concerns the mode of behaviour of the parties. Parties may be necessary to modern democratic government, but Australia's major parties, by their dominance, arrogance and chauvinism, are hindrances to the democratic process.

Justification for party reform flows from the thesis that 'the infirmities of party make government infirm'.[53] The 'infirmities' in Australia are obvious: almost total discipline; almost total confrontation and adversary party behaviour; almost total emphasis on 'anti-other parties', rather than on the formulation and debate of policies; the maintenance of oligarchy; and, above all, a seemingly inexorable tendency for party to overwhelm responsible government and parliamentary democracy. Australian parties act as factions, not as parties:

> The difference is...that parties are instrumental to collective benefits, to an end that is not merely the private benefit of the contestants. Parties link people to a government, while factions do not. Parties enhance a set of system capabilities while factions do not.[54]

It was this distinction, Chapter 3 noted, which led some theorists to see parties outside the framework of pluralist group competition. Unfortunately, in Australia, the distinction is difficult to maintain. Australia's major parties have abrogated the whole of politics to themselves, and have done so with purposes which seek to benefit themselves first, and the polity second. Party in Australia has become a matter of conflict, of confrontation, of a refusal to compromise. There is little evidence of any commitment to impartiality, representation, or responsibility to the society. Reform is unlikely to emerge from within the hegemonic parties. The process of self-protection, confrontation and internal discipline is too entrenched. Reforms can come only from the voters themselves; by increasing involvement in political life, by greater awareness of political events, structures and processes, by a willingness to go beyond the 'how to vote' cards at elections, by a realisation that politics *does* impinge on virtually every aspect of life—in short, by a decrease in the level of apathy. In the final analysis, party reform can only come from below, from a conviction in the electorate that reform is necessary. The hope is that the voters in Australia are not overwhelmed by cynicism before this can emerge.

FIVE
COMMONWEALTH BUREAUCRACY

The popular view

WRITERS ON THE Australian public service have commented time and again on the ambivalent attitude with which it is regarded by the citizenry.[1] Chapter 2 noted how Hancock, in his classic statement, foreshadowed this ambiguity. Australian democrats, it will be remembered, came to look upon the state as a vast public utility charged with providing the greatest happiness for the greatest number. The state, moreover, represented collective power in the interests of individual rights. It followed, therefore, that the state was looked to for its utility-maximising potential, and yet was distrusted because of its capacity to trample on people's rights. This utilitarian ambivalence was not just an import from Britain, but had its roots in the major role played by the state in actually creating civil society in the first place. As Encel put it:

> The ambiguity of Australian attitudes towards authority, and bureaucratic authority in particular, is itself a reflection of the paradox that the quest for equality has been satisfied to a large extent by the establishment of bureaucratic institutions. Equality and authority, egalitarianism and authoritarianism, are twin sides of one coin.[2]
> Bureaucracy 'is the very model of the regime which acts by the rule of equality'. Herein lies the paradox of egalitarianism in Australia: the search for equality of the redistributive kind breeds bureaucracy; bureaucracy breeds authority; and authority undermines the equality which bred it.[3]

Encel's observations expose the core of the popular view of the Australian bureaucracy. Encel starts by quoting Hancock:

> Democratić sentiment applauds the sound argument that every

office boy should have a chance to become a manager, and perverts it into a practical rule that no one should become a manager who has not been an office boy.[4]

Everyone, therefore, should start at the bottom. Those 'high flyers' who are not prepared to may go elsewhere. The result, in the popular view, is a public service characterised by mediocrity. This mediocrity is reinforced by the practice of only granting promotion on the basis of seniority. After all, if policy was made by governments and all public servants did was administer, why should special qualifications be needed? The only rewards given should be on the basis of faithfully mastering the procedures for policy-implementation; such are not gained by study but by time-serving. A consequence of a rigid seniority system, the popular view maintains, is that the public service is dominated by old people who have lost any capacity for innovation. At middle levels, flexibility is only achieved by the provision of an ever more complicated system of overlapping classifications. The Australian public service is integrated not in human terms (by people with certain institutionally-approved qualities) but technologically according to roles and structures; this makes career-development very difficult. Flexibility may only be achieved by redefining 'work-value' with the aid of public service unions. In performing this role, such unions are welded into a corporate mass with little regard for the interests of the labour movement outside the public service.

The popular view of bureaucracy, therefore, is of a relatively stable hierarchy which maintains a shifting equilibrium between gerontocracy and meritocratic pressures.[5] The meritocratic pressures, however, are not quite the same as may be found in Britain. Right from the mid-nineteenth century the British civil service began to recruit an administrative grade (of people 'born to rule') and merit was defined (theoretically) in terms of administrative talent as well as purely technical expertise. In Australia the absence of the thin 'ruling class' layer supposedly gives far more power to those who possess technical expertise and who are able to enter the public service after certification. Because these experts are professionals in the worst sense of the word (they define people outside their profession according to the values of their own profession) the public service develops factions and professional syndicalism. The public service, then, is dominated by time-servers and narrow-minded professionals. What is missing are people of all-round education in the humanities and the social sciences who are capable of seeing many sides of a problem and setting public policy in its social setting. In so far as this deficiency is perceived by public service heads, the popular view maintains, it is met by the desire for more economists. Economists are supposed to possess training in logical thought, an ability to sort out what is important in a mass of material and the ability to see all sides of a question.[6] Alas very few do; what a training in economics usually does for the mediocre and unimaginative is to reinforce that mediocrity and buttress a lack of imagination by a belief in an extremely narrow-minded positivism. Thus, a public service, founded on utilitarianism, seeks refuge in that most utilitarian of disciplines which deals not with real people but ahistorical reified utility-maximising packages.

From the Age of Reconstruction to the Menzies era

The above popular view contains elements of truth but applies more to State-level bureaucracies, and even there can be very misleading. As Encel sees it, if there was any truth in the trajectory of office boy to permanent head, in the Commonwealth public service, it ceased to have any relevance after 1939. In the ten years after the beginning of the war, there was considerable lateral movement into the public service and the development of a leadership core in many departments which was very far from mediocre. Significantly, many outstanding figures in that core were actually *economists* whose understanding of the Keynesian revolution was different from that of the adherents to the neo-classical orthodoxy of today (the purveyors of what Joan Robinson calls 'bastard Keynesianism'). Their vision was not narrow utilitarianism but the social liberalism discussed in Chapters 1 and 2. Though lip-service continued to be paid to the Westminster myth of governments making policy and the public service engaging in administration, what developed was a relationship of partnership between Cabinet and bureaucracy with a lot of initiative coming from the latter. In Encel's view, the creative role of the public service in those years should not be underestimated. The achievements included:

> Policies dealing with full employment, large-scale immigration, a national health scheme, housing, the expansion and stabilisation of rural industry, the establishment of the Australian Regular Army, the administration of Papua and New Guinea, large scale mineral exploration, the establishment of an aluminium industry, the Snowy Mountains scheme, Commonwealth involvement in tertiary education, restructuring of the arbitration system, the setting up of the Joint Coal Board, the first steps toward a nuclear energy industry, the expansion of C.S.I.R.O., railway unification, a national overseas airline, the establishment of T.A.A., overseas

telecommunications, the setting up of an Australian diplomatic service—all these and many smaller actions provided the framework for postwar development. They were accompanied by a fundamental shift of relations between the Commonwealth and the States as a result of the Uniform Tax Case of 1942 and the massive growth of the Commonwealth administrative machine.[7]

Virtually none of the above achievements had figured in Labor Party policy when it came to office in 1941. Most derived from a creative interaction of government and bureaucracy. A public service dominated by inflexible time-servers and narrow specialists could not have achieved all that. Nor, indeed, could it have done so much if public service unions had really pursued reactionary egalitarianism to ensure the 'survival of the thickest'. It was in this heyday of social liberalism that Karl Mannheim, ideologist par excellence of the 'Age of Reconstruction', agreed with Gaetano Mosca that the opposition of concepts like 'state' and 'society' were out of date. 'This dualism usually equates "state" with "bureaucracy" and society with the conglomeration of vigorous organisations which successfully claim the epithets "free" and "private"'.[8] There was, after all, no crucial distinction between public and private organisations: 'public responsibility is interwoven in the whole fabric of society'.[9] If there was no real distinction between state and society, then there really could not be any between government and public service. Traditionally both of these were part of the state; but the government was supposed to be responsible to society whereas the public service was responsible to government. Once the distinction between state and society was seen to have broken down, then the public service was just as responsible to the citizens as to the government. It was not at all clear just how public responsibility might have been interwoven in the whole fabric of society. None the less, this was a dominant view celebrated for nearly a decade; and, though one might be unclear about its theoretical coherence, it did attest to a vigorous public service. It, moreover, provided a basis for considering something students of public administration had known for a very long time, that the distinction between policy and administration was very difficult to make.

The achievements of the Age of Reconstruction were just as much those of the public service as of the Labor Government. The contribution made by the Labor Government was in providing a co-operative atmosphere for the reception of advice from new recruits into that service. There is no reason to suppose that a Liberal Government would not have been so receptive. In her recent discussion of Liberal Party ideology, Marian Simms describes, with some force, the ideological switch which occurred on the right of politics during the demise of the United Australia Party and the rise of the new Liberal Party.[10] Like Labor, the new Liberals responded to the ideologists of reconstruction, and could find in their own ancestry a coherent social liberal vision in which the public service played a major creative role. There were, of course, differences in ideology. The Liberals always maintained a small *laissez faire* fringe and tended to temper Keynes with Hayek rather then Mannheim. It was possible to do this not by examining Hayek's economics (though at one stage even Keynes himself thought himself to be in agreement with the Austrian school) but by the anti-socialist arguments of Hayek's *Road to Serfdom*. Hayek argued that the state should *regulate* but not *control*; but then so did Keynes; and so did the Labor Party. But some mileage could be got out of the Liberal stress on free enterprise (distinguished from *laissez faire*) and eventually the Communist can could be kicked for all it was worth. This, together with the mobilisation of resentment against rationing and the mobilisation of fears about bank nationalisation, was sufficient to provide the rhetoric to support a change in government. But, in many respects, the reconstructionist ideology held and so did the need for an active, creative public service. Encel, however, disagrees. After 1949:

> This bureaucratic revolution fell into the hands of a political party which like the Bourbons in France in 1815 had learnt nothing about the new world emerging from the political and social whirlwinds of the 1930s and 1940s. The Liberal Party was elected on a platform dedicated to the myths of free enterprise, State Rights and loyalty to the British Empire.[11]

To be sure this was the Liberal platform. Yet Simms is undoubtedly correct; free enterprise is not the same as *laissez faire* and it is quite consistent with the reconstructionist ideology. *Laissez faire* is a product of a relatively simple competitive capitalist economy. In this more complicated age, the state will intervene in the interests of regulating competition (or if one likes 'free enterprise'). This requires a large bureaucracy. The Menzies Government was quite aware of that feature of the 'new world emerging from the political and social whirlwinds of the 1930s'.

Encel's argument is that the anachronistic Menzies Government inherited a bureaucratic machine which was already too powerful for its government controllers. The government, however, had been elected on the programme of cutting down the public service, and this it tried to do in 1951. It failed! It had also promised to cut down overlapping bureaucratic functions between Commonwealth and States. This it also failed to do. Indeed, all it was able to do was to ensure that the massive bureaucratic machine ran in low gear and occasionally to 'apply the brakes to the discomfort of the passengers'. Meanwhile the Commonwealth bureaucracy went on growing (if at a slower rate than previously). In 1949, it numbered 150 000, and by 1970 reached 225 000. Its growth led to a series of reorganisations and eventually to a meritocracy of officials in the second division. Through this period, the public service did not distinguish itself in carrying out government policies, because such policies were few and far between. Neither did the public service itself initiate many policies to be adopted by government due to the obstruction of interest groups which had the ear of the government. Indeed, the locus of policy-making was outside government (within political parties, business groups etc.), producing pluralism in the worst sense of the word without the saving grace of diffusing power. This, together with the development of ministerial satrapies and the 'abuse' of public service secrecy by government, led to a demoralisation of the public service, which remained a powerful instrument without adequate employment.[12]

The above is an indication of government incompetence. But what is not clear is the degree of bureaucratic incompetence. Caiden might be correct in his observation that, in the climate of the 'Long Boom', bureaucratic bungles might have been overlooked and that government was not particularly worried about the growth of a complacent meritocratic elite in the public service.[13] Yet, for all that, a strong and large public service was required to implement the policies set in motion by the previous Labor Government, to provide the facilities and infrastructural development without which foreign capital could not be attracted—in short, to stimulate the programme which the Liberals identified as national development. Rather than economic policy simply emanating from interest groups etc., the role of the Treasury was very important, especially when its advice went against the perceived interests of certain manufacturing and other business groups.

Whatever the truth about the lack of initiative in the public service during the long years of Liberal rule, it was clear that, by the 1970s, much of the old view of the public service had crumbled. A significant section of the bureaucratic elite consisted of people who had not worked their way up from the ranks and had pursued professional careers before entering the public service. Typically the higher reaches of the Commonwealth public service were staffed by people who came from a very similar socio-economic background and who were educated at the same schools. Though less of an 'Establishment' than its British counterpart, this group was closely integrated and constituted an elite in the literal sense of the word.

As the events of the early 1970s showed, the group was relatively inflexible, though one can not be certain that this inflexibility was due to long-service on the bureaucratic treadmill or to ideological conviction produced by background and long habituation to the norms of the years of Liberal Country Party government.[14] At middle levels, the bureaucratic complexity caused by the classification system was denser than ever. Professional fragmentation was indeed a problem, as was the degeneration of economics from its temporary exciting role in reconstructionist ideology to its more customary role as 'the dismal science'. At lower levels, there was some truth in the popular view described above; but it was clear that the bureaucracy would soon have to cope with the climate of reform which swept Australia in the early 1970s.

The failure of a reform government

The reformist Labor Government, which achieved office in 1972, reflected most clearly the ambiguity noted at the beginning of this chapter—a distrust of bureaucracy combined with a simultaneous fascination about the possibility for using that bureaucracy to promote change. By 1972, enough had been written, especially about Britain which maintained a not too dissimilar bureaucratic apparatus, to establish good grounds for that suspicion. Ralph Miliband's *The State in Capitalist Society*, published in 1969, which was amongst the most sophisticated of Marxist works adhering to an instrumental view of the state, had already become required reading in many universities, and was not unknown amongst the group of top advisors surrounding the new government and 'irregularly' appointed permanent heads fostered by the new administration. Miliband's arguments were not very new, but he expressed himself most clearly:

> As for the manner in which this power is exercised, the notion of 'neutrality' which is often attached to it is surely in the highest degree misleading; indeed, a moment's reflection must suggest that it is absurd: men who are deeply immersed in public affairs and who play a major role not only in the application but in the determination of policy, as these men undoubtedly do, are not likely to be free of certain definite ideological inclinations, however little they may themselves be conscious of them; and these inclinations cannot but affect the whole character and orientation of the advice they proffer, and the way in which they approach their administrative tasks.... Nor can there be much doubt as to where these ideological inclinations lie: higher civil servants in the countries of advanced capitalism may generally be expected to

play a conservative role in the councils of the state, to reinforce the conservative propensities of governments in which these propensities are already well developed, and to serve as an inhibiting element in regard to governments in which they are less pronounced.[15]

If one grants that Miliband is using the word 'conservative' in a narrow behavioural way rather than in the manner used in Chapter 1, then this description applies also to Australia. Miliband goes on to argue that the good relations enjoyed between social democratic governments and their public services were less a measure of the latter's neutrality than the fact that social democratic governments quickly became 'socialised' by those public services.[16]

At first sight, then, the changes made to the public service by the Whitlam Government would seem to reflect ways of overcoming public service 'conservatism'.[17] A number of departments were abolished and created, in part to disrupt departmental empires which had pursued department strategies in opposition to Labor policies. There was a proliferation of statutory authorities and co-ordinating bodies, an influx of new people into key decision-making roles, the appointment of task forces and commissions of enquiry to speed up policy implementation, provisions made for more 'open government' and the setting up of a Royal Commission (RCAGA), under Dr H.C. Coombs, one of the leading lights of the earlier reconstructionist period, to investigate the possibilities of public service reform. But how much of all this was due to a desire to overcome bureaucratic obstacles in the way of reform and how much due to a technocratic concern to improve the efficiency of what Encel saw as the vast under-used machine? In so far as it was the latter, the old myths of neutrality were preserved. The old ambiguity between the suspicion of unresponsive hierarchy and fascination with the possibilities for bureaucracy in a new 'technocratic' Age of Reconstruction remained. This ambiguity was indeed reflected in the orientation of Prime Minister Whitlam, who had been 'socialised', in Miliband's terms, before he ever entered politics, but who was also responsive to the sociological critique of bureaucracy.

Arguments about whether the Whitlam Government was more concerned to limit capitalism or to promote a new invigorated capitalism through the medium of a streamlined corporate state apparatus have been much debated. As Chapter 2 noted, these sometimes take the form of a debate between the characterisation of Labor as 'democratic socialist' or 'technocratic labourist', or perhaps even as a special case of what Berki sees as the perennial struggle between egalitarian and technocratic impulses in the Labor project.[18]

This chapter will not go into that debate. Suffice it to say that the Labor Government was pulled in different directions. As Wilenski has documented, the rearrangement of departmental functions foundered on the rocks of departmental opposition.[19] The ambitiously conceived Department of Urban and Regional Development (DURD) never achieved the status required to assume the tasks set for it. Many of the statutory bodies managed to generate considerable turbulence. A number of newly established key co-ordinating bodies (such as the Priorities Review Staff) failed to live up to expectations. The new staff brought in to enliven the bureaucracy were often opposed by entrenched bureaucrats. Task forces soon degenerated into old-style inter-departmental committees, described by Sexton as 'like mincers': '(they) take proposals of various shapes and sizes and produce bland consistency'.[20] Moves toward open government foundered on the principles of confidentiality enshrined in the Westminster myth. The Treasury, moreover, was felt for a time to be obstructing what it considered to be irresponsible programmes of government spending (a clear case of an exercise of power in Lukes' 'second dimension'). Finally, the report of the Royal Commission appeared only to be considered by a government of a very different political complexion.

The bureaucratic reforms of the Whitlam years achieved much less than was originally envisaged. The question remains, however, as to how much the failures were due to bureaucratic opposition, as Labor ideologues maintain, and how much to the failure of will on the part of the Government. As Wilenski sees it, the lack of crucial support was due to the permanent crisis situation experienced by a government faced by a hostile Senate and the onset of a major economic recession.[21] Yet Wilenski might concur with the argument, made more forcibly by other writers, that the main problem of the Whitlam years was the lack of sufficiently coherent leadership from Cabinet. As Sexton described it, Cabinet, during those years, was a disparate collection of individuals:

> Like a computer with 27 programmers, Cabinet produced thousands of unrelated decisions on specific submissions but seldom considered their implications for the government electorally or how they interacted within its long-term policies.[22]

In so far as the heads of the public service were concerned with coherence and long-term implications, there is little wonder that the policy-implementation record of the Labor Government was not all that impressive. In the face of what seems to be the lack of a concerted will on the part of government to control the public service, it is very difficult to evaluate the strength of public service obstruction. To counter a 'conservative' conception of 'the public interest' on the part of the public service, a reforming government must have an equally coherent conception of its reformed notion of 'the public interest' and must have ministers with the determination and knowledge to articulate it. This seems not to have been the case even in Britain, where the period of office of a Labour government had been much longer. Lord Armstrong, on his retirement as head of the British Treasury, had made the following oft-quoted remark about his power (Lukes' 'second dimension'):

> Obviously I had a great influence. The biggest and most pervasive influence is in setting the framework within which the questions of policy are raised. We, while I was in the Treasury, had a framework of the economy basically neo-Keynesian. We set the questions which we asked ministers to decide arising out of that framework and it would have been enormously difficult for any minister to change the framework, so to that extent we had great power. I don't think it was used maliciously or malignly. I think we chose that framework because we thought it was the best one going. We were very ready to explain it to anybody who was interested, but most ministers were not interested, were just prepared to take the questions as we offered them which came out of the framework without going back into the preconceptions of them.[23]

Lord Armstrong was talking about what was referred to earlier as 'bastard Keynesianism'. It is doubtful whether many British ministers, including the economist Harold Wilson, would have been too sure about the implications of alternative frameworks (for example, ultra-Keynesianism or socialist theories). This was even more the case in Australia where various kinds of neo-classical frameworks bumped against the naive-Keynesianism of Jim Cairns and seemed to change from budget to budget. That Bill Hayden should finally emerge as an 'economic expert', when few were certain about what his economic framework actually was, testifies to the problem. In such a situation, it is not surprising that Treasury should have stood out against what seemed to be the forays of dilettantes. That some of those forays might have had behind them a consistent body of theory was hidden by the cacophony of discordant voices which substituted for coherent economic policy in those years. One may understand the attitude of Treasury and towards Treasury noted in the Coombs' Report:

> It was argued that Treasury held a substantial monopoly as the source of economic and financial advice and that, partly as a consequence, it had developed an almost doctrinal attitude about the theoretical basis on which policy should be developed. This, it

was suggested, had led to its being insensitive to government priorities; to a failure to present ministers with a full range of options; to an isolation of policy from the influences of other departments, of professional economists outside government, and of the community—especially those sections of it actively engaged in production and commerce. While the Commission accepted that this criticism, certainly in such a bald and oversimplified form, was at least exaggerated, it could not ignore the strength and persistence with which it emerged.[24]

But could one expect change when Labor did not get its act together? If Cabinet had been united, then perhaps Treasury might have been split up in a way more radical than that carried out by the Fraser Liberal Government (by the creation of a separate Department of Finance in 1976). Perhaps, also, effective institutions might have been created to offer alternative economic advice, such as those proposed, too late, by Coombs,[25] and eventually established by the Hawke Government. As it was, Cabinet was not united, and ministers occasionally actually abetted public service rivalries. Hugh Stretton gives a clear example of such rivalries:

> One department of the Federal Government moved to create an Australian Housing Corporation. A rival department believed in that sort of enterprise, but couldn't bear to see it in alien hands, so tried to kill it. They half-succeeded. In its final mangled form, the Act provided that the Australian Housing Corporation could not buy an acre, build a house or lend a dollar without six or nine months of bureaucratic preliminaries including the consent of the Treasury and both Houses of Parliament, with those procedures to be repeated for each line of business. The day the Act was gazetted, the Prime Minister transferred responsibility for the new-born monster from the department that had created it to the department that had decisively crippled it.[26]

The above example is a matter of public record. Stretton notes, however, that there were many examples of that sort of behaviour which were not made public. Ministers did not seem to have the will to correct a situation in which the status of some permanent heads were measured by the 'fear and destruction' which they could inflict.[27] To be sure, a few ministers were at daggers drawn with their departments (not always for good reasons), though more commonly ministers found themselves temporarily 'socialised' by their own department's views and at odds with their colleagues. When ministers did a *volte face*, as the paradigm within which Cabinet policy changed, they lost face in their ministry. Perhaps the saddest case of all was when a minister found himself arguing in Cabinet against a policy document emanating from his department (Treasury) which he had unwittingly signed.[28] But even if Labor had got its act together, it would surely have always been bedevilled by never being sure how to resolve the ambiguity in its thinking between the 'conservative' nature of the state machine and the instrumental role of a relatively 'neutral' bureaucracy in pursuing social change. In this, memories of the Age of Reconstruction could have been highly misleading. As Chapters 2 and 3 suggested, the war at that time had mobilised the whole nation behind a single goal. In the post-war situation, experiments in 'national development' had to be pursued by all if disaster was to be avoided. The crisis of the 1970s was pale by comparison. It may also have been true that the public service, in 1939, was really something which did correspond more to the picture of mediocrity with which this chapter began. The public service in the 1970s was by no means mediocre.[29] Its experts were not just engineers and technicians of the former age but people who really did feel that they understood the dynamics of modern society.

Yet a very powerful case may be made that they, in fact, misunderstood those dynamics. This was particularly the case with Treasury. By the 1970s, the discipline of economics had ceased to be the vehicle for the revitalisation of staid officialdom. The economics of the Keynesian revolution, with its occasional socialist admixture, had paled before what Hughes, in his memorable pun, calls 'the economics of the Stone age'.[30] With Lord Armstrong, one may call this neo-Keynesianism, but that term nowadays is used to cover almost anything. As John Edwards saw it, the 'Treasury view' was:

> opposed to attempts to control prices and incomes directly, because this is 'interference' which distorts the market mechanism in ways that are ultimately self-defeating; it is opposed to indexation as the 'quid pro quo' for wage restraint, though it advises a strong government line against wage increases in the Arbitration Commission; it is temperamentally opposed to government spending, particularly to higher government spending at this time as a solution to unemployment; it is, or was up to September last year (1974), in favour of demand deflation through higher taxes and lower government spending; it dislikes barriers against foreign investment; it is in favour of lower tariffs and more competition, though it maintains that these decisions should be made slowly and with proper provision for the consequences.[31]

Keynes would have been depressed! And yet Treasury officials consistently argued that Treasury did not have a coherent view. All that was consistent, some public servants remarked, was the tradition of saying 'no'. The Secretary to the Treasury put the following case which is a classic positivist statement in conformity with the Westminster myth:

I frankly think it is nonsense to imagine that there is an identifiable Treasury view on economic theory and principles. I do, however, claim that we have a doctrine of another kind to which we adhere quite firmly, and that is to the extent possible all issues should be looked at on the basis of hard work. That is to say, really turning propositions over, collecting the relevant data and testing them rather than merely tossing them about at a high level of generality unalloyed by hard detailed examination...if you like, a tradition of not ignoring the realities of life that bob up at one stage or another. But I do not in any way accept that there is a doctrinal attitude to which you must conform before you can gain entrance to Treasury. It is demonstratively not so.[32]

Keynes would have been amused! One only has to recall his remark that those positivists who claimed not to have an economic view were really the unconscious purveyors of outdated economic orthodoxy. This orthodoxy was pre-Keynesian and very far from the ultra-Keynesianism which, in recent years, has done much to revitalise and supplement the work commenced by Keynes' *General Theory*. Needless to say, it is even more implacably anti-socialist however one defines the term. The Canberra mood was captured by Hugh Stretton, commenting on his extremely frustrating experience as an advisor to the Whitlam Government:

As advisors to any government, but especially to a Labor government, most of those people seemed technically and politically absurd. But it was marvellous to behold how they rationalised their prejudices. Day after day I sat around coffee tables and conference tables with public servants and private consultants who banked Commonwealth, flew Qantas and British Airways and T.A.A., enjoyed high-speed trains and geometrically designed superhighways, trusted the radio beams in the sky and the admiralty charts at sea and the ordnance maps in the bush, used government loans to buy government houses framed and lined with government softwood, preferred public to private superannuation, shot their children with Salk and Sabin, smoked Gauloises and fuelled their Leylands and Renaults with B.P.—but still knew in their bones as a fact of life, beyond any rational dispute whatever, that the private sector is the only productive sector and that public ownership and management are always, everywhere and incurably inefficient.[33]

To say that the dynamics of the economy were misunderstood, is, however, not to say that people in the higher reaches of the public service were mediocre. The vices of the public service lay elsewhere. In the words of the Coombs' Commission:

While many of the individual criticisms expressed from outside the Service are exaggerated and based as much upon prejudice as upon knowledge, there is no doubt that government service is, with notable exceptions within it, like many other large organisations, excessively centralised, excessively hierarchical, excessively rigid and inflexible, and excessively resistant to organisational change.[34]

RCAGA and beyond

The monumental Coombs' Report of 1976 stimulated, for a couple of years, a lively discussion on the possibilities for public service reform.[35] Of all the Royal Commissions up to that time, RCAGA probed more deeply into the contradictions underlying the public service. It did not resolve many of them; nor could it be expected to because those contradictions were, at root, not just public service contradictions but contradictions at the heart of the polity itself. In Spann's words, the contradictions lay between three models: a 'political' model based on the notions of responsible government enshrined in the Westminster myth, an 'accountable management' model deriving from current thinking on public administration and a 'participatory' model aiming to improve public access and the responsiveness of lower levels in contact with the public.[36] While acknowledging the inadequacy of the Westminster doctrine of ministerial responsibility,[37] it is quite clear that RCAGA retained its core and tended to interpret accountability more in terms of accountability *upwards* (to a 'responsible' Cabinet) than *downwards* (directly towards the public). The mechanisms for greater popular participation, moreover, were always constrained by the above notion of accountability within the Westminster myth. That the Coombs' Report seems to have been shorn of its substance, because of alleged radicalism, does not elicit much confidence about the prospects for reform. This feeling is strengthened by comparing that report with the rather pallid *Review of Commonwealth Administration* (Reid Report) of 1983,[38] though one must acknowledge that some moves proposed by the Hawke government offer the prospect of limited reforms.

Since the purpose of this book is to unpack some of the myths which underpin government in Australia, this section will examine some of the key arguments in the RCAGA Report, the problems they give rise to and what has been done to solve those problems in the years which followed. To avoid repetition, it will commence not by focussing on the Westminster myth but on accountable management and participation.

First what is accountability for? A democratic theorist could give a lot of answers to that question and might indeed consider the role of accountability in fostering the personal qualities of officials and citizens. RCAGA and most official thinking on accountability does not do that. Reading the report, one comes to the conclusion that accountability is sometimes seen as separate from efficiency and at other times efficiency is defined to include accountability. Here there is great scope for confusion. But what is efficiency? As RCAGA sees it, efficiency must include effectiveness (the equivalence of means and ends or what Weber calls 'formal rationality'), the economical use of resources (financial and human) and a mysterious third ingredient which is only approached by simile. The efficiency of the public servant is to be like that of the medical practitioner 'whose objectives in relation to an individual client's problem must take into account the client's general welfare and family and social relations, as well as social and political considerations relating to the practitioner himself'.[39] Here efficiency can only be seen in relation to accountability *downwards*, because how else but by being accountable would the public servant know about the client's general welfare, family and social relations which are to be taken into account?[40] Yet accountability *downwards*, according to the medical practitioner analogy, could militate against that other element of efficiency—the economical use of resources. Using the medical analogy, one might consider discussions about the 'economical' use of kidney machines; arguments about the economical use of resources often lead to the conclusion that certain people with kidney diseases should be allowed to die; but they would not be allowed to do so if the kidney specialists were fully accountable to their clients. The economical use of resources, moreover, might militate against the recommendation that the public service should more closely reflect the social composition of the citizenry[41]— against social justice. One must distinguish between the various components of efficiency and between them and accountability and social justice. What follows will explore the implications of that distinction.

Formal rationality

Let us first consider formal rationality (effectiveness). It is a good thing? This question is begged in a lot of the literature on public administration because rationality is confused with efficiency, of which it is one (and by no means a necessary) part. Max Weber is held to be the apostle of efficiency when in fact he had little to say about it; the error here lies in rationality being wrongly translated as efficiency.[42] For the economist, efficiency is defined in terms of the relationships between inputs and outputs or more broadly as the economical use of resources.[43] Most sociologists would go further than that and interpret efficiency as the attainment of a particular goal with the least possible detriment to other goals.[44] Formal rationality, on the other hand, is the equivalence of means and ends within a clear set of rules. It is possible, therefore, to have a bureaucratic system which is efficient (in the above sociological sense) but which consistently violates the norms of formal rationality. This is surely what Weber had in mind, when, in 1909, he commented that the rational German bureaucratic machine had achieved much less than the relatively corrupt bureaucracies of France and America.[45] In times of severe financial restraint, moreover, the pursuit of efficiency often leads to irrationality which is countered by redefining the means and goals which constitute formal rationality. This might make 'efficiency-auditing' extremely difficult or, worse, misleading.

An example will help. Suppose staff ceilings are imposed upon the Commonwealth Employment Service so that it may not service its clients adequately (efficiency in input-output terms is achieved at the cost of rationality); the goal of catering for the needs of the unemployed is then met by redefining (restricting) those who are eligible for unemployment benefit. This redefinition is now said to be more rational in relation to a higher end—providing the incentive to go out and look for a job. This process may go on *ad infinitum*. The relationship between rationality and efficiency is extremely complex. At this point, all one need observe is that an error basic to public service thinking in Australia is that it is felt that to make a system more efficient is to make it more rational and to make it more rational is to make it more efficient.

This was very clearly the thinking which informed RCAGA and Reid. If to be efficient is to be formally rational and if formal rationality consists in the formulation of appropriate means for the attainment of goals, then the system is more rational (and more efficient) if those goals are clearly stated. This was the first criterion for Coombs' efficiency.[46] Yet goals set by government in Australia are notoriously unclear and for very good reasons. By keeping goals unclear it is much easier for government to evade election promises and to respond to the changing power and salience of pressure groups—a feature which has always frustrated rational processes such as 'programme budgeting'. A more rational public service will result in greater disharmony between elected and appointed officials. Can one achieve greater clarity in setting goals without changing the political system? As it is, goals are frequently set in the context of interaction between Cabinet and public service. Ends, therefore, are often given by the means available to achieve them rather than means being worked out by the public service after the ends have been formulated by Cabinet. Indeed, Sir Geoffrey Vickers and R.F.I. Smith wonder whether the policy process ought to be seen in terms of the setting of goals at all. According to Vickers:

> I have described policy-making as the setting of government relations or norms, rather than in the more usual terms as the setting of goals, objectives or ends. The difference is not merely verbal; I regard it as fundamental[47]... *The goals we seek are changes in our relations or in the opportunities for relating but the bulk of our activity consists in the 'relating' itself.*[48]

Collegiality

Though the RCAGA Report, the Reid Report and public service thinking in Australia generally operate within the parameters of Weberian legal-rationality, there are areas in which the Weberian model has been challenged. One of these is the area of collegial decision-making. Weberian ideas about bureaucracy were formulated at a time when the old Prussian collegial bureaucracy, for which Hegel had high hopes, had been replaced by a discrete hierarchy with formal responsibility assigned to each role. In recent years, there has been much criticism of the formal system described by Weber. This is accompanied by considerable advocacy of more collegiality. Modern writers do not talk in terms of the bureaucracy's ability to embody social ethics (perhaps they ought to) but talk about co-ordination. Such thinking pervades the RCAGA Report and all sorts of measures were proposed to involve a wide spectrum of departmental heads with each other in policy boards supervising a cluster of departments[49], and with members of Cabinet in the formulation of overall policy. Despite RCAGA's call for clearer specification of departmental responsibility, one might even be tempted to suppose that this is some modern equivalent of the Prussian collegial bureaucracy interpreting and formulating the sovereign's will. Indeed, to push the analogy further, the sovereign's function of educating officials, was now spelt out in the following way:

> Each minister has a continuous teaching function to perform in his department, pointing out where and how his government needs to be served as a collective entity.[50]

Presumably, this teaching function can best be served if heads of departments are involved in the earlier Cabinet committee discussions on a truly co-operative basis. But how realistic is this? At root there is a notion, central to the Westminister myth, that Cabinet is coherent in its decision-making and that ministers have the ability and the opportunity to perform an educative role.[51] One knows enough (at least in retrospect) about how most Cabinets work seriously to doubt coherence and to suspect that ministers would not like their ignorance and indecisiveness to be exposed to their senior public servants. Secondly, as Spann narrates, most of the permanent heads he talked to complained not about the overbearing behaviour or interference of ministers but about their inaccessibility, indecisiveness, laziness or double-dealing. Are such ministers likely to be able to perform an educative role, much less the unfortunate minister reported by his permanent head as being a 'slow reader'?[52] In any case, given the most conscientious minister in the world, who had achieved the impossible—a coherent articulation of a coherent sovereign's will—how would he or she find the time to devote to a greatly expanded process of policy-formulation?[53]

The development of a more collegial style of policy-formulation should involve not only Cabinet and senior public servants but also parliament. Both the RCAGA Report and the Reid Report devoted some attention to the relationship between parliament and public service, noting the important role which parliamentary committees might serve in scrutinising the activities of the public service.[54] Chapter 4 noted that the parliamentary committee system was one area in which the role of parliament might be strengthened. Such a development, however, has been inhibited by continuing adherence to the Westminster myth. Public servants appear before parliamentary committees as witnesses to 'facts'; and it is by no means clear as to the extent to which they may be prevented from doing so by a minister who may claim that their appearance undermines the Westminister conventions.[55] Both the RCAGA Report and the Reid Report were still locked into those conventions. What is needed, surely, is more thinking on how parliamentary committees may interact with public servants and Cabinet in the formulation of policy.

In the light of what was said in Chapter 4 about the role of political parties, the above might sound utopian; suffice it to repeat, if there is any hope of bi-partisanship it must be in the committees. In so far as effective policy-making occurs in party committees rather than Cabinet, there is clearly a need also to continue the practice of involving public servants in the deliberations of those committees. But here it is very difficult to envisage the role of the public servant in any way other than that of the expert witness appearing with the permission of the appropriate minister.[56] The same obviously applies to pre-election consultations with the Leader of the Opposition.[57]

Chapter 4 has already put forward the case for party appointees to play a role in delegated legislation. Such appointments raise major questions about traditional ideas concerning a career service. The RCAGA Report devoted much space to this question and the present Hawke Government is taking steps to open up recruitment into the public service at various levels. Clearly, the traditional idea of a separate career service, enshrined in the Westminster myth, is outdated.

Decentralisation and control

When it came to discuss the economical use of resources, RCAGA entered the extremely murky set of arguments concerning the relationship between decentralisation and control. At the moment, the Commission noted:

> The prevailing pattern of organisation within the administration is unduly centralised and hierarchical. This involves a waste of human capacity in the middle and lower levels of staff and frequently creates a sense of frustration and lack of purpose.[58]

To remedy this situation, RCAGA recommended that authority over the use of personnel and funds be decentralised, thereby reducing the control functions of the Public Service Board and Treasury. There are three types of decentralisation which could have been considered. The first two (not advocated by RCAGA) are variants of the Swedish system where much smaller ministries simply perform a broad policy-making role whilst statutory boards are concerned with administration.[59] These are surely what Hawker has in mind in calling for the replacement of the present system of staff-line organisation by a system of functional leadership. Hawker advocates the separation of policy units from administrative units, with a different system of accountability applying to each. Policy units would exercise leadership over specific functions performed by a range of lower level administrative units, and not (as in a staff-line system) over all activities of a limited number of subordinate units. Such an overlapping system of authority would help to combat departmentalism and would enhance flexibility.[60] Evidence from socialist countries, however, would suggest that such a system may lead to confused leadership, an inability to locate responsibility and the need for horizontal co-ordinating mechanisms. At the root of the problem lies the difficulty of separating policy from administration.

A variant of Hawker's proposal is that, whilst policy functions remain with the ministries, the decentralised operational unit takes the form of a statutory authority with a considerable degree of independence. It differs from the first model in that leadership from the policy body is indirect. Australia has a long history of this form of organisation, though the nature of statutory bodies has changed with time. In the days before reponsible government in the colonies, boards staffed·by amateurs were responsible for a wide range of functions. In the heyday of the celebration of the British Constitution in the 1880s, however, the functions of most of these boards were transferred to regular ministerial departments and it was not until the mid-twentieth century that a counter-reaction developed.[61]

Modern professionally-oriented statutory authorities are popularly termed 'quangos' (quasi-non-government organisations). As has often been remarked, there is a dearth of theory governing such bodies,[62] with various commentators not being able to agree on just what a quango might be. It seems there is a continuum between 'go' (government organisation) and 'nongo' (non-government organisation), with various species of quango and quago (quasi-government organisation) in between.[63] In any case, regardless of whether they would all qualify as quangos, there were, in 1979, more than 200 statutory authorities at Commonwealth level, employing 271 000 people (compared with 119 000 in Commonwealth ministerial departments); these authorities employed 5.4% of the total Australian work-force.[64] The statutory authorities varied in the degree to which they were formally responsible to ministers or to parliament. They differed also in their degree of financial independence and in their status at law.

As some people see it, there are clear advantages in the statutory authority form of organisation. Quangos are usually more capable than ministerial departments of adopting efficient and business-like approaches to problems. Their relative independence allows for greater impartiality, for greater *esprit de corps* and for the development of a professional ethos. They allow for intervention in areas under state jurisdiction which may be seen as more legitimate than that of formal government bodies. They are usually better able to deal with matters of controversy between parties suspicious of government.[65] In so far as the statutory authorities are set up for limited purposes, they are more likely to act according to what Weber called substantive rationality, rather than remaining content with the mere interpretation of rules, the purpose of which may have been forgotten. They may, moreover, offer a more convenient management structure for public participation than formal public service bodies.

The above view seems to be that of a minority. Many more people are appalled at what they see as 'quangocracy'[66] (an analogue of bureaucratism). Statutory authorities are seen as representing a commercialisation of the public sector, and do not even compare with that sector in the probity of their appointment procedures. Indeed, it is often claimed, they may be used to further a system of political patronage in a way denied to business or ministerial departments.

Secondly, it is by no means clear that statutory bodies are always more independent than the formal public service.[67] In so far as they might be more independent, moreover, it is not always clear that such is a good thing. In 1977, for example, as Spann narrates, the Prices Justification Tribunal ignored the stated policy of the government; the Conciliation and Arbitration Commission refused to take full account of the government's view that wage rises were the primary causes of inflation and unemployment; the Industries Assistance Commission adopted a stand on free trade different from the government; and the Schools Commission and Public Service Board were not loath to criticise the government on matters of policy.[68] One might wish to applaud some of the above displays of independence on ideological grounds; but one has to admit that they do create problems for theories of responsible government. The above examples are all matters of policy. But could one save responsibility by stipulating that the independence of statutory authorities should be confined to administration? As has been remarked, such might only be achieved if one were able to draw a line of demarcation between policy and administration clearer than most public administration theorists deem to be possible.

In the meantime, the press derives much copy from the many scandals or alleged scandals deriving from excessive or insufficient independence. Reactions against attempts to muzzle the Australian Broadcasting Commission were used to advance the case for greater independence, whilst the lack of control over the Australian Dairy Corporation concerning its Asian subsidiaries was used to advance the opposite case. What is sorely needed is a body of coherent theory about which activities are best administered by statutory authorities and which by ministerial departments. Only when that is worked out will one be able to specify the span of mutual responsibility (upwards and downwards) and permissable degrees of independence from ministerial direction. Only then will parliamentary committees be able to refer to guidelines about the proper activities of such bodies (demanded in the Reid Report).[69] In the meantime, one may understand the reserve shown both by RCAGA (which noted the lack of any explicit rationale in the creation of quite a few statutory authorities)[70] and the Reid Report, which recommended that the statutory authority form should only be adopted when regular public service departments could not do the job.[71] Only when such a body of theory is worked out may one have general legislation governing different types of authority or even something as modest as an Australian equivalent of the British Nationalised Industries Act.[72]

The situation will probably get worse before it gets better. The knee-jerk response of the Queensland Government to the High Court validation of federal control over a Tasmanian statutory authority, in the Dams (Franklin River) Case, was to talk of putting many of its own statutory authorities under direct ministerial control. The considerations were narrowly political rather than deriving from any concern about the public interest. Success in clearing the muddy waters probably depends upon continued recovery from the recent economic recession. One consequence of a major depression might be that it will become impossible to distinguish between private corporations publicly funded to keep them afloat, and public corporations which are partially privately financed. The classical political economists felt that a consequence of downturns in the business cycle would be a tendency towards monopoly. Nowadays, such considerations must take into account the role of the state. Instead of corporatism, discussed in Chapter 3, and instead of Mannheim's 'public responsibility interwoven in the whole fabric of society', one might see an ailing part of the private sector made more responsible to government whilst successful statutory authorities become more irresponsible within a framework where the big powerful private firms which call the tune are totally irresponsible. For all that, the statutory authority form of administration might offer scope for downward accountability, given a government sufficiently astute to chart a new form of (non-Westminster) accountability.

A third type of decentralisation was that advocated by RCAGA. It was simply the devolution of authority to lower levels within the existing structure of ministerial departments. Once authority had been devolved, public servants were to develop an 'entrepreneurial role', performance at which would provide the basis for promotion.[73] This devolution, it was felt, together with improved managerial techniques, would help lower-level public servants identify with the objectives towards which personal efforts were directed.[74] The process of developing the entrepreneurial style was to be facilitated by long-term (three year) forward estimates in which departments could negotiate their own staff and funding requirements with Cabinet.[75] In this way, ministers might become more directly involved in assessing departmental needs and better able to understand intra-departmental problems. Department heads

(RCAGA's term for permanent heads no longer permanent), for their part, would understand the nature of budgetary constraints and would be able to engage in long-term planning. The level of staffing, moreover, could be rationally decided instead of by recourse to the current method of staff ceilings which resulted in considerable imbalances between units.[76] Ultimate supervision of the whole process would rest in the first instance with Treasury, the Public Service Board and in particular the Auditor General[77], and in the last instance with Cabinet. In all this, whatever happened to that other 'co-ordinating' body—the Department of the Prime Minister and Cabinet? Its supervising role, which had been growing in importance in recent years, could not be greatly increased because that would only exacerbate the trend towards 'presidential style of government'.[78] The Westminster myth, indeed, has a tremendous tenacity.[79] Nevertheless, as events turned out, the co-ordinating role of that department was to grow considerably as the power of Treasury declined, especially after it was divided in 1976.

Forward estimates, the core of the above proposals, have been attempted in several countries with a remarkable lack of success. They are either excessively vague or excessively rigid. They were, however, promoted by the Liberal Government in the late 1970s, and for reasons suggested earlier in the discussion of goals, seemed to fall into the vague category. By 1983, features such as staff ceilings, about which RCAGA complained, were seen as a 'fact of life' and a 'necessary discipline'.[80]

A major problem here is that neither governments nor public services are usually very good at planning. As has been noted, governments are unwilling to engage in long-term planning due to electoral considerations and a reluctance to specify clear goals on which they may be pinned down. Most senior public servants, it is argued, do not make good planners 'because they are trained to concern themselves with the immediately practicable. The practical administrator is often highly conscious of the need to simplify problems and to seize on one or two essential points; the planner is freer to elaborate and cost alternatives'.[81] Both RCAGA and Spann reject this latter point though, for all the talk of planning in recent years, policy-making in Australia is still characterised by incrementalism and scepticism about favourable outcomes.

When one considers planning together with administrative decentralisation, in the manner of RCAGA, it is instructive to consider some of the experiences of socialist countries. These show that, even when a functional system of leadership is not adopted, the attempt to combine long-term planning with administrative decentralisation leads to administrative fragmentation and to violation of the conditions of the long-term plan. Tremendous pressure is then put on supervisory agencies both at central and regional levels. When fragmentation persists, these supervisory agencies change their role and become directing agencies.

Now what are the implications for Australia? RCAGA proposed that the relatively easy directing functions of the Commonwealth Public Service Board (over personnel and classification) and Treasury (over the provision of funds) would be replaced by a supervisory role.[82] How would these bodies operate if administrative fragmentation occurred? It is likely that the Public Service Board would do very little. After all, it always possessed a supervisory role which it was loath to exercise.[83] Treasury, on the other hand, which has always been powerful, would probably attempt to change its co-ordinating role back to the old role of direction. Its ability to do this, however, would be countered by that department which is really growing in power and prestige—that of Prime Minister and Cabinet. Some argue that it would have been better to have created a new supervisory body, unhampered by either an old tradition of inertia or by long experience of actual control. Opinion on this is divided. RCAGA set its mind firmly against the creation of new bodies[84], with one exception—the Department of Industries and the Economy.[85] Although this department was not even to be a supervisory organ in the above sense, the proposal managed to incur the bitter opposition of Treasury which regarded the proposed department as dangerous because it might provide an alternative source of economic advice.[86] One might imagine what friction would have been caused had the proposal not been done to death and how much more animosity might have been generated by any new supervisory body. It is possible, however, that a government with sufficient will and power could have created a new supervisory organ which might have policed decentralised power. But one should call a spade a spade! Such an organ would *supervise* not co-ordinate! Co-ordinating agencies in socialist countries tend to be, at bottom, agencies charged with exercising a differently based form of *control*. The same is probably true in Australia. Peres puts the case most forcefully:

> Co-ordination is one of the fraudulent words of politics and administration. It dresses neutrally to disguise what nakedly is pure political form. Co-ordination is a political process by which the co-ordinated are made to change their value positions, their policy conceptions and their behaviour to conform with the conceptions and expectations of the co-ordinator.[87]

RCAGA, noting that too much power was centred in Canberra,

proposed that a senior representative be located in each of the States to 'co-ordinate' activities at that level and that the Department of Prime Minister and Cabinet set up a 'co-ordinating' unit for decentralisation.[88] At the basic level co-ordination might be achieved by experiments such as that at Coburg, where the delivery of services of a number of departments might be located under one roof, 'the one stop shop'.[89] Such experiments were endorsed by the subsequent Liberal Government. One may, however, envisage major 'co-ordinating' problems exacerbated by the centripetal tendencies so entrenched in the public service; and it was evident in the 1983 Reid Report that such tendencies are as strong as ever.[90] However committed a department might be to promotion on the basis of merit, there is nothing like face to face relationships for those who want to get ahead. It is a fundamental mistake to underrate the importance of the informal bureaucratic network when it comes to upward mobility. People of talent have to be *seen* as people of talent. Short of a total reconstruction of the system, they have to be seen as pillars of the central bureaucratic citadel itself: in Canberra.

The argument above, concerning the relationship between planning and administrative devolution, has been stated somewhat abstractly. One may envisage all sorts of concrete problems. What, for example, happens when the Auditor General or a supervisory body finds that there has been financial mismanagement in a department? How is responsibility located? The old Westminster myth says that the minister is responsible. Is the head of department (permanent head) now responsible?[91] Surely, under the doctrine of devolved responsibility, the head of department might point to some lower echelon which was responsible. But suppose RCAGA's recommendations about collective decision-making were implemented,[92] could one locate responsibility at all? And what happens when one considers that body of literature on organisational decision-making which talks about 'spans of decision', where proposals grow almost imperceptibly into decisions with no one actually being responsible and responsibility being merely determined by arbitrary rule. Or is the situation as described by Schaffer: 'decisions are convenient labels given *post hoc* to the mythical precedents of the apparent outcomes of uncertain conflicts'.[93] Again, experience with systems of responsibility in socialist countries suggests that attempts to codify responsibility are effective merely in satisfying political authorities that there is always someone to 'carry the can'. They rarely locate real responsibility and where someone who was barely responsible for a wrong decision is actually made to 'carry the can', the loss of morale may be considerable.

The relationship between responsibility and morale is a very important one. Both RCAGA and Reid were aware of this, yet one can not help feeling that the question was dealt with somewhat blandly. As might be expected, the discipline which informed the reports, and thinking in the public service in general, has been that of personnel management rather than organisational sociology. Clearly, identification of officials with policies is achieved if management is project-oriented[94] and if personal qualities necessary to carry out the project are rated more highly than job specifications. Clearly also, the abolition of the old division structure,[95] and top management being regularly moved around and supplemented by contract appointments,[96] could have an effect on the morale of lower upwardly-mobile public servants. Furthermore, staff participation in decision-making at all levels could reinforce commitment. At least, organisational psychology says that such may be the case. The problem is how to create organisational structures in which those objectives are to be achieved. One suspects that project management will work well in the new departments where there are fewer established structures. The prospects for 'organisational development' in the short-lived Department of Urban and Regional Development, for example, encouraged the participation of people with missionary zeal. What would project management look like in Treasury and where could its missionaries be found? In DURD personal qualities could be rated more highly because the details of job specifications were to a large degree created by enterprising officials. There was no time-honoured hierarchy of slots into which people had to be fitted. The abolition of the old division structure might do much to motivate junior staff. So indeed might the rotation of permanent heads. This latter proposal was put forward in both the RCAGA Report and the Reid Report, although the latter recommended against fixed-term appointments.[97] Now the Hawke Government has proposed a much more comprehensive system of appointment. Problems, however, could arise concerning the placement of heads of department who had completed the prescribed five to seven years. Would they possess the necessary expertise to head another department? In 1976 the Fraser Government legislated to remove 'non-established' heads (after five years or a change of government). But what about established heads? Perhaps they might become 'advisors'. Yet can Australia afford a huge corps of advisors who could become divorced from the reality of day to day administration and become the purveyors of outdated orthodoxy?[98] This problem is, however, probably over-stated. Statistics released in the Reid Report show that, of 79 permanent heads appointed between 1972 and 1982, 22 were transferred to other permanent headships and only 17 came from the department to which they were being appointed. Indeed, in January 1983, it was found that only one permanent head had served in his present position for more than seven years and only one other for more than five years.[99]

As for participation in decision-making, can it have any substance until the hierarchical structures which constrain it are fundamentally changed? Attempts to introduce it in a structure which is unreformed will probably lead to it being considered a human relations gimmick and a technique of control.[100] By now the argument of this section should be crystal clear. The change in behaviour, envisaged by RCAGA, required far more radical organisational change than the Commission imagined or than that envisaged by most current exponents or modern personnel management.

Participation

The reforms considered above all bear on the questions of efficiency and accountability. The question remains: what is the relationship between accountability *upwards* and accountability *downwards*? As has been noted, despite its acknowledgement of the unreality of the old notion of responsible government, RCAGA still seemed to assume that, by making the public service more accountable to Cabinet, it would thus be more responsible to the people. A similar assumption was made about accountability to parliament, though the Report noted that only 1% of clients interviewed sought assistance in handling grievances through their MP, and less than half the people interviewed by surveys (the people most likely to be in need) were aware of the role of an MP in taking up grievances concerning the public service.[101] Bearing this in mind, RCAGA did make some recommendations concerning direct accountability and these merit attention. In the words of the Report:

> We suggest...that an official should see it as proper to be 'responsive' to those who seek to participate; at least to perform his tasks in a more open style, to be accessible and to be a good listener; behaving in effect as if his accountability to the minister required also, as does the minister's, an accountability directly to the community.[102]

To say, however, that an official should respond to public pressure is very different from saying that an official should be accountable to the public. At root here is the old distinction between responsiveness and responsibility. The public service (and for that matter Cabinet) responds not to *the public* but to pressure groups (a lot of little publics which are in reality *private*), which may be discounted by the public service as only representing partial interests. If the public service is to be accountable to *the public*, then there needs to be an institutional structure which will encourage a hitherto passive citizenry to scrutinise the activities of officials. As Painter points out, the requirement simply to be responsive could simply result in critical pressure groups being co-opted by officialdom—the corporatist scenario. Painter is most dissatisfied with RCAGA's discussion of participation:

> The commission's discussion of participation falls into this trap of treating participation as if it were a primary goal of outsider groups, and many of their suggestions could hence with some justification be considered as tokenism and symbolic reassurance. Discussion focusses on who should participate in what kinds of structures and the problems that most worry RCAGA concern imbalance in representation or expertise. In discussing representation of client groups they are concerned to 'keep the membership of the body under review'. The report in other words concentrates on forms of participatory structures and on participation as an end, not a means to concrete goals. And even here, although they claim sympathies with participation as an alternative, their main allegiance is to tradition. The discussion of advisory groups in the policy process ends with the proviso that all their deliberations must be firmly locked into the central budgeting process and the normal procedures of accountability. We seem to be back to square one.[103]

RCAGA's recommendations resemble British experiments with 'joint consultation'.[104] How can one go beyond that? Perhaps government could establish real *policy-making* rather than mere advisory bodies at various levels in the public service. Using the formula made famous by the Webbs, these bodies might consist of representatives of 'producers, consumers and citizens'. The representation of producers was a call for industrial democracy. In the bureaucratic context, this requires rank and file representation at the higher-reaches of the public service. In industry, however, such advocacy has created tensions between participatory bodies, which appear to mask the clash of interest between employers and employees, and unions dedicated only to furthering the interests of employees. Could one anticipate a similar development in the public service? As for the representation of 'consumers' and citizens, these policy-making bodies could include representatives of clients served by the department (nominated by particular interest groups—for example, tax-payers association or unemployed workers union) and representatives of the citizens, nominated by local government.

There will, of course, be a certain amount of arbitrariness in how the representatives of clients are selected. This was recognised by RCAGA but not regarded as an insuperable barrier.[105] The problem of a diffused constituency, moreover, would probably preclude elections. If nominated, however, the nomination should surely rest with local government rather than the public service itself. Though the above proposals might seem quite radical in the context of RCAGA, they are merely an extension of practices which apply in embryonic form in few statutory bodies.

Commenting on staff and outsider participation in governing statutory bodies, RCAGA was very cautious. It called merely for current practices to be evaluated and Burkean, rather than delegate, principles of representation to be implemented.[106] Participation should go further than that! Perhaps one may envisage an extension to other fields of the long-term plans for Aboriginal involvement in the Department of Aboriginal Affairs.[107] But would a system of participation at the local level work in a federal structure in which local government is a State concern? Although problems would arise, experiments should be undertaken. In any case, Chapter 6 will argue, one of the most powerful arguments against the federal system is the difficulty in co-ordinating services at the basic level. It is probably the case that a policy-making body in charge of a one stop shop which embraces both Commonwealth and State functions would always be hampered. But there are more immediate problems than that.

Let us state the case baldly. Participation should not be seen as an end in itself.[108] The purpose of outsider participation in the policy-making of the public service is not just to educate people as citizens in the social liberal tradition but to make sure that all the people are efficiently and equitably served. Two major factors frustrate this. The first is bureaucratic structure. Access research conducted by RCAGA showed that people were frustrated not only by the conduct of basic-level staff but also by procedural red tape at higher levels of the structure.[109] Participatory bodies might make counter staff the most efficient and courteous people in the world, but a lot more is required to remedy the structural causes of frustration. The second factor is social. The class structure, and social structure in general, is such that simple participation will not guarantee efficient and equitable service; it might even militate against it. School councillors, for example, will easily acknowledge that there are many groups of parents whose interests are never represented. Many migrant groups, underprivileged groups etc., for a myriad of cultural reasons, do not seek representation on such bodies, and any notion of 'virtual' representation is absurd. But even if there was equitable representation, how might one guarantee that informed discussion and deliberation will follow? How many times do school councils find themselves with a majority of outsiders who have not considered education since they themselves were at school, who swallow nonsense about the pernicious influences of more 'liberal' policies and seek remedy in stricter discipline and an overwhelming concentration on 'the three Rs'. This is a central problem of democratic theory—one which lay at the core of the thinking of John Stuart Mill. Inputs of experts are necessary, and ways must be found to see that those experts are provided by sources other than the institution the democratic body is to supervise.

A further problem of democratic participation lies in the all too frequent disjunction between the organised groups represented and the number of people to be served. This was all too obvious in the Coburg experiment. There, a policy committee, with outside participants, decided not to approve the inclusion of a full unemployment benefits unit at the centre because the growing number of people to be served would take up too much space and crowd out the various voluntary groups using it.[110] Disproportionate influence, it seems, will always be exercised by those groups which are best able to organise. This problem, which lies at the heart of pluralist theory, has been discussed in Chapter 3. Suffice it here just to underline one point; if organisation is the key to effective participation, then who organises the unorganised? Should the state pay professional agitators and would they be credible?[111]

Administrative law

The above problems of participation were merely touched upon by RCAGA and largely ignored in the Reid Report of 1983.[112] RCAGA, and indeed most official thinking, has tended to focus on responsiveness rather than democratic policy-making, and particularly on how to handle grievances rather than anything wider. Since RCAGA, such considerations have informed a body of legislation—the Ombudsman Act (1976), and the Administrative Decisions (Judicial Review) Act (1977). These, together with the earlier Administrative Appeals Tribunal Act (1975), represent Australia's recent attempt to create a body of administrative law.[113] The 1976 Act established a tribunal for the appointment of a Commonwealth Ombudsman who was to investigate complaints of maladministration on the part of Commonwealth officials, to rectify errors with the co-operation of officials, to notify parliament of his or her actions and if necessary to appeal directly to the Prime Minister. The 1977 Act provided for the new Federal Court to review the lawfulness of administrative decisions, its scope being much wider than the Act of 1975. Though the above are welcome steps, one must point out that judicial bodies are notoriously slow and their operation is extremely expensive—a point stressed time and again in the Reid Report.[114] It is possible also that the establishment of bodies to redress grievances might result in even further bureaucratism.[115] The activities of the Ombudsman, moreover, really depend on the goodwill of officials. If sufficient deadlocks were to occur (and they do not appear to have as yet) then there is no way a Prime Minister would have the time to sort them out. At most, one might expect that the deterrent of public exposure through the report to parliament would keep the public service cooperative.

The question of administrative law is new in Australia and one has yet to see how it will develop. There is much to be learned from overseas experience. Take for example the question of financial redress from state maladministration. Provisions for this have been introduced in Australia,[116] though the whole question is limited by medieval notions about Crown immunity. As far as the courts are concerned, an invalid decision causing loss does not provide cause for an action for damages against the government unless the invalidity is accompanied by a civil wrong. Mr Justice Kirby believes this should be modified along lines which pertain in France. The following quote from Duguit is laudable:

> The activity of the state is carried out in the interests of the entire community; the burdens that it entails should not weigh more heavily on some than on others. If then state action results in individual damage to particular citizens, the state should make redress, whether or not there be fault committed by the public officers concerned. The state is, in some ways, an insurer of what is called social risk (*risque social*).[117]

Perhaps a French lawyer would be content to interpret the above. A political theorist, however, cannot but observe that, if the above was carried out to the letter, the whole country would be in a continuous state of litigation. Unless one makes a rather spurious (and legalistic) distinction between collective and individual, then one must admit that state action is causing some damage to the vast majority of the population.

Though administrative law is liable to evince the incredulity of political theorists, its advent is to be welcomed. A little accountability is better than none. The same goes for the recognition, implicit in the provision of administrative law, that the Westminster notion of ministerial responsibility is out of date. For decades, 'administrative law' was considered to be rather 'foreign' and unnecessary in a political system in which public accountability was considered to be sufficiently achieved through ministers responsible to the people through parliament. The real world is now confronted! But one can not fail to note that the advent of the new administrative law has occasioned a formidable backlash. The 1983 Reid Report, echoing the comments of Sir Zelman Cowen whilst Governor General,[118] maintained:

> There is an increasing realisation in a number of quarters that the complex framework of administrative law which has developed in recent years, may have gone too far. There should be an independent assessment of its costs and the relationship of those costs to the community benefits produced. In the interests of helping citizens in resolving their differences with bureaucracy, the framework should be simplified. Access to this machinery for airing public service personnel matters should be modified—private sector employers are not subject to this sort of surveillance of employer/employee relationships and public service staff rights would be more than adequately protected without it.[119]

Such a conclusion is questionable! Surely, public service reforms should be the pace-setter for reforms in the private sector rather than the latter being taken as the norm.

Clearly, if a minimum level of accountability to the citizens is to be enjoyed, then there must be freedom of information. During the decade since 1972, there has been much discussion of proposed legislation but the eventual Act fell short of the American model of 1967 (amended 1974) and very short of the Swedish model. Though, clearly, the legislation was disliked by significant sections of the public service, and eloquent arguments were put forward concerning costs ($18 million per annum to cover staff and overheads),[120] most of the protracted discussions concerned the extent to which such legislation might undermine elements of the Westminster myth.[121] What was particularly guarded was the flow of information between minister and public service department. It is as yet too early to assess the effect of the various clauses relating to information which may be released and how the public service will perform its task in releasing information. One should not hold out many hopes, though clearly some legislation is better than none. Similarly, it is too early to come to any conclusions about the recently established Human Rights Commission. The Commission's task is to monitor the extent to which Commonwealth departments and agencies and general activities in the ACT adhere to the International Covenant on Civil and Political Rights and to international declarations on the rights of various groups. Its achievements so far have been modest but very worthwhile.

Social justice

The final observation in this chapter concerns the relationship between efficiency, accountability and social justice. People like Hayek, in the old classical liberal tradition, argue that there is no such thing as social justice. There are merely 'just' individuals, who are 'just' in so far as they fulfil the prescriptions of the 'higher' law.[122] Most academic thinking in Australia, in recent years, is highly critical of Hayekian views. So indeed must be the Australian Government, which in adhering to some of the international human rights conventions, also affirms a notion of social justice. As far as bureaucracy is concerned, social justice demands that the composition of the public service reflects the composition of society at large. This was a primary concern of RCAGA which noted the relative paucity of numbers of various groups in the public service.[123] Clearly, in a class society and a society in which there is a woeful maldistribution of skills among various groups, there can only be a modest move in the direction of social justice. Why are special avenues into the public service not provided for migrants and Aborigines? It is an open question as to whether a more socially representative bureaucracy now under consideration by the Hawke Government would be more capable of responding to marginalised groups or whether it would be more efficient. It may indeed be *less* efficient; but after all that has been said, would that necessarily be a bad thing? In any case, social justice has intrinsic rather than purely instrumental merits. But how far does one go? Notions of affirmative action or positive discrimination in favour of women and under–represented groups will surely attack the sacred cows of bureaucracy—particularly one which is more and more concerned with meritocratic values. But so be it!

One must not be too sanguine about moves along such lines. Whatever might be done to redress the imbalance at lower levels, short of a fundamental change in the *political* system, the higher reaches will probably continue to be drawn from the most privileged sections of society; their position will be buttressed by a complicated structure of informal networks which link government and business and they will continue to administer the status quo.

Conclusion

One is now in a position to list some of the myths which sustain the position of, and limit the accessibility to, bureaucracy. The Westminster myth protects senior administrators from accountability downward (as it protects government from public scrutiny of its incompetence). The myth, moreover, allows the exercise of power to proceed under the guise of official anonymity (though this is changing). The myth has also been used to hamper moves towards freedom of information and effective devolution of power. The myth which separates policy from administration, repudiated by RCAGA[124] though not always consistently, likewise hides official power and, in so far as it prevents the location of decision-making, impedes accountability. Perhaps the most misleading feature of both the Westminster myth and the separation of policy from administration is that they foster the belief that the point of decision may always be located. Why can it not be admitted that this is often impossible, and why can not the notion of collective responsibility be accepted in place of that of ministerial responsibility? The doctrines of accountable management, likewise, encourage a number of myths. They often hide the fact that efficiency and rationality might be in contradiction. They often hide the fact that co-ordination is often a form of control, and the task of co-ordinating agencies is not so much to foster harmony among dispersed groups as to resolve the contradiction between different interests. They often encourage the mistaken belief that personnel management is a skill separate from organisational sociology, and that the right attitudes might be achieved without major structural reform. Most regrettably, they foster 'participatory' schemes which may easily be dismissed as a 'human relations gimmick'.

Despite the criticism of RCAGA in this chapter, it must be conceded, with hindsight, that there were elements in the Report which should have led to constructive thinking about radical change, directed at making the bureaucracy not only more accountable or more responsive to the people it was to serve but also more responsible. Unfortunately, the excitement generated by its advent declined during the Fraser years. The document, completed under the chairmanship of Reid, was pallid in comparison. One may only hope that the present Labor Government will carry on where RCAGA left off. Here, as yet, there are only a few signs.

SIX
FEDERALISM IN AUSTRALIA
'E PLURIBUS PLURA'

FEDERATION IN 1901 was a compromise. Like most compromises it was an attempt to satisfy sets of contradictory interests. Chapter 4 discussed the contradiction between the bicameral system, designed originally to safeguard States' rights, and the British system of responsible government. This contradiction was one aspect of a much broader contradiction—between a centralised (perhaps even a unitary) form of government and a desire to retain the sovereignty of the former colonies. This contradiction bedevils all federations and has led some commentators to conclude that federations are inherently unstable and must either become more and more centralised to the point of becoming unitary states or else dissolve into their component parts. Considering the steps towards unification, it is sometimes argued that federations pass through three stages—co-ordinate federalism (where distinct powers are specified for centre and regions and provisions are made for the role of the 'state as a whole')[1], co-operative federalism (where centre and regions enter into co-operative agreements concerning overlapping functions) and organic federalism (where the centre takes over most important policy making roles but delegates operational decision-making to the regions, for example, Austria[2]). This final stage is very close to a unitary state. Indeed, it is very difficult to tell the difference between, for example, the federal Austrian state and the British unitary state which delegates powers to some regions. Australia has not adhered to such a progression. Though clearly the Australian economy has become more centralised in the last eighty years, there has not been the automatic growth of any organic federalism nor moves toward a unitary state. Holmes and Sharman, after surveying attitudinal differences among the States on a whole range of questions and arguing that Australia manifests a 'federal culture', conclude:

Once a federal system of government is accepted as the legitimate governing arrangement, it comes in turn to exercise a force upon the political habits of the polity. Sometimes a federal system may tend towards unity, and at other times the pendulum swings towards decentralisation, but this is not to say that it is necessarily moving away from a federal continuum. Movements towards greater and lesser asymmetry and symmetry between the various units in the federal system fuel the swings in the pendulum, but withal the system still exhibits the federal characteristic of a system of checks and balances limiting central government powers within prescribed constitutional boundaries. Regional values and local autonomies are entrenched and constitutionally protected, and barriers are raised to the radical relocation of values by the central government.[3]

Holmes and Sharman are undoubtedly correct. But what one person sees as checks and balances another might see as obstacles in the path of efficiency, on the one hand, and social justice, on the other.

The problem of the Australian federal system, it will be argued, is not that it is unstable, as many of the old commentators argued that all federal systems must be, but that it *is* stable—stable to the point of inertia. Contrary to Holmes and Sharman, who fear the 'totalitarian streak inherent in big government', this chapter will argue that moves must be undertaken to counter the inertia. The need is to create a new legal skeleton upon which the Australian body politic might grow. Such a skeleton (in Sawer's words) should resemble that of the mammal; it should be internal and supportive rather than external and restricting like that of the sea urchin.[4]

The myth of co-ordinate federalism

The original federation drew ideas from America, Canada and Switzerland (for the referendum process) and was specifically designed as a form of co-ordinate federalism, providing both central and State governments with their own sovereignty. It was apparently to satisfy something like the strict test subsequently made famous by Wheare:

Does a system of government embody predominantly a division of powers between general and regional authorities each of which in its own sphere is co-ordinate with the others and independent of them.[5]

Though the inspiration came from a number of sources, the model was more American than anything else and was devised by people well versed in American constitutional law. The Constitution expressly specified a number of powers to be exercised by the central government and allowed the residue to be exercised by the States. Put crudely, it differed from the Canadian model in which the Constitution allocated specific powers to the regions (provinces) and gave the residue to the centre. The American model was preferred because it provided checks on the possible tyranny of a central government. Indeed, it was considered that the powers of the central government would not be all that great. In America, the argument about checks and balances had been the subject of much eloquent political philosophy and had been celebrated in the classic *Federalist Papers*. For James Madison, the American federal scheme was part of a grand design in which powers would be separated and interests divided. This would allow the central government to direct policy in *the public interest* by selecting all that was best in the various private and regional interests which were represented at the centre. Earlier chapters noted that Madison's grand design collapsed in the pluralist era of the twentieth century, and the public interest became celebrated as no more than the balance of private interests. They noted also that the Australian Commonwealth was born at a time of social liberal fervour in Australia, which reflected a British concern with the public interest (usually referred to as the 'common good'). Yet despite the role of prominent social liberals such as Deakin in its formulation, that Act of the British Parliament which became the Australian Constitution is remarkably devoid of social liberal concerns. Reading the Australian Constitution, it is difficult to see how such a document could be used effectively in promoting the self-development of citizens towards the common good. The document is merely a set of rules specifying the dimensions of co-ordinate federalism.

A positivist may say that a constitution can be no more than a set of rules and the law is itself nothing but an elaborate set of rules. Critics of positivism, however, note that the United States Constitution is much more than a set of rules. It contains a number of principles from which rights may be derived. Indeed, its first thirteen amendments are precisely a Bill of Rights. As Dworkin so eloquently argues, the pretensions of legal positivism that the law can be no more than a set of rules is both false and dangerous.[6] It is false because judges inevitably invoke principles, and it is dangerous because there is felt to be no need to lay those principles down. In a co-ordinate federal system judges might apply different and inconsistent principles in the centre and regions and might feel justified in doing so 'according to the rules'. McMillan, Evans and Storey point out some of the unfortunate consequences of this in Australia:

Section 51(31) requires that any acquisition of property by the Commonwealth be on 'just terms'. The section has been interpreted such that it does not prevent a State from compulsorily acquiring land otherwise than on just terms and subsequently transferring it to the Commonwealth; nor does it prevent the Commonwealth taking land otherwise than on just terms in a Territory.

Section 80 guarantees a trial by jury for any person charged with an indictable Commonwealth offence. The Commonwealth can avoid that guarantee, simply by providing that an offence shall be triable summarily rather than by indictment.

Section 116 guarantees the free exercise of religion. During wartime the section did not protect the activity of Jehovah's Witnesses in preaching non co-operation with the Commonwealth in terms of military obligation.

Section 117 prohibits States from discriminating against interstate residents. The section has not invalidated State legislation requiring a period of local residence as a prerequisite for admission to a profession.[7]

Of course, the same problems arise in the United States. But there, at least, one does have appeal to constitutional principles which have allowed people to elaborate standards for adjudication at a national level. Commenting on the various methods devised to use rationally the waters of the River Murray, Clark observes that if differences of opinion were to occur in the United States:

> The traditional means of resolving such differences would be first to resort to litigation to obtain a declaration of the respective quantitative and qualitative entitlements of the contending States and then, by an 'aftermath compact', an inter-State Commission would be created to administer the resource in a manner consistent with the prior judicial determination. This has been possible because the United States Supreme Court has developed a doctrine of 'equitable apportionment' which allows the Court to apportion the available resource between contending States... Since 1911, however, the (Australian) High Court has denied its capacity to make similar awards. It regards its jurisdiction as confined to matters which are capable of resolution by pre-existing rules of law. The American doctrine of 'equitable apportionment' requires the application of principles of equity, comity, politics and international law in addition to rules of law, which in the view of Isaacs J. would be 'outside the pale of sober thought' in the Australian context. If there is an inter-State common law to apply to a dispute between the States over the River Murray—which is itself a matter of doubt—it would probably only empower the High Court to declare particular activities as exceeding the reasonable

share of one State. It would not support a prospective determination of entitlements upon which it would then be possible to build a rational co-operative administrative structure.[8]

One needs, therefore, to draft principles and to state explicitly principles which are currently only implicit. It may be possible to order these principles in terms of a single standard. But if one does not agree with Dworkin that principles and rights may be derived from the one basic right of citizens to equality of respect[9] and still adheres to legal positivism, one surely has to agree with Hart that one needs not only rules which grant rights and impose obligations upon members of society (primary rules), but also secondary rules which stipulate how and by whom primary rules may be formed, recognised, modified, or extinguished.[10] Section 51 of the Australian Constitution provides such secondary rules (so essential for any notion of co-ordinate federalism), but they are contradictory and leave citizens bemused as to what secondary rules take priority. The High Court, moreover, over time, has changed its interpretation of the rules of recognition. For example, in 1982 the High Court upheld (by a majority of four to three) the validity of the Racial Discrimination Act (1975) by invoking Section 51(29)—the external affairs power (the Koowarta Case). It was decided that the Commonwealth had the power to legislate on any matter of international concern in which failure to act might affect Australia's relations with other countries (apparently regardless of whether Australia was bound by an international treaty). By a single act, the High Court changed the rules of recognition usually applied to Section 51. Such a change was underlined in the subsequent Dams Case (by reference, amongst other things, to Australia's obligations under the World Heritage Convention). One might now anticipate no successful challenge to legislation concerning the discrimination of women, reference being made to the International Covenant on the Elimination of All Forms of Discrimination against Women. Precedents have been established for guaranteeing legislation protecting the rights of indigenous minorities (under ILO Convention 107) and the enactment of human rights legislation.[11] Evidently the 1983 Attorney General, Gareth Evans, thought that such is the case,[12] though the opposition is formidable and frightening in its emotional crudity. One has only to consider advertisements in the national press calling on people to voice their protest at government consideration of the convention governing discrimination against women for this to be abundantly clear.[13] It was argued that ratification of that convention implied domination of Australia by *Soviet*-inspired legislation, and one may envisage a repetition of the situation where '95 percent of women are forced into the workplace'. That such a ludicrous claim is taken seriously is testimony to the earlier argument about the woeful lack of attention given to political education by either of the major political parties. Anyone claiming to be progressive must regard the anticipated use of the Koowarta and Dams precedents with optimism; but that optimism should not detract from the point that the High Court action was only possible because the rules of recognition concerning federal and State jurisdictions in the Constitution are confused. This is a problem well known in the United States and applies to all federal constitutions, though in Australia the waters are made more muddy by medieval British notions such as the Crown 'single and indivisible'. There is, and can be, no such thing as co-ordinate federalism in a modern state.

Nowadays it is mainly judges who talk the language of co-ordinate federalism. Political theorists have been most eloquent in their denunciation of Wheare's test. Friedrich, for example, criticises his excessive legalism and the demand for a total demarcation of functions. According to Friedrich, federalism 'should not be seen only as a static pattern or design characterized by a particular and precisely fixed division of powers',[14] and that 'the idea of a compact is inherent'. Friedrich here is talking about what is usually known as co-operative federalism. His sense of a compact includes consensus, discussion and an intention to arrive at a mutually acceptable solution. Yet it is Wheare's test rather than Friedrich's arguments which are more commonly celebrated in the rhetoric about federalism. It is easy to see why the rhetoric is encouraged by lawyers trained in a positivistic discipline which reduces law to rules. It is easy also to see why hidebound politicians offer similar encouragement, for it provides a ready rationalisation of the status quo. It is less easy to see why the rhetoric is adhered to by more progressive legislators. To attempt an answer one must return to the discussion of responsible government in Chapter 4. Clearly the participation of any minister in any of the institutions of co-operative federalism must involve a modification of the responsibility of that minister to his or her parliament. Indeed, the decisions of a co-operative body, such as the Loan Council, might be quite irresponsible. Take for example Section 105A of the Constitution, inserted as a result of the referendum of 1928. Referring to agreements between the Commonwealth and the States with respect to the public debts of the States, the fifth clause reads:

> Every such agreement and any such variation thereof shall be binding upon the Commonwealth and the State parties thereto,

notwithstanding anything contained in this Constitution or the Constitution of the several States or in any law of the Parliament of the Commonwealth or of any State.

Commenting on that clause Sir Edward Mitchell remarked in 1931:

> The provisions of that sub-section (5) are probably unique in the whole legal history of all English-speaking communities with parliamentary institutions, and have the effect of putting both the existing financial agreements on a higher plane as regards enforcing its obligations, than the Commonwealth Constitution, hitherto described as the supreme law of Australia.[15]

Back in 1927, the Commonwealth Government held that there was no danger of the Loan Council becoming 'some sort of super parliament'; it 'could never be regarded as an authority superior to the Commonwealth parliament or to the State parliaments'.[16] A literal reading of the above clause, however, suggests the opposite, and the only safeguard against such an interpretation seems to be a 'gentleman's agreement'. It was a concern over irresponsibility which led Sawer to oppose the Petroleum (Submerged Lands) Bill of 1967. His arguments deserve to be quoted:

> The State Ministers who will make all the crucial decisions are in no way answerable to the Commonwealth Parliament, whose legislation provides the main basis for their powers... One could easily imagine the readiness with which any Commonwealth Minister will wriggle out of answering parliamentary questions and criticisms... Meanwhile, in the State Parliaments, the relevant Minister will wriggle out of responsibility just as easily... The ultimate responsibility for these decisions could and should have been placed squarely with the Commonwealth Minister.[17]

After all that has been said about the irresponsible nature of Australian parliaments this would seem merely an academic argument, but it does point to a reason why politicians prefer to talk the language of co-ordinate federalism. They are not prepared to admit to irresponsibility! Once concessions are made, however, the myth of co-ordinate federalism plays into the hands of people who attack the manifest justice of decisions in the Koowarta and Dams cases on the grounds that the principles of co-ordinate sovereignty have been violated.

The nightwatchman state

One may have little doubt that many of the founding fathers of the Australian Constitution would have been most surprised at the use of Section 51 (29) in the Koowarta decision, even though some of the social liberals at that time might have supported it (but not many in a prevailing racist environment). This is because the Constitution is a set of rules for what, in classical liberal theory, is called 'the nightwatchman state'. Not only was the Commonwealth given a limited set of powers which it was felt impractical for the States to perform, but, as has been noted, Commonwealth powers themselves reflect a limited role for government in general. The role of government in the classical liberal tradition was to do as little as possible consistent with holding the ring for the interplay of market forces. As Herbert Spencer put it, the scope of government should be the minimum consistent with the continued existence of trade in an ordered society. There were, of course, some exceptions here, notably the corporations power (S 51[2]), which few people seemed to understand, and the conciliation and arbitration power (S 51[25]), which everybody pretended to understand but understood differently. In general, though, the blueprint was in the classical liberal vein and even contained some classical liberal pieties which could not possibly mean what they said—for example the famous Section 92:

> On the imposition of uniform duties of customs, trade, commerce and intercourse among the States, whether by means of internal carriage or ocean navigation, shall be absolutely free.

One does not have to be a philosopher to acknowledge that, in the absence of a predicate specifying freedom with regard to what, the notion of absolute freedom is literally nonsense[18] and can only be there to serve an ideological purpose. Were this not the case, one would have expected a more specific formulation of the conditions necessary for a common market. As Sawer notes, Section 92 was concocted in 1891 by Sir Henry Parkes, 'a non-lawyer and an execrable minor poet, who was not present in 1897–8 to explain his rhetoric'.[19] One might, however, understand the use of the phrase by reference to the intentions of the founding fathers, but the High Court has ruled against such reasoning in legal decisions.

It might be interesting to dwell on why a classical liberal set of rules was adopted at a time when the main currents of political thought in Australia were utilitarianism (which called for a centralised regulator state), populism (which wanted to mine the state for its own ends) and social liberalism (which wanted to use the state to advance to the good life). Suffice it to say that, if classical liberalism was ever a real option for Australia (in which the state has always played a more powerful role than in most other capitalist countries) it certainly had less and less relevance as the twentieth century wore on. In Australia, it is now the preserve of the libertarian right, which may have influenced the rhetoric but not the policies of the former Liberal Country Party Government. The need for change is obvious, yet one is stuck with a document constructed in the model of a perpetual motion machine; indeed, since the American Revolution, classical liberals have been obsessed with the machine analogy, and machines, unlike 'the body politic', do not evolve.

The formal mechanisms for change

Clearly the founding fathers of the Australian Constitution did not believe that their machine would operate without modification for all time. They did, however, lay down formidable barriers to change. These were all well understood by the federal planners, but have become more resistant to change since the formation of the party system. The proposal for change should ideally pass both houses of parliament by an absolute majority; but, if is rejected by one house or if one house fails to pass it within three months, the Governor General may submit the proposal to the electors. The Governor General would presumably only so act on the advice of the government. When submitted to referendum, the proposal must be supported by a majority of the Australian electorate and be supported by a majority of the electorate in four of the six States. Such were formidable obstacles in 1901. When one considers the confrontational style of Australian politics since then, they have become almost insuperable.

It was not until 1974 that an attempt was made to ease the formal constraint against change. In May of that year, the Whitlam Labor Government proposed, as one question out of four, that amendment of the Constitution should require a majority of Australians and a majority in only three States. This received only 48% support overall, and a majority 'yes' only in New South Wales.

Of the various attempts to hold referendums, the majority have foundered in the parliament. Thirty-eight questions have reached the referendum stage and only eight were carried by the double majority. These eight proposals were either non-controversial questions to improve the running of the constitutional machine, or were questions on which there was strong and bi-partisan majority opinion long before the referendum. An example of the latter would be the referendum of 1967 giving the Federal Government the right to legislate on behalf of all Aborigines.

The proposals which failed to pass were of three types—those designed to increase the formal powers of the Federal Government, those designed to change the legal position of certain economic or social groups, (including those which could be interpreted as affecting the class structure), and those on which the major political parties were in disagreement *at the time of submission to a referendum.* This third category highlights the important role political parties have come to play in a process which was devised *before a party system had formed.* The role of those parties in seeking their own short-term advantage is striking. For example, a referendum was put to the electorate by the Whitlam Labor Government, in 1974, to ensure that Senate elections should be held at the same time as elections to the House of Representatives. This question was opposed by the Liberal Country Party Coalition. The proposal was accepted by 48% of the electorate, but by a majority of voters in only one State—New South Wales. In 1977, the Liberal Country Party in government supported the same proposal and 62% of the voters supported it, but the amendment was defeated in three States—Queensland, Western Australia and Tasmania—where the State divisions of the Liberal and Country Parties had vehemently opposed it. In 1984, the proposal, opposed by the Liberal and National Parties, was rejected once again.

The role of political parties and the cumbersome procedures for change laid down in section 128 of the Constitution are, indeed, important barriers to change. A third explanation has also been advanced for the lack of reform and this must be taken most seriously; it is alleged that the hidebound Australian electorate just does not want any change and any democrat just has to face that fact. This is the kind of argument considered in Chapter 4. It is reasonable to expect that the electorate, consistently treated as idiots by political parties, would be suspicious of those who wanted to change the rules which govern them. Most referendum campaigns have been filled with emotional rhetoric and extravagant bombast. Electors quite naturally just resign themselves to a cosy identification with their own State.

Identification with the States and the proposal for new States

But how does one explain why it is the State rather than any other entity which continues to engender primary loyalty? The question here is akin to the one which has concerned students of nationalism. Why does the nation in Europe produce an identification stronger than region, city or anything larger than the nation? Just why do the citizens of many African 'nations' fight with such vigour for the integrity of what were, after all, boundaries created in the course of conflict between nineteenth century imperial powers (boundaries, moreover, which often cut across ethnic lines). There are few satisfactory answers to such questions. It could perhaps be suggested that such identification was the result of a perceived threat. Thus, nineteenth century New South Wales might be carved up into separate self-governing colonies, but twentieth century New South Wales could not cede territory to new states in the Riverina and New England. This was because such action would weaken the power of the original State against the Commonwealth. Such an argument does not seem very convincing. A more down-to-earth answer is that existing State Governments do not want to lose economic assets. One wonders, then, whether opposition would be mitigated in the case of the Commonwealth compensating an original State for the loss of tax revenue on the creation of a new one. There is, moreover, a psychological dimension here which needs much more research.

In any case, the constitutional provisions for the creation of new states are both rigid and vague. They are rigid in that the Constitution demands the consent of the parliament of the original State(s) concerned and a majority of the voters in a referendum for any modifications to present boundaries. They are vague in that the Constitution is not at all clear as to whether any new state would enjoy equal status with existing States. Section 121 provides that, upon the admission or establishment of a new state, the Commonwealth Parliament might 'make or impose such terms and conditions, including the extent of representation in either House of the Parliament, as it thinks fit'. The creation of new states seems to be a risky business indeed, but it is generally believed that, at some time in the not too distant future, the Northern Territory will take that path.

Federalism and local government

It is doubtful whether the cause of bringing government closer to the people will be served by the creation of new states. What is needed is a process of administrative devolution within a more centralised economic and legal structure. But that seems even more unlikely at the moment than the creation of new states. This is both because of constitutional inertia and a belief system which makes people suspicious of the centre and just uninformed about and uninterested in grass-roots local government, in which people might participate in the manner prescribed by both socialists and social liberals.

It is sometimes argued that participatory democracy does not depend upon powerful local (municipal, shire or district) government. For Spann:

FEDERALISM

Even if we were to identify democracy with participation, such a democratic tradition has not depended here in any important way on local councils. Self-government, self-determination and responsibility for political decisions can be developed in a number of ways. Because Australian local authorities are in important respects the administrative agents of State government, the politically active may pursue their claims by participation in State or federal politics; or by working through any of the numerous associations and organisations that may present claims at any level of government. Enthusiasm for local councils may wane not because democracy is dying, but because even those interested in participation choose other avenues for their activities.[20]

Chapter 3 has already outlined criticisms of the above pluralist approach. One should not start from a consideration of people who are already politically-active, who are already 'free to choose' at what level to exercise their activism. The point is to shape the institutions of daily life in such a way as to develop people's political efficacy. Democracy in the work-place might be one way. Strengthening local government might be another. This, it will be remembered, was the concern of the Webbs some three-quarters of a century ago.

As it is, local government in Australia is less significant politically than in comparable countries. This is clear when one considers the ratios of federal, State and local government expenditures. These, in the early 1970s, were 48:44:8 in Australia, compared with 60:14:26 in the United States and 40:32:28 in Canada.[21] A large number of functions performed by local government in these other federations are performed in Australia by the State Governments. The fact that the United States and Canada are both federations would suggest that lack of local government power is not due to federalism. Yet one might concede that point whilst acknowledging that the inertia of the present federal system is such that attempts by a reforming central government to change the power relationship between State and local government will have limited effect.

Though enhanced local government power is a necessary condition for fostering citizen competence, it is obviously not a sufficient one. One only has to look at Britain where local governments have much more power than in Australia and where the central government can directly affect the powers of local government for that to be quite clear. In Britain, the contribution of local government to democracy has been minimal. In addition to mechanisms which may alter the situation where local councils are simply agents of State government, one needs political parties dedicated to altering the consciousness of ordinary citizens. As earlier chapters have noted, neither of the major parties in Australia are so predisposed. This is particularly regrettable when one considers that, in the days of the short-lived Department of Urban and Regional Development, the ALP did, for a time at least, appear to appreciate the problem.

Changes in the federal process

Though there have been few changes in the formal structure of Australian federalism, there have clearly been major changes in the actual processes of central-regional relations. Some of these have come about because States have referred powers they hold to the national government. An example here would be the transfer, in 1977, by South Australia and Tasmania of ownership of those States' country rail systems. A more important example would be the recent decision by all the States not to refer cases to the Judicial Committee of the Privy Council in London and to respect the Australian High Court as the highest court of appeal. In the latter case consistency was achieved; but the former case, it might be argued, was an example of creating a situation where the federal division of powers varied from State to State. A similar situation could be the product of the reverse process. In Western Australia, for example, a State family court came to administer both Commonwealth and State family law—a provision explicitly refused by all the other States. One doubts that uniformly rational administration may be achieved within the ambit of co-operative federal arrangements. Even the modest referendum proposal to assist this by allowing for the interchange of powers between Commonwealth and States was defeated in late 1984.

The most significant changes in the processes of federalism have come about through the actions of the High Court. Much of law in Australia has actually been *created* by that court. This is a point which legal positivists consistently fail to appreciate. According to that theory, judges only interpret the law, leaving legislators the task of actually creating it. Thus judges are supposed not to discuss rules in terms of their content but in terms of their pedigree—the conventions which sustain them and the explicit constitutional powers which allow them. This doctrine in Sir Owen Dixon's words, should be mainly negative and restraining in its function, not initiating or constructive.[22]

This is not to suggest that all High Court Justices have taken this position. Compare the following quote from Dixon with that of Isaacs, an earlier High Court judge. The polarisation could not be greater:[23]

> The Court's sole function is to interpret a constitutional description of power or restraint upon power and say whether a given

measure falls on one side of a line consequently drawn or on the other, and that is nothing whatever to do with the merits or demerits of the measure. Such a function has led us all, I think, to believe that close adherence to legal reasoning is the only way to maintain the confidence of all parties in federal conflicts. It may be that the Court is thought to be excessively legalistic. I should be sorry to think that it is anything else. There is no other safe guide to judicial decisions in great conflicts than a strict and complete legalism.

Owen Dixon, 1952

It is the duty of the judiciary to recognise the development of the Nation and to apply established principles to the positions which the Nation in its progress from time to time assumes. The judicial organ would otherwise separate itself from the progressive life of the community and act as a clog upon the legislative and executive departments rather than as an interpreter.

Isaac Isaacs, 1922

As indicated earlier, judges often decide cases according to principles and then seek constitutional justification. In the first two decades after Federation, the doctrines of implied prohibitions and implied immunity of instrumentalities (that neither the Commonwealth nor the States could make laws binding on each other) were both derived from the principle that the Commonwealth was the creature of the States, designed to serve their ends and that the interests of limited government would best be served by stressing the powers reserved to the States. It could be argued that this principle did boil down to a literal interpretation of the Constitution. The Engineers Case of 1920, however, completely overturned this interpretation. Instead of implied prohibitions and implied immunities, the powers explicitly laid down in the Constitution were to be given full force and were able to bind State governments. This was the application of a *new principle* which lawyers, according to the positivist tradition, had to *justify* according to its constitutional pedigree. Following Dworkin, however, one has to admit that this was not just mere interpretation but the creation of new law. The High Court had, in fact, deprived the States of much of their status as 'legal personalities'.[24]

For the next 30 years, a whole series of decisions were taken in the spirit of the new principle which greatly increased the powers of the central government especially with regard to financial matters. Many new powers were created and justified, in the positivist tradition, according to existing powers. The primacy of Commonwealth industrial awards was justified according to the inconsistency clause

(Section 109) in a manner which would have shocked the founding fathers. The funds of the Lang Government were seized in a way unforeseen by the lawyers of 1901. National control was established over broadcasting under Section 51(5) covering postal, telegraphic, telephone and other like services (and who knows what the founding fathers would have thought about radio). The Commonwealth, moreover, moved to regulate the use of airspace within the boundaries of a State (and who in 1900 had ever heard the concept 'airspace'). Finally, in 1942, in the First Uniform Tax Case, the use of the 'defence power' changed the whole fiscal management of the country—a situation never reversed in peace time. All the above should be seen as the actual creation of new law, which positivist considerations and the axioms of the Westminister myth should not hide.

The Second World War was followed by a severe modification of the centralising trend in High Court decisions (in which attempts were made to give back substance to the legal personality of the States) followed in the 1970s by a less consistent line. As the discussion earlier suggested, the initial backlash is clearly associated in the public mind with the person of Sir Owen Dixon who had a personal dislike of the Engineers decision. This highlights the very important role of individual High Court judges in making (or failing to make) new constitutional law. It is for this reason that both major political parties have been most concerned about the party allegiences of High Court judges. In 1974, the appointment of Labor Senator Lionel Murphy as a Justice brought a strong criticism from the Liberal Party; the Labor Government was accused of 'stacking the court'. In 1964, the Menzies Liberal Government appointed one of its ministers, Garfield Barwick, as Chief Justice, and this brought similar criticism from the Labor Party. Clearly the affiliations of judges is important since in certain areas only they are capable of legislating (and the word is stressed). But this should not be an unqualified endorsement of the view that great men make history. One has to see both the centralising tendencies and the reaction against them in the context of war, boom and depression. The earlier centralising set of tendencies were a response to a nation rapidly industrialising and having to cope with national emergencies. The reaction, though originating at a time of reconstruction (and indeed causing considerable trouble), could in the long-term be seen in the general context of the reaction against explicit central controls during the 'Long Boom'. The ambivalence since reflects the patchy nature of the repeated recessions which have plagued Australia and the rest of the world. One should, therefore, not be surprised at the advent of what seemed to be a new centralising trend in the recent recession. But judgement on this issue must wait upon the conclusion of a new agreement between Commonwealth and the States on taxing powers.

Another quasi-formal means by which the federal processes have been modified is unchallenged legislation. Occasionally, a blind eye is turned by the States to national intrusion on State authority. The very existence of the Snowy Mountains Scheme, the CSIRO and the Commonwealth Employment Service are just three examples of a deliberate decision by the States not to enforce their constitutional authority within the federal structure.

Every occasion of unchallenged legislation establishes a convention of federalism—a generally accepted agreement that the formal rules of the federal structure should be ignored. In a wider sense, federal conventions, like constitutional conventions, are the informal agreements which allow an anachronistic structure to function— even if not at its most effective and efficient. Chapter 4 raised a number of problems about the status of conventions. How, one may ask, could one obtain agreement on conventions which explicitly violate the Constitution?

The Loan Council and the Premiers Conference are two quasi-formal 'conventions' of federalism, designed to modify the essentially exclusive and hence potentially confrontationist dual structure of power into a more co-operative federalism. The anachronistic nature of these conventions is revealed in the continued use of sexist terms such as 'gentlemen's agreement'. Both conventions have become just as internally divided as the other components of the federal process, and the recent history of both reinforces the conclusion that power within the federal compact has moved to the national government. The agenda for both are set by the Commonwealth Government and (Holmes and Sharman notwithstanding) the whole proceedings are inevitably dominated by the Prime Minister. The Loan Council, for its part, has been described merely as a forum for the government to announce its unilateral decisions, though the role of that council in controlling capital funds raised by the States has declined considerably in the last three decades and especially in the most recent past.

The role of the Senate as a guardian of the conventions of federalism has already been discussed. Indeed, if the time devoted to the Senate in the Constitutional Conventions is any guide, then the federal upper house was perceived as the lynch pin of the whole federal edifice. There is no need to repeat here the earlier discussion of the change in function of the Senate due to the growth of the party system and its failure to import local concerns into the centre (a move which Sawer sees as towards rather than away from co-ordinate federalism).[25] It need merely be noted that the Senate is clearly one of the important areas where, despite a continuity of structure, the processes of federalism have undergone considerable change.

The overall impact of the (minimal) changes in the structure of federalism and the (considerable and important) changes in the processes of federalism has been a seemingly inexorable transfer of power to the national government. This has not come about, as some States' righters constantly assert, because of the desire of centralists (which usually refers to the ALP) deliberately to set out to consolidate power in Canberra. Such assertions are for party or electoral effect rather than offered as explanation. In fact, the drift of functions and power to the national government has occurred as much, if not more, under Liberal Country Party governments as under Labor.

The trend has occurred because society, the social system and the economic system have changed. The sparsely-populated, essentially agricultural society has changed to one with relatively densely-populated urban complexes; something like a developed industrial and commercial nation has come into being. The 'tyranny of distance' has been partly overcome by a network of transport and communication—much of which was not even envisaged by the constitution-makers. Small business has become large; craft unions have become national trade unions; new urban and rural issues and problems have emerged, many demanding the expenditure of vast amounts of money; the fragmented society of the 1890s has developed into one with interlocking national, State and local demands and problems concerning political, social and economic issues.

New federalisms

One result of these changes in the society, the polity and the economy, was that the *practices* of federal politics increasingly showed a trend to *interdependence*, rather than the *independence* of the original plan. As the society became more complex, so the sovereign division of powers became more and more blurred. Issues such as education, health, welfare, transport, development and communications cross State boundaries and affect all levels of government. By the 1960s, through necessity—but not without political disagreement, even party confrontation—the neat, vertical division of powers between national, State and local governments, had become a complex and confusing mix of inter-relationships. For example, national, State and local authorities had all become involved in the provision of health services; ministers and departments of education existed both at national and State levels; constant conferences and meetings between national and State governments and authorities were held to co-ordinate activity in these fields. Along with the original vertical division of powers, there had developed a system of horizontal co-operation. Such developments caused strains within the system as some governments either sought more responsibility and power, or attempted to retain power in the face of actual or perceived involvement by another level of government. It is not surprising, then, that the 1970s saw the emergence not only of the perennial question of how best to organise politics in a federal system, but of two *apparently* contradictory answers.

The 'New Federalisms' of Whitlam and Fraser were, at first sight, dramatically opposed one to another. Before this apparent contrast is spelt out, however, it is important to note that both emerged from the ideology of the major political parties.

The idea of 'New Federalism' was introduced into contemporary Australian political debate by Whitlam in a 1957 paper, and in 1971 when as Leader of the Opposition he outlined the concept:

> Ideally, our continent should have neither so few State Governments nor so many local government units. We should have a federal system of overlapping parliaments and a delegated but supervised system of local government. We should have a House of Representatives for international matters and nationwide matters, an assembly for the affairs of each of our dozen largest cities and regional assemblies for the few scarce areas of rural production and resource development outside those cities. Vested interests and legal complexities should not discourage or deter us from attempts to modernise and nationalise our inherited structure.[26]

In essence, the Whitlam plan was designed as a move towards organic federalism. It aimed to replace the three-tier system of federal government in Australia with a two-tier system and recognised that the locus of the *processes* of federalism had moved inexorably to the centre. It was a statement that the existing State boundaries, drawn in London in the early nineteenth century, did not reflect distinctive social and economic communities, but more often than not divided such communities. Finally, it was based on the belief that the *structure* of dual sovereignty was not adequate for the social, economic and industrial situation of the 1970s. The aim of Labor's New Federalism was to integrate the efforts of national and regional governments to deal with social and economic problems; the purpose of dual sovereignty was to *divide* such efforts.

There is no need to repeat in detail the story of how every strategy used by the Whitlam Government to bring this concept to fruition was resisted, and ultimately defeated, by a changing constellation of opponents which included the Liberal Country Party Coalition, the State governments, local governments, and even some state branches of the ALP. Whitlam's attempts to change the *structure* of federalism in his 1973 and 1974 referendums were soundly defeated, partly because of tactical errors by the national government. The attempts to change the *processes* of federalism by means of direct grants to local authorities, by tied grants to States, and by the creation of institutions such as the Australian Assistance Plan, the Schools Commission, and the Department of Urban and Rural Development, were resisted at every step and, if inaugurated, were short-lived.

One of the more innovative moves of those years was the attempt to revive the Interstate Commission, allowed for under Section 101 of the Constitution. This body had existed in the second decade of the twentieth century, playing a function in examining tariffs and restrictive trade practices. When, however, it started issuing judgements about State laws which it felt infringed the Constitution, its activities were challenged in the High Court. In the famous Wheat Case of 1915, the High Court ruled that the powers of adjudication allowed for under Section 101 were not of a judicial nature (a piece of linguistic nonsense if there ever was one), and the Commission soon went out of existence. An attempt was made in 1975 to legislate for a new commission which initially was to regulate interstate transport. The Bill, however, was adulterated in 1975 by a hostile Senate which removed all regulatory powers and just left powers of investigation; the pallid Act which remained was never proclaimed by the incoming Liberal Government. Apparently, opposition to the recreation of the Interstate Commission derived not from any hostility on the part of the Liberal Party to regulation but from sustained pressure by various interest groups. Such opposition was rationalised in terms of the extent to which the Commission might violate parliamentary responsibility and in anticipation of a future High Court veto along the lines of the current interpretation of Section 92. As a consequence, the transport system in Australia is rational only in so far as co-operative agreements have been made in which uniformity costs very little.[27] It has already been noted, moreover, that without some body like the Interstate Commission with regulatory powers the River Murray Waters Agreement is a totally inadequate vehicle to impose a management required for the whole basin.[28]

Perhaps the major act in the tragedy of Whitlam's New Federalism, was the inauguration of the first full-scale Constitutional Convention since Federation. Planned to be the source of constitutional reform, the deliberations were rapidly overtaken by party politics, the virulent advocacy of States' rights and internal bickering. After three years of constant efforts, Whitlam's New Federalism had failed on all counts. The Liberal and Country Parties most firmly opposed the attempts by the Whitlam Government to change either the *structure* or the *process* of federalism. But dissent came from all States and cut across party lines. Indeed, opposition from Labor Premiers was an indication of how deep the concept of States' rights is in the Australian belief system. Significantly, Whitlam's move to a more organic federalism was branded by its critics 'coercive federalism'. As one example, and one not too far out of the mainstream of the reactions, consider the following statement by Premier Bjelke-Petersen:

> Every parent in this country will need to consider very carefully whether any extension of federal power, any denigration of the Crown's role and functions in our particular form of federal democracy will not within our children's lifetime lead to a system of government involving fear and the midnight doorknock.[29]

The 'New Federalism' of the Fraser Government, announced in 1976, was, in part, a reaction to Whitlam's policies and actions. The then Liberal Premier of New South Wales, T.L. Lewis, summarised the reactions of the States and the Liberal and Country Parties:

> My theme has been federalism, genuine federalism, that is a division of government functions, responsibilities and power in Australia between the Commonwealth and the States... We need to return to the basic issues. We do have a federal system. It reflected the wisdom of quite great men who put it together. The Australian people...do not want it changed... We must make federalism work... But we will only achieve this by returning from the new centralism to the original concept of federalism.[30]

But this commitment to the original 1890s concept of dual sovereignty has been an integral, in fact a key, component of Liberal ideology ever since the formation of the party in 1909. The Liberal platform emphasised:

1 The distribution of power and responsibility between Commonwealth and State governments and local authorities to ensure the maximum participation of the individual citizen in the decision-making processes and as an essential safeguard against authoritarianism.
2 The clear and contemporary delineation of powers as between

Commonwealth and State parliaments with safeguards to ensure that State parliaments have adequate and assured sources of revenue over which they have full responsibility
3 A spirit of co-operation between Commonwealth, State and local authorities, particularly in areas where Commonwealth or State governments have essential but different obligations.

Fraser's New Federalism was introduced in two stages: a guarantee that States would receive a certain proportion of income-tax revenue from the national government and a return to the States of a real right to levy their own income tax. The cautious acceptance of stage one by the Premiers who, regardless of party, had been seeking a guaranteed share of income-tax revenue, became vocal opposition when it became clear that the States would not only suffer a decrease in real income, but might have to apply stage two and levy a second income tax to maintain existing levels of development. By the conclusion of a series of Premiers' Conferences, it was apparent to the leaders of the States that this New Federalism may have been fine in theory, but contained many problems in practice.

Fraser described stage two as being a means of ensuring that those governments which seek to spend public money should also face the responsibility of raising the money and justifying such expenditure directly to their electorates. Another interpretation can be made, one which is more in the spirit and actuality of the history of the federal process. If one assumes that no State government would risk introducing a second income tax on the grounds of certain electoral reaction, then Fraser's New Federalism was a very effective method of *imposing* a political and economic policy on the States. The rhetoric of his 'federalism' might have included dual sovereignty, co-operation and political and economic responsibility. The reality could have been that Fraser found a means to continue the process of increasing the power of the national government, a means to oppose Whitlam's 'centralism' in rhetoric, but actually to impose a *coerceive* federalism. As Peachment and Reid put it:

> Mr. Whitlam's New Federalism put a federalist gloss on policies which sought the expansion of the power of the central government. Mr. Fraser's initiatives claimed an intention to reverse 'the flow of power to Canberra' and to restore federalism. In office, however, Mr. Fraser's government has sought to conquer the powers of the States by means which some students of politics would call subtle, and others would call devious.[31]

Fraser's New Federalism undoubtedly served the cause of greater central control. But it should be pointed out that certain features of that 'New Federalism' showed that the Federal Government was, in certain areas, unwilling to exercise the control it already had. This chapter has already mentioned the decline in importance of the Loan Council in recent decades. As part of the 'New Federalism', in 1982, Fraser brought about changes in Loan Council guidelines giving State electricity authorities more freedom to borrow on their own behalf, and recently this freedom has been extended by the Labor Government to other areas. Following the recommendation of the Campbell Committee, such freedom might lead to competition between States with different degrees of resource security (the very situation the Loan Council was designed to prevent). It is too early to predict what the limits of Federal Government control might be. It is possible that a completely new system of Federal-State financial arrangements will emerge and that the Loan Council might be supplemented or replaced by new co-operative bodies. All one may say at this stage is that the negotiating style seems to have changed. Apparently instead of the 'take it or leave it' approach of the Fraser Government, there has been a return to a bargaining approach analogous to that which occurs in a one-sided industrial dispute. According to Prime Minister Hawke, one has seen 'a rare and historic development which highlighted the unanimous endorsement by the States of the correct course the government was taking in the area of economic management'. Perhaps the spirit of 'compromise and consensus' reigns; yet one must also be mindful of the comment of the (Acting) Labor Premier of New South Wales, 'when you are looking down the barrel, what option have you got'.[32] Compromise at gun-point may not be real compromise but is there any other option? As the Hawke Government enters its second term it is clear that any Hawke-style 'New Federalism' will be very difficult to bring about. The defeat of the transfer of powers referendum made that quite clear.

The case against federalism

Politicking in, around and through, federalism has occurred constantly since 1901. But the events of the 1970s seem to have taken this politicking to the point where Riker has been proven correct, 'federalism is no more than a constitutional legal fiction which can be given whatever content seems appropriate at the moment'.[33] The question of federal politics has engendered intense debate during the past decade, more so than at any previous time since Federation. In 1960, federal inter-relations appeared to S.R. Davis as relatively settled. Referring to the national and State governments, he was able to:

hazard the guess that at no other time in the past have their relations appeared so permanently settled as they do now, and at no time has there been a more mature understanding of each other's needs. Except for the annual feuding and fussing over the division of the tax spoils, the Commonwealth and the States have bedded down with sympathy and resignation, if without great love... The States are neither as unhappy as they say, nor the Commonwealth as imperialistic as some believe. If there are many oddities still in the system what is important is that most of those who work it have come to understand the complexities and learnt to live with them without great discomfort.[34]

Just one decade later the stable and inert edifice of federalism was under attack and it continues to be so.

Many works have been written arguing why constitutional change is needed of which McMillan, Evans and Storey's *Australia's Constitution: Time for Change* is an eloquent example. The recent euphoria surrounding the Dams Case has highlighted many of the points made in that volume, though one suspects that the book's educative effect might be blunted out of consideration of the electoral concerns of State Labor governments. Interestingly here, the current Prime Minister's Boyer Lectures which advocate a unitary state have been quietly buried.[35] This book is not so constrained; the case outlined in these works deserves to be restated.[36]

This chapter has argued that, through constitutional means, the Commonwealth Government has acquired economic power far greater than that envisaged by the founding fathers. It has control over tariffs, subsidies, income tax, State borrowing and expenditure (through the provision of grants) and has established central banking controls. It has not the power, however, to impose a prices and incomes policy; all it was able to do in the 1983 wage pause was to control the salaries of Commonwealth public servants and rely on the force of persuasion to influence the States and the private sector. It has, moreover, only indirect control over interest rates and the non-banking activities of banks. Though the Commonwealth Government has considerable power to regulate business activities, it is often only able to make this effective with the co-operation of the States. Section 51(1), which grants the Commonwealth power over trade and commerce with other countries and among the States, falls far short of the United States Commerce Clause, which in that country enables the Federal Government to enact regulation on almost any activity so long as it is 'co-mingled with' or has 'some effect on' interstate and foreign commerce. As was noted in the earlier discussion of the fate of the Interstate Commission, the power in Australia is heavily circumscribed by

Section 92 guaranteeing 'absolute' freedom of trade, and by a rigid distinction between interstate and intrastate trade which is clearly artificial. Though recent High Court interpretations of Section 51(20), specifying Commonwealth power to regulate 'foreign corporations and trading and financial corporations formed within the limits of the Commonwealth', could make the hitherto mysterious corporations power into a powerful regulatory weapon, the extent to which it extends to mining or manufacturing, the activities of stock exchanges or matters which might be considered to be ones of 'internal organisation' is not clear.

In short, it may be argued that the present federal structure denies to the Commonwealth power adequate to conduct economic planning or even the modest guidance advocated by Keynesians and the like. Of course, it could be argued that there are a lot of agreements between the States and the Commonwealth which do, in fact, already give the Federal Government considerable powers, but these might be sabotaged at any time by the withdrawal of any State government from a co-operative arrangement. Given a crisis situation, co-operative federalism might easily dissolve into combative federalism.

There are, after all, limits beyond which co-operation does not extend. A rational and efficient distribution of manufacturing and processing industry can not develop in a situation where States compete one with another to have various plants located within their borders. The result is unnecessary duplication and, as Chapter 3 noted, the provision by tax-payers of an unnecessary amount of infrastructural expense. Such a situation may only be rectified by some central planning body which has the power to outmanoeuvre State governments.

Perhaps the most insidious effects of federalism concern minerals and energy. The distribution of such resources has enriched Queensland and Western Australia at the expense of the States in which the majority of the population is located. As Stevenson puts it:

> Because the States control mineral resources, and because mineral resources are now so important to the Australian economy, the State level of government has acquired vitally important functions and responsibilities... Under the impact of mineral resource development, a gradual shift of wealth, population and economic and political power is taking place in the direction of Queensland and Western Australia, the States which control most of Australia's mineral reserves and which are also the States most dependent upon mining. Since local attachments and hostility to the federal government have always been stronger

in these remote States than in the two large States, and since these traditional sentiments are now reinforced by economic self-interest, the outlying hinterland States can be expected to exert their growing influence in favour of decentralisation.[37]

Without necessarily subscribing to 'stamocap' theory, outlined in Chapter 3, one must concede that it is likely that the external linkages of those States with huge transnational corporations will grow at the expense of links with the manufacturing States and Australia in general.[38] These transnational corporations, with more economic muscle than even the Federal Government, are allowed to get away with extremely favourable terms when dealing with the much smaller States.[39] Federalism has made it difficult to create a single system of resources tax. To be fair, however, it is arguable that the abolition of federalism would offer no ready made panacea. The Commonwealth Government already has considerable taxing power which it has used to create incentives for mining and to discourage the use of petroleum. The Commonwealth has control over the export of minerals mined in Australia and is actively involved through the AIDC in guiding the development of resources projects. As noted earlier in discussing the diminished role of the Loan Council, the inequities which have resulted are as much the fault of the Federal Government as that of the States. On the other hand, it might be argued that the mere possibility of State opposition has inhibited the actions of the Commonwealth. Why, one might ask, did it take a Federal election for a Commonwealth Government even to attempt to use the 'external affairs' power (amongst others) to determine the direction of a State's hydro-electric policy?

The fact that the Commonwealth Government has had to use the 'external affairs' power to stop the Tasmanian dams and the 'trade and commerce power' to stop sand mining on Fraser Island is ludicrous. In this day and age, when the world environment is so dangerously threatened, it is archaic for a modern state not to have an 'environment and conservation power' built into its constitution. The issue here is not merely national heritage but world heritage. It probably is the case that the Dams decision implies that serious cases of environmental damage might be countered by Commonwealth action, but it is unlikely that the 'external affairs' power could be used for less serious cases of environmental damage. What is needed is a national environmental policy, policed by a central body, which has the power to override the considerations of local government for short-term economic development. It is unlikely that this could be achieved under the rubric of co-operative federalism.

It could be argued that co-operative federalism is most successful in the field of industrial relations. After all, most State tribunals tend to follow the lead of the Australian Conciliation and Arbitration Commission, and a fair degree of co-operation exists between federal and State bodies concerned with industrial relations. Such might be the case; but when one looks at the trade union structure at federal and State level, one beholds an administrative nightmare. Since an award covering all members of a union often can not be obtained from one tribunal, unions often have to operate at both federal and State levels where they are in fact two separate legal entities. This is of more than mere academic interest when different factions of the union operate at the different levels. It is also not always the case that federal and State awards keep in step. This leads to dissatisfaction and leap-frogging claims. Thirdly, it is sometimes the case that disputes confined to one State in industries covered by a federal award might create problems as to which tribunal should exercise jurisdiction. Indeed, a lot of unnecessary effort is expended by unions ensuring that disputes are 'national'. A number of measures have been taken in recent years to solve these problems within the scope of co-operative federalism (joint sittings of tribunals, cross-vesting of State and federal jurisdiction etc.), but the success of such measures depends upon the continuing goodwill of the various parties. It is also possible that the proposal to set up an integrated national court system could be emulated in the sphere of industrial relations. This would clearly be a major step in the direction of organic federalism. But why not go the whole hog? For the unions unity is strength, and big unions operating uniformly at a national level will achieve more than fragmented unions operating at two levels (however co-operatively). The same argument may be put with equal force for the other side in industrial disputes.

In the fields of urban and regional development and health and welfare, there is no doubt that the Commonwealth already has considerable power through the use of Section 81 grants, and considerable use was made of these during the Whitlam administration in pursuance of his 'New Federalism'. It is not at all clear, however, just how far the use of Section 81 grants may be extended. Nor is it at all clear how the federal structure might inhibit the provision of a national scheme for accident compensation and national standards for health and safety.

A further set of problems arises from the fact that different legal provisions covering the same activity apply at Commonwealth level and in the various States. Some co-operation is doubtless quite effective and some model laws specifying a unified standard have been enacted in the various States. Nevertheless, there are manifest disjunctions between federal legislation governing family law and the various State laws governing property and the custody of children. There is a greater likelihood of imprisonment for certain offences in some States than others. There are wide disparities in the compensation available to the victims of crimes. There are different State traffic laws, laws governing the possession of firearms, laws governing defamation and those specifying censorship. Different standards apply covering biotechnology, food and drugs and, of course, different interpretations of human rights.

Finally, it has been argued that the various public services which operate in Australia differ markedly in the quality of their personnel and the effectiveness with which services are provided. The case for unified standards in recruitment, promotion and centralisation is overwhelming. The most efficient move in this regard would be to establish a single public service.

The prospects for reform

It will be clear from the previous discussion that the Australian Constitution should be assessed as a product of the 1890s reflecting the interests of the founding fathers—the agricultural and commercial elites of the colonies which saw central government as a threat. In Encel's words it is not surprising that the 1901 compromise was 'permeated by the conservatism, parochialism and pettiness that characterised the Australian colonies at the end of the nineteenth century'.[40] The surviving structure in 1985 is still so characterised. For Colin Howard, one of Australia's foremost constitutional lawyers.

> We blandly ignore the twentieth century. Such an approach to life in any other context would be seen as self-evident folly. All that is different in the constitutional context is that the folly has become so entrenched and familiar as to seem part of the natural order of things.[41]

It is clear also that the major methods for constitutional change do not hold out much chances for success. The sad history of change through Section 128 referendums and the reference power specified in Section 51(37) has already been considered. If one could take seriously the current rhetoric about national reconciliation and consensus, there might be some hope for the constructive and rational use of the reference power. But the reality of the party system is that confrontation, conflict and division stems directly from political parties not being able to see beyond immediate electoral advantage. This was clearly illustrated in the case of the 1984 referendums. Moreover, underlying the debate about States' rights is the concern of parties and groups about the possible effects on the class structure. Though Sir Joh Bjelke-Peterson probably does not completely believe his association of central government in Australia with the growth of the police state, he probably perceives very well that States' rights serve better the large primary producers he represents and the transnational corporations with which he has cordial relations. On the other side of the political spectrum are those who opposed the national referendum to give the Commonwealth power over prices and incomes on the grounds that this would help big business the more effectively to 'collude'. Such considerations are not irrational and do reflect very real cleavages and calculations of class interest. But one should not despair and say that no change is possible so long as those cleavages exist. It is silly just to sit and wait for a situation where the class structure alters and somehow political parties disappear. The effect of waiting and doing nothing might be to exacerbate regional and social disparities in wealth, income and the provision of services. If such developments generate conflict, there could be more and more pressure for a unitary state. Such a state might be brought about by stealth (for example, using the 'defence power' against mythical foreign subversion). But few would advocate a unitary state created for the sake of preserving the privileges of a rich minority. Action should be taken now to create a different kind of unitary state which might forestall and inhibit such authoritarianism. It is difficult to see how this could be brought about by using the existing referendum power, by using the reference power or by invoking other mysterious clauses in the current Constitution (the 'joint venture power', for example, specified in Section 51[38] which few people claim to understand).

It may well be that the necessary constitutional changes will only be brought about by revolutionary methods, but such revolutions might result in other unforeseen changes, and it is not fruitful to speculate on the possible scenarios. The various legal methods have been canvassed by McMillan, Evans and Storey.[42] These include first the drafting of new constitutional provisions by a bipartisan parliamentary committee. Previous experience here shows that, however cordial and co-operative the discussions of such a committee might be, its deliberations founder on the rocks of party confrontation once the parliamentary and referendum stages are entered into. Secondly, the use of parliamentarians' conventions (as witnessed in Adelaide in 1983) is bedevilled by party confrontation and State obstruction right from the start. Thirdly, the provision of an independent drafting commission (as in Sweden) might be entertained, though this is not expected to capture the popular imagination so necessary if the referendum hurdle is to be overcome.

Perhaps one could even entertain suspending the existing Constitution so that it is impossible for obstructionists to campaign for the status quo. Following the recent agreement between the British and Australian governments one can not be sure what the role of the United Kingdom Parliament would be in such a situation. Nevertheless, it might be possible directly to legislate for a popularly elected constitutive assembly which may deliberate on a constitutional draft, to legislate on the establishment of a caretaker administration, and to specify the mechanisms of referendum, making clear that the choice is for a new constitution or no constitution at all. Preparations might be made for an Act of Independence which would require the United Kingdom to remove the Australian Constitution from its statute book.

The value of a popularly elected body in drafting a new constitution is that it might be able to generate an awareness among the citizens which could offset cynical reactions to party machinations. McMillan, Evans and Storey opt for a new model convention which would be partially elected and partially nominated by existing legislatures.[43] But why not a return to something like the model of 1897–98 (where only the Western Australian delegation was nominated)? Clearly, the deliberations of the constitution-drafting body will reflect the power of parties and be the site of considerable machinations and intrigue; the deliberations will certainly not be like those at the turn of the century. For all that, direct popular election may both stimulate popular interest and give a power and confidence to the assembly that appointment by parliaments might not achieve. That rationale was commented on most clearly by Quick and Garran at the time of the original Constitution.[44]

The above scenario is clearly far more wide-ranging than that which happened in Canada in that there the federal nature of the constitution was retained. Clearly, any abolition of the Australian States would require application by those States to the United Kingdom Parliament to have the State Constitutions revoked. Perhaps all this is utopian. But how else would one achieve a change in people's consciousness except through the medium of a national constituent assembly?

An appeal to United Kingdom legislation should involve no loss of national self-respect. It certainly did not in the case of Canada (though there the mechanisms were different). One suspects, however, that the whole issue will be bedevilled by discussions of republicanism. The kind of reforms suggested above do not hinge on Australia becoming a republic; indeed, in the light of the considerations above it does not matter very much whether the formal head of state is the Queen (via the Governor General), or a president; what is important is not the status of the head of state but the reserve powers exercised by that head of state. So long as these are constitutionally established, one could call the head of state what one likes.

Surely questions of symbolic importance, such as those involved in making Australia a republic, should be less weighty than matters of substantial reform. Alas, such questions of symbolic importance are major ones in the electorate. It is sad to comment that many people would fight to the death for the Queen yet show no interest at all in the inequities of constitutional provisions. It would be most distressing if the popular awareness, which a constituent assembly was supposed to generate, foundered on the rocks of a symbolic battle between monarchists and their opponents. Perhaps an intelligent reformist party should actually profess an adherence to monarchy to pre-empt that challenge and proceed with the really important constitutional reform.

A new Australian constitution should clearly be of a 'we the people...' type (and even this may be bent to accommodate formal monarchy). It should specify a number of principles from which citizen rights may be derived. These principles should be ordered so that judges, who will continue to make the law as well as interpret it, may be provided with a philosophical yardstick. Perhaps it could begin with Dworkin's argument about the primacy of equality of respect and treatment as equals rather than philosophically vacuous general principles about liberty. In recognising that judges make law and do not just interpret it, there need to be a number of laws of recognition, specifying not the detailed lines of demarcation between legislative and judiciary but the principles under which competence might be decided.

In discussing the structure of the central legislature, there need to be provisions governing not just formal mechanisms but the meaning of representative and responsible government and how that responsibility might be monitored. There must be clear principles specifying what powers are devolved to regions under what headings and for what purposes. A unitary state is clearly superior to a federal state in that a region defined for one purpose need not be coterminous with a region defined for another. In some cases and for some purposes, such regions might be the same as the old States, though there should be no question that sovereign power lies with the centre. An acknowledgement that different kinds of local authorities are needed for different kinds of services should lead to a very detailed provision of local authority competence (a feature entirely absent in the existing Constitution).

Perhaps most important: there has to be clear provision in the

Constitution for amending its provisions. A simple referendum formula for all questions is absurd. It should be much easier, for example, to change a constitutional provision for the devolution of power over sewerage than an infringement on the right to free speech. Smooth and effective change, moreover, may best be achieved by the provision of some permanent independent review body open to advice from all quarters.

Conclusion

This chapter has argued against federalism. In the nineteenth century, James Bryce discussed the merits and demerits of modern federalism in America.[45] The merits were eight in number: a nation with state identities, flexibility, prevention of despotism, interest in and better local government, increased potential for political experimentation, political stability and efficient government.

It is by no means certain that these are all merits nor whether those that can be considered merits apply in Australia. There are State identities but these have often overwhelmed the nation. Except in times of crisis such as the world wars, it has been parochial States' rights which have been dominant. Flexibility is undoubtedly a virtue but it is merely implied at the level of formal structure; the practices of Australian politics are bedevilled by inflexibility. There is little evidence, moreover, that the three-tiered system of government has brought better government; and it seemed to be the conviction of the Whitlam administration that only by circumventing the State structure could one make local government more efficient. As for experimentation, a very good case could be made that the Federal Government has served as an impediment. Doubtless the Australian polity is very stable; but one should remember that one person's stability is another person's inflexibility. Bryce's claim about efficiency is also rather suspect. As Bryce saw it:

> Creating many local legislatures with wide powers relieves the national legislature of a part of that large mass of functions which might otherwise prove too heavy for it. Thus business is more promptly despatched, and the great central council of the nation has time to deliberate on those questions that most nearly touch the whole country.[46]

Bryce would have been amazed at contemporary Australia. Finally, concerning Bryce's point about preventing despotism, one doubts whether Bryce was correct about the United States, but certainly a good argument may be made that in Australia federalism has *allowed* rather than placed barriers on the emergence of despots.

One has only to look at Queensland today! Certainly despotism at a national level has been absent in Australia; but the same cannot be said for the federal structure in Brazil or for that matter the federal structure in the Soviet Union.

Turning to the demerits of federalism suggested by Bryce, it is obvious that all but the first apply to Australia:

1 Weakness in the conduct of foreign affairs
2 Weakness in home government, that is to say deficient authority over the component States and the individual citizens
3 Liability to dissolution by the secession or rebellion of States
4 Liability to division into groups and factions by the formation of separate combinations of the component States
5 Want of uniformity among the States in legislation and administration
6 Trouble, expense and delay due to the complexity of a double system of legislation and administration.[47]

Given that the 'positive advantages' of federalism are no longer evident in Australia (if they ever were) and that the demerits are entrenched and more and more obvious, the question of whether federalism has outlived its usefulness needs to be faced. On the whole, it seems that the disadvantages of a federal structure have been exacerbated in Australia by the nature of politics and the limitations of such a system now outweigh the merits.

Following McMillan, Evans and Storey, this chapter has argued that the time has come for major reform. Australia needs a unitary state which incorporates *constitutionalism* into its processes. One hesitates to use that word because, as Chapter 4 remarked, it has become the catch-cry of the *laissez faire* right, which wishes to return to some idea of a minimal state in which the rights of property are supreme. But constitutionalism did not always mean, and should not mean, that. It should not be considered a right-wing rallying cry or a dirty word. All that it means is that there should be some means effectively to govern the government and that certain considerations, which outweigh the interests of those 'with the numbers', should be entrenched in fundamental law. Those considerations, however, will be shaped by those in power and by the institutions of property. The challenge for the reformer is to make certain that those considerations change in accordance with values which define citizens as part of a common evolving humanity rather than those which serve the ends of particular vested interests. This was the hope of the Enlightenment thinkers, many socialists, many social liberals and many modern Marxists. It should be the prime consideration of those who may come to draft, discuss and ratify a new Australian Constitution.

PART FOUR
ELECTORAL SYSTEMS

SEVEN
ELECTORAL POLITICS
THE ROOTS OF APATHY AND CYNICISM

FEW PEOPLE IN Australia would deny the importance of elections, since elections are a vital prerequisite for representative government. Chapter 4 argued that government in Australia does not adequately represent the people, but that observation should not lead one to conclude that elections are a waste of time. There are a few 'Marxists' who argue that elections are not important, because they consist merely in a chance for the oppressed classes to decide which members of the dominant class should sit in parliament to oppress them under the guise of representation, but such 'Marxists' are few and far between. Marx, to be sure, did not have any illusions about the representative nature of what he saw as 'bourgeois democracy', but he certainly preferred bourgeois democracy to current forms of European authoritarianism and consistently campaigned for constitutional reform on bourgeois lines. Nowadays, explicitly Leninist parties, such as the Socialist Party of Australia, and 'Eurocommunist'-type Marxist parties, such as the Communist Party of Australia, regularly take part in elections, and only the Communist Party of Australia (Marxist-Leninist) remains aloof from electoral politics. A few anarchist groups have mounted a challenge to the electoral process. Indeed, as Chapter 4 noted, anarchist opposition to parliaments and elections have shown a consistency since the time of Godwin at the end of the eighteenth century. One suspects that quite a few people today would agree with Godwin's conclusions, yet in very few cases does this lead to a demand that elections be boycotted. There is, after all, a crucial difference between cynicism about parliament plus not having extravagant illusions about the role of elections in producing political change and boycotting elections altogether.

Previous chapters have not been enthusiastic about the state of representative government in Australia. At the descriptive level, the arguments of Schumpeter make some sense; democracy, as it is practised, often does mean that elections are just opportunities for the citizens to authorise or (more commonly) veto self-selected groups of people who aspire to rule them.[1] What Chapter 2 criticised, it will be remembered, was the slide of Schumpeter and his followers from description to prescription. Following Pateman,[2] one might be critical also of Schumpeter's supposed demolition of 'classical democratic theory'. Such 'classical theory', according to Schumpeter, was based on an activist model of participation which required a level of rationality on the part of ordinary voters which was just not possible. Yet classical theorists, like Bentham and the two Mills, were not so naive as to believe that individual voters would sit down and work out what was in their best interests independent of propaganda and influence. Indeed, the 'classical' model attacked by Schumpeter was not classical at all but (like the 'British Constitution') a product of the late nineteenth century. It found expression in the view that the explosion of information available to the ordinary citizen, especially in print, would supply the materials for voters to be truly judgemental.

The rationally-activist mood enjoyed a very brief life and much of the 'behavioural revolution', which followed Schumpeter's work, was dedicated to discrediting that mood. For the behaviouralists, the voter was revealed as essentially a creature of habit with low levels of information, interest, motivation and participation. But can one jump from a generalisation based on behaviour to a statement about essence? If voters were as the behaviouralists said they were, one must then go on to ask why. One reasonable conclusion is that apathy is the most rational response to the political system as it is, and the citizen might direct his or her activism into areas which offer a much better return than politics. This is a theme which has recurred several times in this book. To paraphrase Marx: behaviouralists have merely interpreted the surface of the world; the point is to change the conditions which give rise to behaviour.

Before examining the evidence about electoral behaviour in Australia, this chapter must look at the structures within which that behaviour takes place, for it may only be by structural change that behavioural change might come about.

Electoral systems

The structures of the Australian electoral systems offer a wide range of participation for the citizen. In fact, the old adage that representative elections should be free, fair and frequent needs to be modified slightly to describe the Australian situation. Elections and systems show a remarkable frequency, complexity, and diversity. It is not unlikely that Australian voters could face a series of elections and referendums which would demand the use of at least five different electoral systems and at least three methods of voting. In comparison with Britain or New Zealand, where elections to a single house of parliament are based on a simple plurality system, Australian elections have been complicated by federalism, bicameralism, and a diversity of electoral methods and laws. Australian electors, in any three-year period, will be asked to vote for the Australian Senate with one electoral system, for the House of Representatives with a different system, for their two State houses with the possibility of different systems for each, and for their local government with yet another system. As well, they may be asked to decide on federal or State referendum questions, again with a different system of voting. They will be asked on one occasion to mark their ballot paper with sequential numbers—filling all available boxes; on another occasion they might be required to use a system of limited optional preferences; on yet another occasion they might be asked to put a cross in any one square; and on referendums they will be required, to write 'yes' or 'no'. Is it any wonder that voters are confused? Is it any wonder that, regularly, many Australian voters produce an informal ballot, whether by accident or design? Perhaps the reverse question could be asked. Is it not a wonder that many more voters are not so confused?

Any analysis of theory and practice in Australian politics has to confront the disjunctions in the electoral processes, and consider qualitative as well as quantitative issues. The structures, methods and processes of elections impinge on the wider political context. They affect, and are affected by, the ideologies, intentions and behaviour of individuals, groups and political parties, and by the concepts of political representation currently in vogue. And, of course, they can be, have been, and are being, used by political parties to seek and win office by means which are, at least, questionable.

There are at least four related groups of issues which need to be considered. The first concerns who should have the right to vote. The second concerns the mechanics of election systems, the relation of votes to seats. The third, and usually the most controversial, is the question of the justice, fairness and degree of representation in electoral systems. The fourth set of issues concerns the relationship between electoral and party systems. There are no simple answers to any of these questions because there is no single body of opinion about the purposes of elections, the concept of 'fairness' in electoral systems, and the relationship between elections, election systems, parties and party systems. The problem is exacerbated by the fact that no two electoral systems are the same in all details. Nevertheless, there are some broad lines of agreement on what constitutes a democratic electoral system, and there are means of comparing systems and their effects. These broad lines form the basis of a comparison of theory and practice in Australia.

The right to vote

In the nineteenth century, the Australian States were pioneers in the extension of voting rights, but in the twentieth century the pace of reform has been very slow. Indeed, it was not until the mid 1970s that South Australia abandoned its property-based restrictive franchise for its upper house, and not until the late 1970s that popular election was introduced for the upper house in New South Wales.

But Australian electoral laws go further than a right to vote. Most incorporate three aspects of compulsion, backed by a legal sanction—compulsory enrolment, 'compulsory voting' and compulsory preferences. (The Senate, and the Legislative Council systems of New South Wales and South Australia incorporate a modified system of optional preferences, and the latter has retained voluntary voting.)

Compulsory enrolment is obviously useful in ensuring one person-one vote, and is an efficient and effective means of obtaining data necessary, for example, for redistributions. But is 'compulsory voting' justified? This question becomes more important when it is realised that compulsory voting can not be enforced. What the Electoral Act can enforce is compulsory attendance. What voters do, once their name has been ticked off, is their own affair. Given the secrecy of the vote, there is no way of compelling a person to vote. Of course, for the overwhelming majority, compulsory attendance is in effect 'compulsory voting', and this is assumed in the relevant arguments.

It can be argued that a duty to vote denies the right to vote. If citizens are forced to vote, then they lose the right to choose whether or not to vote. Perhaps, as Joan Rydon somewhat infelicitously argued, the consequence might be that 'in Australia where the apathetic and ill-informed are forced to the polls by law, it is...likely that the scum and dregs of political life will decide who is to govern the country'.[3] Australia also demands compulsory preferences in most elections, thus forcing voters either to express preferences for candidates they may not wish to support at all or to cast an informal ballot. In theory, at least, a 'democratic' election system should offer the widest range of choice. And that suggests voluntary voting and optional preferences.

Why have these elements of compulsion been retained? It is a consequence of political parties not just accommodating themselves to the system, but learning to use it to their advantage. Compulsory voting clearly aids pollsters, psephologists and parties in their quest to predict and analyse voting patterns. More importantly, it has eased the burden of the political parties in their quest for power. They have been relieved of the task of 'getting out the vote', and have been able to concentrate on the second problem—that of getting the vote to them. Thus, compulsion has affected the mode of political campaigns. Assured of the votes of their committed followers, parties seek support among the 'swinging' voters. This has added to the pressures on both Labor and non-Labor to gravitate to the 'centre' of politics in Australia as well as contributing to the debasement of political rhetoric, as noted in Chapter 4. Such rhetoric involves distortion and even deliberate lies. If it is not sufficient in the commercial sector for advertising to be governed by the principle of *caveat emptor*, it is surely not sufficient for parties and voters in an electoral process in which people are legally obliged to be 'consumers'.

There is a need, therefore, to legislate for truthful advertising and to abolish the system of compulsory voting which sustains misrepresention. Liberal, National and Democrat, as well as all minor parties, however, resist any suggestion of optional preferential voting. In both cases, the unstated reason is that the existing compulsion benefits the parties which support it. The parties or, at least, the major parties, have accommodated themselves to the peculiarities of the Australian systems which, of course, they designed and introduced.

Votes and seats

The 'mechanics' of an electoral system, the means of translating votes into seats, have an important bearing on the formation of parliaments and governments. The Australian colonies pioneered such electoral reforms as the secret ballot, male suffrage and, later, adult suffrage, and 'one person, one vote' for the lower houses. Since then, however, the various States have often gone their various ways. New South Wales experimented with a second ballot and proportional representation, Queensland used a form of contingent voting, then a simple plurality system and finally incorporated preferential voting in 1962. South Australia varied from a plurality system to contingent voting to preferential voting, and briefly incorporated a list system for its upper house in the 1970s. Proportional representation is used for the Senate, was used until 1978 in the indirect election of the New South Wales Legislative Council, and has been used continuously since 1907 in Tasmania, the only State which has shown relative stability of choice of system.

Why has there been such kaleidoscopic change? The most direct answer is that parties, in government, have designed and carried into law the electoral system which they perceive to be of the most benefit to them. And, on occasions, the two major parties have agreed that one system is to be preferred because it maintains their hegemony over the whole process of representative government. Both Labor and Liberal, for example, are opposed to proportional representation—not because of any theoretical weaknesses, but because proportional representation would give greater opportunities for minor parties and independents to enter the legislature and disturb the existing two-party hegemony. The sucesses of the DLP in the Senate in the 1960s and until 1974, and of the Australian Democrats since 1977, are perceived by both major parties as solid evidence why proportional representation should be resisted for other elections. Nevertheless, there is pressure within the Labor Party, currently spearheaded by Senator Gietzelt, for that party to adopt proportional representation as its policy for all elections. A calculation of potential Labor benefits and loss, rather than any theory of what are fair electoral mechanics, will decide whether he can convince his colleagues.

Supporters of proportional representation, since the time of Catherine Spence, have pointed to its overcoming the biases, inherent or deliberate, in single-member representative systems. They see multi-member electorates as having positive attributes in that proportional representation offers representation to a wider group of parties and interests, and greatly reduces the problem of wastage of votes. Of the two major variations of proportional representation used in Western nations, the list system, confined mainly to Europe, is designed to provide *parties* with legislative representation proportional to their electoral support. The variation used in the Senate and the Tasmanian Assembly, a modification often referred to as the 'single transferable vote' type of proportional representation, places less emphasis on parties and more on the opportunity for electors to vote for individual candidates. A list system denies this opportunity. The South Australian and New South Wales Legislative Councils now incorporate a modified optional preferential system. Voters are required to cast preferences up to the number or vacancies to be filled, and have a free choice of preferences after that. Under the 1984 Electoral Act, the new

Senate voting system offers voters a choice between a list system, and full preferential voting. The electors can choose to cast a vote for the party of their choice, and allow preferences (if any) to be allocated by that party. Their other alternative is to cast a vote for individual candidates on the lower part of the ballot paper.

Opponents of proportional representation have argued that the system leads to a proliferation of parties in the legislature, and a consequent instability, with government dependent on alliances, 'backroom' arguments, and small-group coalitions. They often point to the Fourth French Republic as epitomising such shortcomings. Yet, such extreme proliferation has not occurred in the Senate, in Tasmania, in South Australia nor in New South Wales. In Tasmania, often pointed to in a rebuttal of Duverger, third parties have consistently failed to get off the ground. In the Senate, the election of DLP, Independent, and Australian Democrat members has been welcomed by supporters of proportional representation on the grounds that a more accurate representation of the electorate is thereby obtained. It is criticised by both major parties, however, on the grounds that a potential balance of power in the hands of a minor party is far from what is intended in a system of responsible government.

The single transferable vote system of proportional representation is complex for voters, parties and electoral officers. Introduced by the Chifley Government in 1949 to overcome previous massive party imbalance in the Senate, it has produced a new shortcoming of its own. This is the possibility, even the probability, given the present system of six-year terms for Senators, of deadlock between parties, of control by small parties, or of deadlock between houses. The system is designed on a principle of election by quota, a proportion of the formal votes calculated by:

$$\frac{\text{Total Votes}}{\text{Seats to be filled} + 1} + 1$$

In a normal election, one producing six senators from each state, the quota for election is 14.3%; in double dissolution elections, the quota is 7.7%. Hence, it is not too difficult for small parties and the occasional independent to win seats. Proportional representation, however, has not brought to Australia the fragmentation and instability of some European countries. Because of entrenched party organisation and the party identification prior to its introduction, the splitting of representation between a number of parties did not occur. Since 1949, party control and party pre-selection have been strengthened. Under normal electoral circumstances, five out of six vacant Senate seats are safe, with the major parties usually assured of at least two each. Hence candidates pay more attention to gaining party support than representing the public. 'How to vote' cards become increasingly important, and informal and 'donkey votes' often decisive. It should also be noted that, under the single transferable vote system, the transfer of surplus votes is on a basis of a 'random selection' which, despite the protestations of statisticians, may not necessarily be a perfectly accurate mirror of the whole vote 'population'.

The preferential system of voting in single-member seats is the most commonly used in Australia—for example, for all mainland lower houses. Its 'mechanics' appear to be relatively simple, but as the following example shows, can have odd results.

Table 7.1 First preference votes, Macmillan (Victoria) 1972

		Votes	Per cent	
Armitage	Lib.	12 025	24.15	
Buchanan	Ind.	3 113	6.25	(Liberal sitting member lost pre-selection)
Hewson	CP	8 282	16.63	
Houlihan	DLP	3 583	7.19	
Mountford	ALP	22 802	45.78	

Under a plurality system, Mountford would have been elected, as he won the largest proportion of the formal primary votes. Nevertheless, actual preference distributions provided the following:

Table 7.2 Preference distribution, Macmillan

	Buchanan eliminated		Houlihan eliminated		Armitage eliminated	
Armitage (Lib.)	12 835	25.77	13 226	26.55		
Hewson (CP)	10 262	20.61	13 406	26.92	26 096	52.40
Houlihan (DLP)	3 721	7.47				
Mountford (ALP)	22 987	46.15	23 173	46.53	23 709	47.60

Hence the candidate who won less than one-sixth of the primary votes, defeated the candidate who won almost half. To extend such a comparison to a national election result begs the question of whether party support would have been the same under a plurality or a proportional system; but even with that qualification in mind, a comparison of actual (preferential) and theoretical (plurality, proportional) results provide striking conclusions for the 1977 and 1983 Federal Elections

Table 7.3 Actual and estimated results, House of Representatives, 1977, 1983

	1977			1983		
	PV	FPP	PR	PV	FPP	PR
Labor	51	50	50	75	72	63
Liberal	54	57	50	33	35	45
National	20	18	13	17	18	11
Democrat	–	–	11	–	–	6
DLP	–	–	1	–	–	–

These two elections produced markedly different actual results—in 1977, a win to the Coalition, with the Liberal Party depending on seven National Party numbers to obtain its governing majority; in 1983, a clear absolute majority for the Labor Party.

A first-past-the-post system would not have varied these results in any significant degree, but proportional representation would have had major effects. In 1977, the Coalition would still have formed a government, but with a very narrow majority. In 1983, the Labor Government's majority would have been reduced. In both elections, the National Party's representation would have been significantly less, and the Australian Democrats would have achieved representation in the House. These data suggest why the Labor, Liberal and National Parties are not in favour of proportional representation.

The simpliest 'mechanics' for voters, parties and officials, are clearly to be found in the first-past-the-post (plurality) system, and this system is the most widely used in Western countries. Proponents of the plurality system (including the ALP in the 1960s and 1970s when DLP preferences were causing problems for the party) have as their prime aim the formation of a strong and stable government, since one party, under normal first-past-the-post circumstances, is able to win an absolute majority of seats. Opponents point to the tendency for the plurality system to elect candidates on less than an absolute majority and to the 'wastage' of votes involved. They put emphasis not on government formation, but on reflection of (party) opinion in the parliament—the closest 'mirror' being achieved by proportional representation.'

One major criticism of the plurality system has been countered in the Australian systems. Preferential voting has ensured that no candidate is elected unless he or she secures an absolute majority (at least 50% plus one vote of the formal votes cast); and compulsory voting has ensured that, except in the closest of results, the member represents a majority of the enrolled adults in his or her district. Nevertheless, the problems of over-representation remain, due both to the concentration of party support in localised areas leading to a considerable 'wastage' of votes, and to the inequalities in the populations of the electoral districts. Even with compulsory preferential voting and equal enrolment districts, there is no guarantee, in any system based on single-member electorates, that a majority of votes will produce a majority of seats, and no assurance that party representation in parliaments will be proportionate to electoral support.

A 'fair' system?

The United States Supreme Court decided in the 1960s that any American electoral system, based on unequal numbers of voters in electoral districts, is against the terms of the Constitution. No such ruling has been made in Australia. As earlier chapters have noted, while lip service has been paid to the concept that all votes should have an equal value—'one vote, one value'—the practice has been that governments have consistently legislated for inequalities in electoral systems, inequalities which have generally favoured the extra-metropolitan areas and hence the non-Labor parties. Such malapportionment in Australia has often been incorrectly termed a gerrymander. Narrowly defined, a gerrymander involves an attempt to maximise the vote of a party by the manipulation of electoral boundaries, and such a practice is easily identified by the existence of convoluted electorates on the map. There is little evidence that a gerrymander—a deliberate electoral inequality based on odd-shaped boundaries drawn to provide partisan advantage—exists in any Australian system. There are, however, electoral systems which involve deliberate malapportionment based on a system of electoral zoning. There is also some 'accidental' malapportionment due to the continuing centralisation of population in major cities unaccompanied by corrective electoral redistributions.

The former was most evident in recent years in South Australia, Queensland and Western Australia, where electoral zones produced massive inequalities. There are two principles used to justify such a situation. One is that distances and scattered populations of the far-flung electorates impose disabilities which should be compensated for; thus, such electorates should have fewer constituents than the geographically smaller urban electorates. But one should be wary of the principle of compensation for disabilities. By the same logic, as Humphrey McQueen points out, one could justify a policy of 'one vote for capitalists, 10 for male workers, 15 for female workers, 20 for working class housewives, 50 for recently arrived migrants and 100 votes for Aborigines'.[4] The second principle is that primary producers and their related market towns have a 'stake in the country' and hence merit greater political power. As the Queensland National Party sees it, disproportions are necessary to obtain equivalence between 'balanced' development and political representation. One is not quite certain what that may mean. Could it be the old classical liberal notion of disproportionate representation of the more productive interests, or is it a covert statement of the populist notion, remarked on in Part I of this book, that the rural areas are the site of 'virtue'?

Malapportionment due to population movements is a continuing process. No system of single-member districts can fully overcome such demographic changes and consequent effects, even by constant redistributions. When a marked change in population distribution has occurred, and no redistribution has been held for some time, distinct partisan advantage can accrue. South Australia provides the best case. A redistribution in 1936 set up a ratio of electorate population which was 2:1 in favour of rural areas. This minimum weighting was retained until 1969, when the basic division between metropolitan and extra-metropolitan areas was modified to take into account the growth of the former. In 1968, the mean enrolments in metropolitan and extra-metropolitan districts were 27 600 and 9600 respectively.

Arguments about the 'fairness' of Australia's electoral systems have been a central focus of political debate since 1855; there is no doubt that they will continue, and remain generally at a rhetorical level. What is actually meant by 'one vote, one value' is a matter of debate, but one aspect is quantifiable—the extent to which 'fairness' can be defined as equality of enrolments.

Malapportionment has been most obvious in the Australian States. As one observer put it:

> It appears that the electoral experience of the Australian States is a mixture of three things—adventure, heterodoxy and knavery. Between them, the States have fathered a crop of electoral devices, confounded their textbook behaviour, and at times and in places used them with a skill which even a funfair poker machine proprietor could admire.[5]

But in the last decade, much of the 'knavery' of deliberate, partisan malapportionment has been successfully attacked and defeated; and in 1984 only Queensland and Western Australia incorporate significant malapportionment.

Table 7.4 Indices of malapportionment

Election		Measure of Malapportionment[a]		
		David-Eisenberg	Dauer-Kelsey	Gini
Tas.	1982	1.05	50.9	0.037
NSW	1981	1.28	48.5	0.039
SA	1982	1.64	46.1	0.090
Aust. Nat.	1983	1.86	46.1	0.070
Vic.	1982	1.84	45.4	0.088
Qld.	1984	3.88	40.4	0.171
WA	1983	5.79	36.1	0.194

Notes: David-Eisenberg 'Perfect' 1.0 larger = malapportionment
Dauer-Kelsey 'Perfect' 50.0 smaller = malapportionment
Gini 'Perfect' 0.0 larger = malapportionment

Source: Extracted from C. Hughes 1977–83 Supplement to A Handbook of Australian Government and Politics 1965–1974 ANU, Research School of Social Sciences, Working Papers in Political Science January, 1984

When it comes to upper houses the levels of malapportionment diverge even more widely.

Table 7.5 Gini index of malapportionment in upper houses

	Gini index
South Australia	.000
New South Wales	.000
Victoria	.133
Tasmania	.220
Western Australia	.560

Source: D. Horne, E. Thompson, D. Jaensch and K. Turner Changing the System Adelaide APSA Monograph, 25, 1981, p. 26

Reform has come exclusively from Labor governments, resistance unanimously from Liberal and National Parties. The proposals for electoral reform—for 'one vote, one value'—by the Dunstan, Wran and Cain Governments, in South Australia (1970s), New South Wales (1970s) and Victoria (1983), were carried into law in the face of opposition from the anti-Labor parties which had benefitted from the previous malapportionment. The Burke Government in Western Australia had its Electoral Reform Bill rejected by the Liberal majority in the Legislative Council in 1984, but is trying again, with a compromise proposal. Tasmania, of course, has had one vote, one value since 1909. Only one case of malapportionment was introduced by, and benefitted, the Labor Party—the 'Gair-mander' in Queensland from 1947 to 1957.

The national electoral system has shown some slight malapportionment in the past, especially through the tolerance of plus or minus 20% granted to Electoral Commissioners, and the consequent slight over-representation of rural areas. But the Whitlam Government carried an Electoral Act reducing this tolerance to plus or minus 10%, a proposal accepted by the Liberal Party (but vehemently opposed by the [then] Country Party), and the 1984 Redistribution Commission was required to take population growth into account. The result is the nearest to 'one vote, one value' possible in a system based on single-member electorates.

That leaves only Queensland, but there the possibility of reform—the abolition of the Bjelke-mander—has been entirely up to the Liberal Party. The Bjelke-mander is unique in Australia's history—designed to favour the National Party to work *against both Labor and Liberal*. Until 1984, its abolition was a simple matter of Liberal and Labor combining on one bill, and one only, to pass an Electoral Reform Act. But this required political courage from the Liberal caucus, and there had been only initial signs of that. The formation of a Bjelke-Petersen National Government in 1984, with the Liberal Party consigned to a small cross-bench rump in the parliament, has removed any chance of electoral reform in Queensland—at least until the ALP wins government or the Liberal Party revives itself. Given the rationale and impact of the Bjelke-mander, neither is a possibility in the near future.

As this book has constantly argued, the major impediment to reform is the highly partisan nature of politics in Australia. For example, the modest referendum proposal of 1974 to amend the Constitution, so that House of Representative electorates in each State would contain the same number of people, was accused of being a 'Labor gerrymander', desinged to take advantage of safe Labor seats containing a large number of migrant non-voters. The failure of that referendum proposal is but another example of the difficulty of achieving change by constitutional means. As has been noted, the High Court here has not played an innovative role. It ruled in 1975, for example, that Section 24 of the Constitution providing for the House of Representatives to be 'chosen by the people' did not necessarily imply the principle of 'one vote, one value'. Here surely was an area where the Court could have *made* law in the manner suggested in Chapter 6. Chapter 4, moreover, has already noted the refusal of the High Court to rule on misleading political advertising.

Consistent with the argument in Chapter 6, a number of principles and rights pertaining to the electoral system should be built into the Constitution in addition to the simple mechanical clauses which currently exist. There is probably no need to specify in any detail how the electoral machinery should be constructed; such would impede flexibility. But there should be at least a set of principles upon which judges could base equitable decisions. Such constitutional principles would be binding on the States and, for that reason, one will expect continued opposition. Indeed, it is arguable that the only way one might achieve a really equitable system is by adopting a unitary system of government. A major source of irrationality is, after all, the requirement that Commonwealth electoral divisions do not cross State borders. Moreover, the very existence of the Senate, that supposed lynch pin of the federal edifice, is a gross affront to any interpretation of the principle of 'one vote, one value'. In Senate elections the vote of a Tasmanian is ten times more 'valuable' than the vote of a Victorian.

Of course, a number of very significant reforms have already been carried out without constitutional change. The emphasis on equi-enrolment electorates with a tolerance of plus or minus 10% in the national electoral system was carried through in the face of some strong opposition from non-Labor elements, notably the National Country Party, and doubtless many other reforms could be carried out more simply. But not every political party would consider voluntary voting, optional preferences, party names on ballot papers and proportional representation in multi-member electorates as 'reforms'. Most States still retain electoral systems which are malapportioned. Queensland receives the most publicity but Western Australia has the greatest maldistribution.

In recent times, the Labor Party has changed its earlier call for a plurality system—a proposal which had its origin in the effectiveness of DLP preferences against Labor in the past—to a system of voluntary preferential voting. The proposal has been strongly resisted by the Liberal and National Country Parties. The DLP, the Australian Democrats and some members of the ALP advocate proportional representation for all elections, and it may be that other political groups will support it. But, as has been noted, it is likely that the major parties will resist proportional representation, not because proportional representation, under a system of single transferable votes in small three or five-member constituencies, does not overcome the problems of malapportionment and consequent party bias, but because the major parties do not favour the intrusion of minor groups. Here one only has to consider the ALP's embarrassment at the advent of the Nuclear Disarmament Party.

Many seemingly convincing 'principles' are put forward by the architects of malapportionment in an attempt to justify the inequalities produced. The defenders of all but one of the malapportioned electoral systems in the history of Australia have rested their cases on a set of 'principles'. These usually include such statements as:

1 The rural voters have a stake in the country and an electoral system has to recognise this
2 Voters in the sparsely settled areas need smaller-enrolment electorates to achieve parity of 'quality' of representation
3 The problems of rural voters in contacting their parliamentary representatives need to be eased
4 The need for any parliamentary representative to be able to service the needs and desires of his or her electors has to be recognised.

The first populist 'principle' discussed earlier in the case of Queensland can be discounted immediately. There is no basis for any case which seeks to argue that all rural residents are 'worth' more than all urban, especially metropolitan, residents. Yet most systems of malapportionment seem to assume this.

The other three 'principles' can be subsumed into one also noted earlier: that dispersed populations in large areas are at a representational disadvantage in comparison with the closely-settled, small-area electorates in the city. They are! But this can be resolved *without* recourse to malapportionment. Provision of a virtual 'open cheque book' for electorate expenses for the rural representatives and electors is a simple means whereby the 'quality' of rural representation could be improved.

The usually unstated 'principle' underlying any system of deliberate malapportionment is advantage to a political party. Once this is recognised, and admitted, then there can be some common grounds for debate. Deliberate malapportionment is designed for one purpose, and one only—to benefit the political party which introduced it.

The Dunstan Labor Government inaugurated a reform which is now a model for the Commonwealth and the States. Until the reform in South Australia in 1975, the redistribution process itself was inaugurated and controlled by the party in power. The government set the terms of reference for a redistribution, and had the authority to demand a re-think, and to reject a redistribution. Under the Dunstan model, the Redistribution Commission is an independent statutory body which inaugurates and carries through a redistribution. Governments and oppositions, parties, groups and individuals can propose, suggest and comment, but the redistribution does not require government or parliamentary approval.

The problem remains: there is no *Australian constitutional* guarantee of the principles of one person, one vote, one value; and the 1983 Constitutional Convention found the Liberal and National Party delegates opposing, and defeating, a proposal that there should be. In 1974, the Whitlam Government proposed to the Australian voters an amendment to the Constitution 'to require memberships of the House of Representatives and all State Houses to be directly elected by equal electorates'. But the referendum received only 47% 'yes' overall, and a majority 'yes' only in New South Wales.

The Hawke Government has managed to achieve substantial reforms. One of the first initiatives of the government was to establish a Joint Select Committee on Electoral Reform, with very wide terms of reference. The Committee reported in September 1983, and the principal recommendations were incorporated into the Electoral Act in 1984. This Act brought into being an Australian Electoral Commission as a statutory authority, replacing the Electoral Department. It also introduced substantive changes, including:

1 The removal of parliamentary, government, or party approval for any redistribution
2 The introduction of public funding of political parties for national elections
3 The parallel requirement for disclosure of donations to political parties or candidates (in excess of $200 to a candidate, in excess of $1000 to a party).

Chapter 4 has already canvassed other arguments for reform such as those supporting fixed-term parliaments and the like. There is no need to repeat them here. Suffice it to conclude with the point noted at the beginning of this chapter; there is no one answer, nor any perfect model of electoral system, and any system will at some time give some advantage to one party or another. The lessons of recent years are that there are glaring weaknesses and limitations in the present systems, and that modifications will have to be carried through. The nature of these depend, in the final analysis, on the political values of parties and governments.

Social factors in electoral change

Even a cursory glance at the history of elections in Australia suggests that, if government and opposition are seen as being produced by 'swings in the political pendulum', then the pendulum has often become stuck for long periods. Rather than swinging fairly evenly between Labor and non-Labor, the Australian national political pendulum has spent much more time on the non-Labor side. From 1910, the history of party government at the national level is a history of short-term Labor governments succeeded by long-term non-Labor governments. Of the 74 years to 1984, Labor held national office for only 20, just over one-quarter of the total. The electoral histories of the States suggest that the pendulum has become stuck even more. It is apparent, as Aitkin noted, that the 'ebb and flow of party support in federal elections have been most subdued and there has not been much drift to minor parties'.[6] At every one of the 31 elections from 1910 to 1984, the Labor and Liberal Parties (Labor and Liberal Country Party Coalition from 1922) won over 80% of the vote, and at 23 elections won over 90%. There has, moreover, been a remarkable stability of support for the three 'old' parties. Labor's share of the overall vote has varied between 30% in 1931 and 51% in 1914, with a mean of 45%, and with the largest shift from 49% in 1929 to 38% in 1931. The Liberal Party has a similar history of relative stability of support. If the nadir of 1943 (the period of fragmentation of the United Australia Party) is excluded, the range is from 30% in 1940 to 54% in 1917, with a mean of 39%. If the remarkably stable pattern of support for the Country Party, a mean of 11%, is added to produce a figure for 'Coalition' support, then the range is (again excluding 1943) from 41% in 1972 to 53% in 1975.

Such patterns show great electoral stability; and especially for the post-war period they are indeed surprising. The relative stability was maintained while the electorate almost quadrupled in size from 2.2 million in 1910 to eight million in 1983. Further, Australian society has been transformed since 1945, from a relatively homogeneous, essentially primary producing nation, to a socially heterogeneous, increasingly urban, industrialised nation. Why have these new social characteristics apparently not affected the general two-party nature of the Australian electoral system?

Clearly a multitude of factors is involved. Aitkin's view that the causes 'are to be found in the adoption, by millions of Australians... of relatively unchanging feelings of loyalty to one or other of the Australian parties'[7], begs the questions of what forms the loyalties, what reinforces them, and what tends to erode them, either at a specific election or over time.

Obviously, some pressures on a voter will be more important than others, and will be more important at one election than at another. Hence, in the study of individual or aggregate electoral behaviour, 'the question becomes less what *can* be measured than what is *most strategic* to measure'.⁸ Without some means of identifying the conditions which in any one election are politically relevant, the analyst is left in a morass.

How then may the multitude of factors be refined? A basic distinction may be made between short-term and long-term factors. The dividing line here might be arbitrary; but it is usual to define the former as those factors which become salient following the formal announcement of an election even though an informal campaign may already have begun. The analysis here focuses on party campaigns, the role of leaders in those campaigns and reporting in the mass media of the campaigns and of the behaviour of candidates. The long-term factors are social cleavages, party identification, and party images. Analysis of social cleavages focus on the politicisation of gender, age, ethnic and regional division. It highlights the politicisation of occupational and status groups and the political relevance of changes in the stratification system. All these divisions should be (but rarely are) related to changes in the overall class structure of society. Analysis of party identification includes the extent and intensity of party allegiances in the electorate, and the degree to which such allegiances are translated into votes. Analysis of party image includes the degree to which parties are associated with the above divisions, the degree to which they have been cohesive or internally divisive since the last election, and the degree to which party leaders have managed to project images of efficient management for themselves and the opposite for their opponents. Such considerations lead to an examination of the mass media and other instruments of political communication and socialisation.

A short chapter of this kind can not examine the relationship between voting patterns and all the above dimensions of social cleavage. Probably more research has been conducted in this area of Australian politics than any other. The result has been considerable confusion, with the same data being used to establish quite different conclusions. The crisis here is not one of reseach methodology but of basic political theory. It is, moreover, not just a matter of detached academic debate. The various and contradictory conclusions have shaped party policies and the images developed by party leaders. The influence, for example, of David Kemp's *Society and Electoral Behaviour in Australia*⁹ on the image projected by the Liberal Party needs little emphasis. To highlight the crisis of theory, consider Kemp's findings.

Kemp's basic point is that the statistical association between occupation category and party identification over the past 30 years has weakened. Now, as a consequence of *embourgeoisement*, many more blue-collar workers vote Liberal than before, and conversely many more white-collar workers vote for the ALP. This is a point made long ago by Alford,[10] and although commentators might disagree about the extent of this process, the general conclusion is widely accepted. But problems begin to arise when one observes that the degree of ALP support amongst manual workers does not constitute a steady decline but fluctuates considerably. Two major troughs stand out, after the split in the mid-1950s and at the time of the Vietnam War election. This suggests that there may be major variations of ALP support which have nothing to do with *embourgeoisement*. Indeed, even if one grants that there has been a long-term trend regardless of fluctuation, one has to acknowledge that the whole *embourgeoisement* thesis has been challenged most eloquently in Britain.[11] In Australia, there has been little change in the distribution of taxable income in the entire post-war period.[12] But, protests Kemp, that is beside the point; what he is measuring is workers' *subjective* feelings of *embourgeoisement*.[13] But, if that is the case, why was the fall in ALP vote steepest amongst the unskilled workers, the stratum least likely to entertain such feelings? As Reynolds point out, British research shows that an inverse relationship between voting Conservative and level of income may only be explained when one considers age; this variable was absent from Kemp's data.[14] So also, it is argued, are a lot of the variables present in British analyses, such as plant size, regionalism or changes in socialisation patterns etc. The Australian evidence is far from clear-cut.

But let us assume Kemp is correct and occupational categories in general are becoming less important in party identification. What conclusions follow from this? Kemp is in no doubt: *class* is becoming less and less significant as a determining factor in voting behaviour. If by class Kemp merely means an aggregation of occupational categories, then one has no more than a tautology. But Kemp also means something else by class. Class has something to do with identification. So one asks people what class they identify with and comes up with the extraordinary conclusion that the working class is in the minority. Since such is the case, the ALP would be well advised to disassociate itself from the trade unions, based in a minority class and purveying the out-dated 'ideology' of working class egalitarianism. Instead the ALP should cultivate its relatively 'non-ideological' white-collar component. Because the ALP is dogmatically unwilling to do this, the future for the Liberals seems secure.

Kemp's use of class here is clearly categorical rather than relational. Objective class is given by a set of occupational categories and subjective class consists in identifying oneself with a particular label. As Chapter 3 observed, this is not the way much mainstream social theory treats class. In the Weberian tradition, 'economic class' was given by the market allocation of life chances. Economic classes and status groups were integrated into 'social classes' which developed 'orientations to action' through the medium of party. Thus, party identification was not just a reflection of external forces but a factor in social class action. As Connell and Goot point out (from a position far from the Weberian) one can not at one level maintain, as Kemp does, that political parties are prime movers in the political system but at election time are merely dependent variables.[15] In the socialist tradition, in the words of Connell and Goot:

> Class analysis is about the creation and control of a social surplus, about power, production and wealth; about the social organisation of production and consumption, and the techniques, tensions and struggles that centre on them; about the formation and transformation of the massive, complex, and constantly changing social groupings that are organised around and by the capital-accumulation process; about the vicissitudes of the struggles that arise from exploitation and oppression, the forms of political mobilisation, the dynamics of culture and consciousness, the intractabilities of social structure and the possibilities of structural change. To take an occupational-prestige dichotomy (or an income or educational classification) as a substitute for *that*—and then to jeer at 'simple class models' of politics as a discredited 'conventional wisdom'—hardly even reaches the level of farce.[16]

This book is not so uncharitable. Kemp does offer a wealth of material on the relationship between occupational status and voting. But surely the connection between occupational categories, class and voting is unproven. To establish such a connection one would have to examine the process whereby white-collar jobs are deskilled. A few Marxists (in the style of Poulantzas), on the basis of a rigid interpretation of Marx's discussion of 'productive labour', would agree that the working class is in the minority[17]; but, in rebuttal, a wealth of literature (both Marxist and non-Marxist) argues that the working class must include many occupations not usually classified as blue-collar.[18]

Many other criticisms of Kemp have been advanced, such as the quality of the questionnaire material etc. There is no need to explore them here. The point has been made. There is probably a growing disassociation of occupational categories and party identification at least at middle levels of the overlapping occupational stratification system. But one is not sure how far we may extrapolate trends. Nor is one at all sure what the key determinants are in this process; and catch-all terms like *embourgeoisement* do not explain very much. Finally, Kemp's data do not help one say anything useful about social class in a Weberian sense or class in a Marxist sense. It is a sign of the immaturity of Australian politics that Kemp's book is taken to be iron-clad proof of the uselessness of analysing class politics. Despite the above criticisms, there is no doubt that the work of behavioural scientists such as Aitkin and Kemp are of immense value in highlighting the complexity of voting behaviour. The task here has merely been to hint at the problems.

The question arises as to what methodology would establish the relationship between class in a Marxist sense and voting behaviour. Of course one should ask questions, and questionnaires are useful. Perhaps one should ask the kind of questions which would elicit answers about real ownership and control of productive wealth, about the power to hire and fire and determine the life chances of others. It is possible that Kemp is correct and that there is a growing dissassociation of voting behaviour and class. But one doubts most strongly that this would apply to those who occupy the pinnacles of economic power. When adult male suffrage was generalised in England in the nineteenth century, Disraeli guessed as much and presided over Conservative administrations with considerable mass support. In those days there was much less doubt about the different cultures of 'the two nations' (classes). In the British conservative tradition, culture was certainly seen as class-dependent; yet for Kemp it is an independent variable.[19]

There is insufficient space here to explore other cleavages which are important in any analysis of voting behaviour. Here again theory is probably as undeveloped and as confusing as that concerning occupational categories. An ageing population might cause a polarisation centering on 'grey power'. Questions of gender, it is felt, have not been satisfactorily handled and will become increasingly important. The tension between rural and urban Australia together with the cleavage between the resource-rich North and the manufacturing South suggests a major dimension of conflict. The emergence of issues such as abortion has led to a new form of politicisation of religious cleavages. Ethnicity also could become a major source of tension. The shadow of 'the bomb', moreover, has already had an impact on the orientations of youth. There are no signs that those cleavages will go away and that Australia will become dominated by issue-politics with constantly shifting alliances, and a new type of instability. Cleavage politics, after all, involve clashes of ideology, and one must be most wary of people who talk about 'the end of ideology' (most recently Kemp himself). As

Chapter 2 observed, the end of ideology is no more than another form of ideology which seeks to mask cleavages.

Party identification and electoral change

In his study of Australian voters in 1967 and 1979, Aitkin concluded that 'the extent to which the electorate accepted a partisan label varied hardly at all over twelve years' and that 'the similarity in structure of these two separate examples of 1967 and 1979, both interviewed in periods of electoral quiet, is most striking'.[20]

These conclusions lead to questions about party identification. Clearly Aitkin and others have produced sufficient evidence to show that party allegiance is strong, and transmitted from one generation to another. What are much more complex, and concern a long-running debate in political science, are questions about the nature, status and salience of party identification. Aitkin's study suggests that party identification is a determining influence on the vote. If commitment and fidelity to party are maintained, even across generations, then it seems logical to assume that party allegiance is an independent variable explaining individual and aggregate voting patterns, and that it retains its potency in different political environments. Certainly much of the early research into voting behaviour (and this is only a recent phenomenon) made the assumption that party identification was causally related to the voters' choices. This assumption provided one means to explain the disjunction between the ideal of the rational, adjudicating voter who weighed issues, events and people before casting a vote, and the apparent stability of patterns of party choice.

This approach was developed overseas in *The American Voter*[21] which proposed that party identification was the key to explaining voter consistency and stability of party choice. Campbell et al proposed a 'funnel of causality' where party identification held the status of a perceptual screen through which all events and issues of the time, and all aspects of the political life of the individual, were forced to pass, and against which they were measured.[22] The tendency, then, is for voters to follow their party identification under all but extreme circumstances. The model was claimed to be the explanation for consistency of voting and for stability of electoral patterns; and party identification (with its correlates — habit and the family) was held to be the causal, determining factor.

More recently, this model and explanation has come under question, especially in America and Britain. Major shifts of electoral opinion in both countries have raised the question that either party identification has weakened significantly, or the causal relationship is not as strong as suggested. Before examining the bases of such a challenge, however, one should note that Australia has *not* shown equivalent electoral shifts. While American voters were swinging widely between Republican and Democrat, and British voters' consistency all but disappeared, the patterns of party support in Australia have been remarkably stable. It may be, then, that the causal relationship *is* strong in Australia.

The most recent challenge to the concept of the causal status of party identification is that by Himmelweit et al[23], based on a 15-year longditudinal study in Britain. On their evidence, the authors reject the model of party identification as *the* over-riding influence. They see, 'no reason to treat the voting decision as different from any other decision by postulating one dominant, permanent source of influence with cognitions relegated to a subsidiary position'.[24] They return to a version of the 'consumer model of voting' where the voter is 'responsive rather than dependent', but (contrary to Schumpeter) is 'active rather than passive',[25] and hence their model relegates party identification to one influence among many. They conclude that party identification has no direct influence on the vote, that it is only one of a multitude of social and issue variables, the effects of all of which will vary.

This 'consumer model' suggests for Britain, as did a study by Pomper et al[26] for America, that voters are less consistent, and voting patterns less stable, because of the emergence of the 'responsive voter'[27] who is not so bound by party identification.

In relating this 'consumer model' to Australia, the first point to make is that the change in consistency and stability, noted elsewhere, has *not* occurred in Australia. A second point is a criticism of the model itself. Himmelweit et al make a clear distinction between two concepts which one feels are not distinct. 'In our model party identification has no direct influence on vote... *The habit of voting for a party, on the other hand, has a direct influence on vote*'.[28] This major distinction between 'habit' and 'identification' is not justified. To the political theorist or analyst, the concepts of 'party identification' and 'habit voting for the same party' are qualitatively different. *But are they so to the average voter?* The basis for all recent models of voting behaviour is the sample survey. But how many respondents would make the distinction between the two concepts? Survey analysts may attempt to make a distinction between identifying with a party but, as Aitkin[29] notes, the concept of party identification is a 'psychological attribute, uncomfortably close to the actual behaviour it is used to explain'. Voters do not make this 'scientific' distinction;

and the 'consumer model', in making this distinction a key to explanation, has not adequately allowed for the cognitive level of the average voter.

When one examines the patterns of party support in Australian elections and compares them to American or British patterns, Australia is distinguished by relative stability. Shifts in aggregate electoral patterns are miniscule compared with the other two nations. To use the terminology of Himmelweit et al, then, the 'habit of voting' in Australia appears to be very strong. Examining and comparing the burgeoning evidence from survey data, one finds that this stability appears to rest, today as in the past (as far as one can establish), on a consistent strength of party identification and its transmission from one generation to another. As Aitkin puts it, 'in contrast with Britain, where the proportion not voting in accordance with party identification increased,... Australian electors did not begin to act out of sympathy with their party identification'.[30]

Hence, while the impact of social cleavages on voting patterns may be declining and the description of elections in Australia as class-based may be questionable, the importance of party identification is reinforced. Himmelweit et al's version of the 'consumer model', and the 'responsive voter', may be appearing in Britain and America, but there is little evidence of this development in Australia. One reason for the change in America could be the erosion of the parties themselves—what has been called the disaggregation of the American electorate. And one reason for the continuing salience of party identification in Australia could be the continuing ubiquity and dominance of the parties and party system. Of course, the two 'levels' are inter-related—party identification and party system reinforce each other to some degree. But there is no evidence in Australia to suggest that party identification is less than a key determining factor in explaining individual voting behaviour and patterns of party support.

The voter and democratic theory

The introduction to this chapter noted that most Australian voters are not the rationally-activist-type celebrated for a few short decades in civics text-books. Certainly there is 'a general attitude...of disinterest qualified by a fatalistic skepticism'. 'Politics is a vacancy, an unused space', with most voters representing 'in the evangelical phrase, the Great Unreached'.[31] 'All this has been said many times and, as Chapter 2 noted, was remarked on by Hancock in 1930; the state was no more than 'a vast public utility'.

But, earlier chapters have argued, something should be done

about the apathy rather than just resigning onself to a theory of 'democratic elitism'. Pateman's plea is relevant here.[32] It is only by developing democratic participation in the work-place or the home— in institutions where most people live most of the time—that one may expect the voter to participate more fully in the life of the polity. Of course such participation could result in a situation where participation at one level reinforces a lack of interest in policies at the national level. The task is to ensure that does not happen, by returning to some of the ideals of what Schumpeter called 'classic democratic theory'. These were never a description of what was; they were a prescription for what could be. One can not afford, in these times of economic instability and major threats to peace, to echo Morris Jones's In Defence of Apathy'.[33]

What, then, can be done to produce an environment where apathy is less obvious, where the Australian voter has the opportunity to be closer to the rational-activist of democratic theory? This is not the place to repeat the textbook list of 'causes of apathy', but one can point to the difficulties involved in 'changing the system'.

One of the major difficulties is the combination of apathy and cynicism evident among the next generation of Australian citizens. To evidence this, one need only refer to two surveys, both of which focussed on young people.

The first has been drawn from an informal survey carried out by the Sydney *Sun* newspaper in 1969:[34]

> Today's Question: Are you interested in the coming federal elections?
>
> Linda Davies, 17, receptionist: No, they are dull. Politics just seems to go on and on. Nothing changes. Everyone votes and nothing happens. Politicians don't seem to try to interest people. You're not going to be much better off no matter who you vote in.
>
> Dierdre Gray, 16, typist clerk: Not really. Nothing exciting ever happens. No one seems to care about politics in Australia. We never talk about politics. The only things I know about elections come from school and even then we didn't talk about them often.
>
> Anne Armitage, 19, hairdresser: No. I'm just not interested. Whoever is in power is going to be blamed for what's going wrong. That's all there is to politics.... Who cares about politics? I don't think I'll even bother about voting.

The second is a very revealing survey carried out by the Australian Electoral Office in 1983. The following extracts are taken from the *Report*:[35]

The single most important reason why young people fail to register to vote is because they do not see any direct link between the government or government institutions and their own lives. They become apathetic and will not take the steps necessary to become enrolled.

The same apathy is responsible for their failure to acquire any real political knowledge leading many young people to feel incapable of recording a meaningful vote. They feel that if they can't vote wisely there is little point in bothering to enrol.

Central to an understanding of enrolment failure in young Australians is the realisation that the majority of this group reach 18 years without any feelings toward or knowledge of our political system and what it means to live in a democracy.

Time and time again they made the statement 'but what does all this have to do with me'. 'It doesn't actually affect anything in my life'.

Who is at fault, and what can be done about it?

It is a common complaint that the Australian mass media is to blame. But is it at fault? If the media 'give the public what the public want' (their constant defence against any critical comment), then can the media be blamed? Is 'reform' of the media dependent on the precondition of 'reform' of the average Australian voter? The debate becomes circular—a veritable 'Catch-22'.

Only recently have some State education systems allowed, let alone encouraged, the teaching of politics in schools; and Victoria, Western Australia and the ACT, where teaching politics has been introduced, have not taken the view that *all* trainee-electors should be given apprenticeship training for an adult political life. Certainly it does seem curious for a society to hope that a person who reaches voting age will suddenly become informed, rational and motivated if there has been no real effort to educate in that direction.

For most people, their party is the fall-back position for any political question. And more often than not it is a case of 'my party right or wrong'. This suggests a considerable responsibility for the political parties to go beyond *realpolitik*—getting the numbers at the polls. But, this chapter has suggested, even the cumbersome electoral machinery is designed by political parties for political parties rather than for the benefit of the voters. It may be, then, that the voters' cynicism about the political system is not unfounded. In the present system apathy might be quite rational. The point is to change the system—and this involves a certain amount of ideological politics. One should rejoice that the end of ideology is not at hand. But who may not be just a little apprehensive of what ideologies might triumph? To ensure that they are ones conducive to the development of specifically human values, political parties must engage now in creating the conditions for citizens' self-education rather than gathering the numbers and thinking of their own short-term electoral ends.

NOTES

Introduction

1. I. Kant 'On the Common Saying: "This May Be True in Theory, But it Does not Apply in Practice"' in H. Reiss (ed.) *Kant's Political Writings* Cambridge University Press, 1970, p. 62
2. E. Erikson *Young Man Luther: A Study in Psychoanalysis and History* New York: Norton, 1962
3. D. Jaensch *The Australian Party System* Sydney: George Allen and Unwin, 1983
4. J. Habermas *Legitimation Crisis* London: Heinemann, 1976

Chapter 1

1. The term is Serle's. See G. Serle *From Deserts the Prophets Come: The Creative Spirit in Australia* Melbourne: Heinemann, 1973, p.2
2. J. Ward *James MacArthur: Colonial Conservative, 1798–1867* Sydney University Press, 1981, pp. 19–20
3. R. Mills *The Colonization of Australia, 1829–42* (1915), Sydney University Press, 1974
4. E. Wakefield *A Letter from Sydney and Other Writings* London: Dent, 1929
5. This theme is traced in D. Pike *Paradise of Dissent: South Australia 1829–1857* (1957), Melbourne University Press, 1967
6. J. Lang *Freedom and Independence for the Golden Lands of Australia: The Right of the Colonies and the Interest of Britain and of the World* London: Longman, Brown, Green and Longman, 1852
7. G. Ionescu and E. Gellner (eds) *Populism: Its Meanings and National Characteristics* London: Weidenfeld and Nicolson, 1969
8. A. Stewart 'The Social Roots' *ibid.*, pp. 187–9
9. D. Waterson *Squatter, Selector and Storekeeper: A History of the Darling Downs* Sydney University Press, 1968, pp. 109–10
10. *ibid.* p. 104
11. This point is made with regard to the ideology of the Country Party by D. Aitken *The Country Party in New South Wales* Canberra: ANU

Press, 1972, pp. 3–20. It ran counter to the conventional wisdom in K. Hancock: *Australia* (1930), Sydney: Australasian Publishing Co. Pty. Ltd., 1945, pp. 194–5

12 Waterson *Squatter, Selector and Storekeeper* pp. 272–6
13 On the development of early agrarian ideology, see B. Graham *The Foundation of the Australian Country Parties* Canberra: ANU Press, 1966, pp. 38–46. Graham offers an interesting comparison with agrarian populist ideologies in North America, *ibid.* pp. 1–30
14 Hancock *Australia* p. 196
15 V. Palmer *The Legend of the Nineties* Melbourne University Press, 1954
16 R. Catley and B. McFarlane *Australian Capitalism in Boom and Depression* Chippendale: APCOL, 1981, pp. 31–4
17 H. George *Progress and Poverty: An Inquiry into the Cause of Industrial Depressions and of Increase of Want with Increase of Wealth—The Remedy* London: Kegan Paul, Trench and Co., 1883. On George's influence, see A. Métin: *Socialism Without Doctrine* (1901 and 1910, trans. R. Ward) Sydney: APCOL, 1977, pp. 21–7
18 Resolution adopted at the 4th Intercolonial Trades Union Congress, Adelaide, 1886, cited in R. Ebbels *The Australian Labor Movement: 1850–1907, Extracts from Contemporary Documents* Melbourne: Cheshire Landsdowne, 1960, p. 99
19 E. Bellamy *Looking Backward: 2000–1887* (1887), Boston: Houghton Mifflin, 1931. On Bellamy's influence, see Ebbels: p. 55
20 T. Rowse *Australian Liberalism and National Character* Melbourne: Kibble Books, 1978, pp. 37–76
21 *ibid.* p. 40
22 *ibid.* pp. 43–52
23 T. Irving and B. Barzins 'History and the New Left: Beyond Radicalism' in R. Gordon (ed.) *The Australian New Left* Melbourne: Heinemann, 1970, pp. 66–94
24 R. Ward *The Australian Legend* Melbourne: Oxford University Press, 1965
25 W. Wertheim *Evolution and Revolution: The Rising Waves of Emancipation* Harmondsworth: Penguin, 1974, pp. 108–10
26 A. Deakin *Federal Politics: The Liberal Party and its Liberal Programme* cited in M. Clark *Sources of Australian History* London: Oxford University Press, 1957, p. 482
27 W. Spence *Australia's Awakening: Thirty Years in the Life of An Australian Agitator* Sydney: The Worker Trustees, 1909 (reprinted 1961) p. 381
28 *ibid.* p. 380
29 S. and B. Webb *A Constitution for the Socialist Commonwealth of Great Britain* 2nd edn, Cambridge University Press, 1975
30 ALP Platform, 1905, from *The Worker* Brisbane, 15 July 1905, in Clark *Sources of Australian History* p. 471
31 A. Deakin 'Speech on the Immigration Restriction Bill' *Commonwealth Parliamentary Debates* 12 September 1901, Vol. IV, cited in Clark *Sources of Australian History* pp. 496–7

32 *ibid.* pp. 498-9
33 *The Argus* 10 May 1909, in Clark *Sources of Australian History* p. 491
34 D. Murphy *T.J. Ryan: A Political Biography* St. Lucia: University of Queensland Press, 1975
35 Métin *Socialism Without Doctrine*
36 Spence *Australia's Awakening* p. 378
37 These terms are used in the sense described by K. Polyani *The Great Transformation: The Political and Economic Origins of Our Time* (1944), Boston: Beacon Books, 1957
38 V. Childe *How Labor Governs* (1923), Melbourne University Press 1964, pp. 131-50
39 The Blackburn Declaration was adopted by the 1921 Federal Conference. See L. Crisp *The Australian Federal Labor Party* Sydney: Hale and Iremonger, 1978, p. 281. On the history of the socialisation objective up to that time see *ibid.* pp. 270-98

Chapter 2

1 M. Dixson *Greater than Lenin: Lang and Labor, 1916-1932*, Melbourne Politics Monograph n.d., esp. pp. 183-9
2 *ibid* pp. 10-11
3 A. Davidson *The Communist Party of Australia: A Short History* Stanford: Hoover Institution Press, 1962
4 R. Cooksey *Lang and Socialism: A Study in the Great Depression*, Canberra: ANU Press, 1971
5 E. Page *Truant Surgeon: The Inside Story of Forty Years of Australian Political Life* Sydney: Angus & Robertson, 1963, pp. 62-111
6 Catley & McFarlane (*Australian Capitalism* p. 43) point out that this term of the 1970s was merely modern jargon for a set of theories which date from the 1890s
7 A concise summary of his views is E. Shann *Bond or Free? Occasional Economic Essays* Sydney: Angus and Robertson, 1930
8 *ibid.* p. 36
9 B. McFarlane *Professor Irvine's Economics in Australian Labour History: 1913-1932* Canberra: Australian Society for the Study of Labour History, 1966, esp. pp. 27-31
10 Hancock *Australia*
11 K. Hancock *Country and Calling* London: Faber & Faber, n.d., pp. 92-3
12 J.S. Mill 'Representative Government' in J.S. Mill *Utilitarianism, Liberty, Representative Government* London: Dent, 1910, pp. 249-56
13 Hancock *Australia*, pp. 223-9. Hancock gives a stimulating comparison with America
14 *ibid.* p. 61
15 *ibid.* p. 229
16 *ibid.* p. 122

17 *ibid.* pp. 88–107
18 Rowse *Australian Liberalism* pp. 77–125
19 P. O'Farrell *The Catholic Church and Community in Australia: A History* Melbourne: Nelson, 1977, pp. 384–7
20 Rowse *Australian Liberalism* pp. 149–56
21 C. Hartley Grattan *Introducing Australia* New York: John Day Company, 1942. Grattan, however, did not believe that the United States would ever top Britain in investment (p. 81) and noted that many Australians felt that a reliance on the United States would be dangerous (pp. 20–1 and 238–45)
22 *ibid.* pp. 256–9
23 J. Burnham *The Managerial Revolution* (1941), Bloomington: Indiana University Press, Midland Books, 1973
24 P. Joske *Sir Robert Menzies: 1894–1978, A New Informal Memoir* Sydney: Angus and Robertson, 1978, p. 69
25 Catley & McFarlane *Australian Capitalism*, p. 66
26 *ibid.* p. 68
27 Rowse *Australian Liberalism* pp. 157–60
28 G. Bolton '1939–51' in F. Crowley *A New History of Australia* Melbourne: Heinemann, 1974, p. 482
29 R. Murray *The Split: Australian Labor in the Fifties* Melbourne: Cheshire, 1972, pp. 44–65
30 An attempt to seek coherence in the eclectic package is D. White *The Philosophy of the Australian Liberal Party* Melbourne: Hutchinson, 1978
31 In 1968 Gorton proposed to hold a Liberal philosophy conference. This apparently made his colleagues somewhat uncomfortable. See G. Freudenberg *A Certain Grandeur: Gough Whitlam in Politics* Melbourne: Sun Books, 1978, p. 142
32 J. Schumpeter *Capitalism, Socialism and Democracy* New York: Harper & Row, 1950, p. 269
33 See the critique in C. Pateman *Participation and Democratic Theory* Cambridge University Press, 1970, esp. pp. 3–5
34 Rowse *Australian Liberalism* pp. 197–203
35 P. Coleman 'The Liberal and Country Parties: Platform, Policies and Performance' in J. Wilkes (ed.) *Forces in Australian Politics* Sydney: Angus and Robertson, 1963, pp. 1–17
36 D. Horne *The Lucky Country, Australia in the Sixties* Harmondsworth: Penguin Books, revised edn, 1967
37 H. Marcuse *One Dimensional Man, The Ideology of Industrial Society* (1964), London: Sphere Books, 1968
38 P. O'Brien 'Some Overseas Comparisons' in R. Gordon (ed.) *The Australian New Left* Melbourne: Heinemann, 1970, pp. 219–34
39 Irving and Barzins 'History and the New Left'
40 J. Sendy *Comrades Come Rally! Recollection of an Australian Communist* Melbourne: Nelson, 1978, pp. 122–7
41 R. Catley and B. McFarlane *From Tweedledum to Tweedledee: The New Labor Government in Australia: A Critique of its Social Model* Sydney: ANZ Book Co., 1974

42 G. Duncan 'The ALP: Socialism in a Bourgeois Society' in G. Duncan (ed.) *Critical Essays in Australian Politics* Melbourne: Edward Arnold, 1978, pp. 77–96
43 D. Dunstan '1970 Labor Policy Speech' cited in D. Jaensch *The Government of South Australia* St. Lucia: University of Queensland Press, 1977, p. 39
44 A. Rand *Capitalism: The Unknown Ideal* New York: Signet Books, 1967, frontespiece
45 H. Lunn *Joh: The Life and Political Adventures of Johannes Bjelke-Petersen* St. Lucia: University of Queensland Press, 1978
46 Lunn *Joh* pp. 95–118
47 Catley & McFarlane *Australian Capitalism*
48 H. Mayer 'Some Conceptions of the Australian Party System, 1910–50' in F.B. Smith & M. Beever (eds) *Historical Studies: Selected Articles* Melbourne University Press, 1967, pp. 217–40
49 Lunn *Joh*, p. 100

Chapter 3

1 Thanks are due to Hugh Stretton for helping to reconcile differences of opinion between the two authors concerning this chapter
2 L. Broom and F. Jones *Opportunity and Attainment in Australia*, Canberra: ANU Press, 1976, p. 50
3 E. Wheelwright *Ownership and Control of Australian Industry* Sydney: Law Book Co., 1957 (5% held 53%); E. Wheelwright and J. Miskelly *Anatomy of Australian Manufacturing Industry* Sydney: Law Book Co., 1967 p. 18 (7% held 58%); T. Sykes 'In a Few Hands' *Australian Financial Review* 12 February 1973–16 February 1973 (4% held 55%), all cited in R. Connell *Ruling Class, Ruling Culture* Cambridge University Press, 1977, p. 41
4 Broom and Jones, *Opportunity and Attainment* p. 50; P. Groenewegen 'Consumer Capitalism' in J. Playford and D. Kirsner *Australian Capitalism*, Ringwood: Penguin, 1972, p. 105. P. Raskall 'Who's Got What in Australia: The Distribution of Wealth' *The Journal of Australian Political Economy* No. 2, June 1978, pp. 3–16
5 N. Podder and N. Kakwani *Distribution of Wealth in Australia* mimeo, University of New South Wales, 1973, cited in Raskall 'Who's Got What in Australia' p. 11
6 M. McMichael 'Australian Boards of Directors: Organisation and Functions' *The Australian Director* August 1976, p. 13
7 This was first raised in B. Fitzpatrick and E. Wheelwright *The Highest Bidder* Melbourne: Landsdowne, 1965, and has figured in Wheelwright's work ever since
8 UNESCO, Commission on Transnational Corporations, 4th Session, 15–26 May 1978 *Transnational Corporations in World Development: A Re-examination* New York 1978, p. 267 and 273
9 *Australian Financial System: Interim Report of the Committee of Inquiry* May 1980 (Campbell Committee) Canberra: AGPS., 1980, p. 79

10 A. Crosland *The Future of Socialism* London: Jonathan Cape, 1956, pp. 150–1
11 R. Tawney *Equality* (1931), London: Unwin Books, 1964
12 M. Weber *Economy and Society* Berkeley: University of California Press, 1978, p. 53
13 An Australian example is G. Wickham 'Power and Power Analysis: Beyond Foucault' *Economy and Society* Vol. XII, No. 4, November 1983, pp. 468–96. For a collection of Foucault's lectures and interviews, see M. Foucault *Power/Knowledge, Selected Interviews and Other Writings, 1972–1977* C. Gordon (ed.) Brighton: Harvester Press, 1980
14 Thanks to Kevin White for this wry comment.
15 H. Emy 'The Diffusion of Power' in A. Parkin, J. Summers and D. Woodward (eds) *Government, Politics and Power in Australia* 2nd edn, Melbourne: Longman Cheshire, 1980, pp. 327–8
16 G. Harman 'Pressure Groups and the Australian Political System' in *ibid*. p. 285
17 C. McGregor 'Patterns of Power' in *ibid*. pp. 295–8
18 S. Lukes *Power: A Radical View* London: Macmillan, 1974, p. 15
19 R. Dahl 'The Concept of Power' in R. Bell, D. Edwards and R. Wagner *Political Power: A Reader in Theory and Research* New York: The Free Press, 1969, p. 80
20 H. Wolfsohn, contribution to 'A Symposium on Power in Australia' *Arena* 6, 1965, p. 10
21 *ibid*.
22 A good summary is D. Austin 'Ideology in Class Society: The Contribution of Max Weber' in P. Hiller (ed.) *Class and Inequality in Australia: Sociological Perspectives and Research* Sydney: Harcourt, Brace Jovanovich Gp., 1981, pp. 28–39
23 For an excellent discussion of Weber's treatment of this, see R. Brubaker *The Limits of Rationality: An Essay on the Social and Moral Thought of Max Weber* London: George Allen and Unwin, 1984
24 Weber *Economy and Society* p. 73.
25 S. Encel *Equality and Authority: A Study of Class, Status and Power in Australia* Melbourne: Cheshire, 3rd edn, 1977, p. 57 and 78
26 See Brubaker *The Limits of Rationality* pp. 104–6
27 *ibid*. pp. 67–8
28 *ibid*. p. 68
29 Habermas *Legitimation Crisis*
30 R. Connell and T. Irving 'A Working Paper Towards a Historical Theory of Class' in Hiller (ed.) *Class and Inequality* p. 10
31 A good summary is B. Jessop *The Capitalist State* Oxford: Martin Robertson, 1982
32 B. Fine and L. Harris *Rereading Capital* New York: Columbia University Press, 1979
33 C. Bulbeck 'State and Capital in Tariff Policy' in B. Head (ed.) *State and Economy in Australia* Melbourne: Oxford University Press, 1983, pp. 219–37
34 N. Poulantzas *Political Power and Social Classes* London: New Left Books, 1973

35 As in the German *Staatsableitung* school. See J. Holloway and S. Picciotto (eds) *State and Capital: A Marxist Debate* London: Edward Arnold, 1978
36 F. Block 'The Ruling Class Does Not Rule: Notes on the Marxist Theory of the State' *Socialist Revolution* 33, 1977, pp. 6–28
37 C.W. Mills *The Power Elite* New York: Oxford University Press, 1959, p. 244
38 Connell and Irving 'A Working Paper', p. 20
39 J. Baily 'Media Power—Is it Inevitable' in ANU, Centre for Continuing Education *Power in Australia: Directions of Change* papers from the National Conference, November 1981, Canberra: ANU, p. 88
40 *ibid*. p. 86
41 N. Abercrombie, S. Hill and B. Turner *The Dominant Ideology Thesis* London: George Allen and Unwin, 1980
42 C. Chamberlain *Class Consciousness in Australia* Sydney: George Allen and Unwin, 1983
43 J. Playford 'Who Rules Australia' in Playford and Kirsner (eds) *Australian Capitalism* pp. 108–55; H. McQueen *Australia's Media Monopolies* Camberwell: Widescope, 1977; A. Theophanous *Australian Democracy in Crisis* Melbourne: Oxford University Press, 1980; K. and E. Windschuttle *Fixing the News: Critical Perspectives on the Australian Media* North Ryde: Cassell, 1981; C. Williams *Open Cut: The Working Class in an Australian Mining Town* Sydney: George Allen and Unwin, 1981; Connell *Ruling Class, Ruling Culture*; R. Connell and T. Irving *Class Structure in Australian History: Documents, Narrative and Argument* Melbourne: Longman Cheshire, 1980
44 R. Wild *Social Stratification in Australia* Sydney: George Allen and Unwin, 1978: R. Kriegler *Working for the Company, Work and Control in the Whyalla Shipyard* Melbourne: Oxford University Press, 1980
45 S. Bowles and H. Gintis *Schooling in Capitalist America* New York: Basic Books, 1976
46 R. Connell, D. Ashenden, S. Kessler and G. Dowsett *Making the Difference: Schools, Families and Social Division* Sydney: George Allen and Unwin, 1982
47 M. Newton 'The Economy' in A. Davies and S. Encel (eds) *Australian Society: A Sociological Introduction*, 1st edn, Melbourne: Cheshire, 1963, pp. 240–1
48 P. Bachrach and M. Baratz 'Two Faces of Power' in F. Castles et. al. *Decisions, Organisations and Society* Harmondsworth: Penguin, 1976, pp. 392–404
49 A. Giddens *The Class Structure of the Advanced Societies* London: Hutchinson, 1973, p. 120
50 Wild *Social Stratification in Australia* p. 114
51 Mills *The Power Elite*
52 J. Higley, D. Deacon and D. Smart *Elites in Australia* London: Routledge and Kegan Paul, 1979, pp. 220–67
53 E. Campbell *The 60 Rich Families Who Own Australia* Sydney: Current Book Distributors, 1963
54 R. Miliband *The State in Capitalist Society* London: Weidenfeld and Nicolson, 1969, p. 54. *passim*

55 Playford 'Who Rules Australia'
56 Encel *Equality and Authority* p. 4
57 R. Putnam *The Comparative Study of Political Elites* Englewood Cliffs, NJ: Prentice Hall, 1976, p. 86
58 Higley et. al. *Elites in Australia* p. 108
59 *ibid*. p. 74
60 For a critique of elite theories see T. B. Bottomore *Elites and Society* Harmondsworth: Penguin, 1966
61 Higley et. al. *Elites in Australia* p. 218
62 *ibid*. p. 263
63 Schumpeter *Capitalism, Socialism and Democracy*
64 P. Bachrach *The Theory of Democratic Elitism: A Critique* University of London Press, 1969
65 P. Schmitter 'Still the Century of Corporatism?' *Review of Politics* Vol. XXXVI, No. 1, January 1974, pp. 93−4
66 P. Loveday 'Corporatist Trends in Australia' *Politics* Vol. XIX, No. 1, May 1984, p. 49
67 These are summarised in Holloway and Picciotto (eds) *State and Capital* pp. 1−31
68 J. O'Connor *The Fiscal Crisis of the State* New York: St. Martins Press, 1973; Habermas *Legitimation Crisis*; C. Offe "'Crises of Crisis Management": Elements of a Political Crisis Theory' *International Journal of Politics* Vol. VI, No. 3, Fall 1976, pp. 29−67. These are discussed in an Australian context by J. Triado 'Corporatism, Democracy and Modernity' *Thesis Eleven* 9, July 1984, pp. 33−51
69 D. Rawson 'Who Wants Union Democracy' in ANU, Centre for Continuing Education *Power in Australia* p. 144
70 B. McFarlane *Economic Policy in Australia* Melbourne: Cheshire: 1968, p. 92
71 Triado 'Corporatism, Democracy and Modernity' p. 34
72 G. Dow, S. Clegg and P. Boreham 'From the Politics of Production to the Production of Politics' *Thesis Eleven* 9, July 1984, p. 24
73 Loveday 'Corporatist Trends in Australia' p. 50. See also T. Matthews 'Business Associations and the State, 1850−1979' in Head (ed.) *State and Economy* pp. 115−49
74 A. Gouldner *The Future of the Intellectuals and the Rise of the New Class* London: Macmillan, 1979
75 D. Apter *Choice and the Politics of Allocation* New Haven: Yale University Press, 1971, p. 73
76 D. Kemp *Society and Electoral Behaviour in Australia* St. Lucia: University of Queensland Press, 1978, pp. 26−7
77 See the argument of Block 'The Ruling Class Does Not Rule'
78 Encel *Equality and Authority*
79 Wild *Social Stratification in Australia* p. 114
80 J. Conybeare 'Politics and Regulation: The Public Choice Approach' *Australian Journal of Public Administration* Vol. XLI, No. 1, March 1982, pp. 39−40
81 R. Parish 'Preface' in G. Tullock, et al. *The Economics of Bureaucracy and Statutory Authorities* St. Leonards, NSW.: The Centre for Indepen-

dent Studies, 1983
82 Conybeare 'Politics and Regulation', p. 38
83 *ibid.* p. 37
84 Offe 'Crises of Crisis Management'

Chapter 4

1 W. Godwin *Enquiry Concerning Political Justice and its Influence on Modern Morals and Happiness* (1789), Harmondsworth: Penguin, 1976
2 S. and B. Webb *A Constitution for the Socialist Commonwealth*
3 L. Crisp *Australian National Government* Croydon: Longmans, 1965, p. 232
4 R. Parker 'Responsible Government in Australia' in P. Weller and D. Jaensch (eds) *Responsible Government in Australia* Richmond: Drummond, 1980, p. 11
5 E. Thompson 'The Washminster Mutation', in *ibid.* p. 32
6 *ibid.*
7 B. Galligan 'The Founders Design and Intentions Regarding Responsible Government' *ibid.* pp. 1–10
8 M. James 'Sovereignty vs. Constitutionalism in Australian Political Thought' in L. Chipman et. al *Constitutional Theory and Australian Practice* conference sponsored by the Centre for Independent Studies (Turramurra), University of Sydney, 23 November 1979, p. 8
9 W. Bagehot *The English Constitution* London: Fontana, 1963
10 A. Dicey *Law of the Constitution* London: Macmillan, 1964
11 J. McMillan, G. Evans and H. Storey *Australia's Constitution: Time for Change* Sydney: George Allen & Unwin, 1983, pp. 211–2
12 R. Dworkin *Taking Rights Seriously* Cambridge Mass: Harvard University Press, 1977, p. 269
13 F. Hayek *Law Legislation and Liberty* Vol. II, *The Mirage of Social Justice* London: Routledge and Kegan Paul, 1976, p. 147. See the discussion in B. Brugger 'Classical British and European Liberalism and Democracy' in N. Wintrop (ed.) *Liberal Democratic Theory and Its Critics* London: Croom Helm, 1983, pp. 38–44
14 James 'Sovereignty vs. Constitutionalism'
15 F. Hayek 'Whither Democracy' in F. Hayek *Social Justice, Socialism and Democracy: Three Australian Lectures* Turramurra: The Centre for Independent Studies (CIS *Occasional Papers* No. 2) 1979, p. 35
16 See the argument in Pateman *Participation and Democratic Theory*
17 Dicey *Law of the Constitution* pp. 171–80
18 H. Emy *The Politics of Australian Democracy* 2nd edn, Melbourne: Macmillan, 1978, pp. 577–82
19 G. Sartori *Parties and Party Systems: A Framework for Analysis* Cambridge University Press, 1976, Vol. I, p. 63
20 T. Lowi 'Party, Policy and Constitution in America' in W. Chambers and W. Burnham (eds) *The American Party Systems: Stages of Political Development* New York: Oxford University Press, 1975, p. 239

21 C. Macpherson *The Life and Times of Liberal Democracy* Oxford University Press, 1977, pp. 64–9
22 Bagehot *The English Constitution* p. 68
23 Parker 'Responsible Government in Australia' p. 13, (emphasis in original)
24 *ibid.*
25 *ibid.* p. 14
26 See G. Reid 'Responsible Government and Ministerial Responsibility' in G. Curnow and R. Wettenhall (eds) *Understanding Public Administration* Sydney: George Allen and Unwin, 1981, pp. 39–55. A comment specifically blaming the decline of responsibility on the growth of the party system is Sir H. Maine 'The Nature of Democracy' in H. Maine *Popular Government* London: John Murray, 1909, pp. 56–126
27 Courtesy A. Bear
28 See J. Uhr 'Parliamentary Reform in Canberra' *The Australian Quarterly* Spring 1982, Vol. LIV, No. 3, pp. 220–2
29 Sir B. Snedden 'Parliament: the Fulcrum of Democracy' in J. Holmes (ed.) *Televising Parliament, Working Papers on Parliament* No. 2, Melbourne University, Department of Political Science in association with the Australasian Study of Parliament Group, 1980, p. 1
30 R. Rose *The Problem of Party Government* London: Macmillan, 1974, pp. 381–3
31 N. Johnson *In Search of the Constitution: Reflections on State and Society in Britain* Oxford: Pergamon Press, 1977, p. 85
32 J. Pettifer (ed.) *House of Representatives Practice* Canberra: AGPS, 1981, p. 557
33 J. Kerin 'Parliament in Contemporary Society' in H. Mayer & H. Nelson (eds) *Australian Politics: A Fourth Reader* Melbourne: Longman Cheshire, 1976, p. 382
34 See M. Indyk 'Making Government Responsible: The Role of Parliamentary Committees' in Weller and Jaensch (eds) *Responsible Government in Australia* pp. 93–109
35 Rose *The Problem of Party Government* pp. 469–70
36 C. Clark 'Parliamentarians by Lot' *Quadrant* Vol. XVIII, No. 3, May-June, 1974, p. 49
37 Crisp *The Australian Federal Labor Party* pp. 9–10
38 See A. Parkin and J. Warhurst (eds) *Machine Politics in the Australian Labor Party* Sydney: George Allen and Unwin, 1983
39 Crisp *The Australian Federal Labor Party* p. 22
40 I. Jennings *Parliament* 2nd edn, Cambridge University Press, 1957, p. 445. See the discussion in Crisp *Australian National Government* pp. 308–9
41 This is argued in D. DeBats 'Liberal-Democratic Theory in America' in Wintrop (ed.) *Liberal Democratic Theory and Its Critics* pp. 71–8
42 A. Deakin, 15 September 1897, Australasian Federal Convention, Second Session, Sydney *Official Debates* Sydney: Govt. Printer, 1897, p. 584

43 See S. Griffith, 4 March 1891, in New South Wales *Official Report of the National Australasian Convention Debates* Sydney: Govt. Printer, 1891, p. 33
44 Thompson 'The Washminster Mutation' pp. 33–4
45 See Uhr 'Parliamentary Reform in Canberra' pp. 224–6
46 Sir B. Snedden .'Ministers in Parliament—A Speaker's Eye View' in Weller and Jaensch (eds) *Responsible Government in Australia* pp. 68–85
47 N. Blewett (1977) cited in MacMillan, Evans and Storey *Australia's Constitution: Time for Change* pp. 223–4
48 Sartori, *Parties and Party Systems* pp. 28–9
49 A. King 'Political Parties in Western Democracies: Some Sceptical Reflections' *Polity* Vol. II, No. 2, Winter 1969, p. 111
50 K. Janda 'Primrose Paths to Political Reform: "Reforming" versus Strengthening American Parties' in W. Crotty (ed.) *Paths to Political Reform* Lexington Mass: Lexington Books, 1980, p. 317
51 J. Jupp *Political Parties* London: Routledge and Kegan Paul, 1968, p. ix
52 L. Webb 'The Australian Party System' in C. Hughes (ed.) *Readings in Australian Government* St. Lucia: University of Queensland Press, 1968, p. 322
53 Rose *The Problem of Party Government* p. 479
54 Sartori, *Parties and Party Systems* p. 25

Chapter 5

1 These are summarised in R. Spann *Government Administration in Australia* Sydney: George Allen and Unwin, 1979, pp. 34–6
2 Encel, *Equality and Authority* p. 78
3 ibid. p. 57
4 Hancock *Australia* p. 118
5 Much of this is based on Encel *Equality and Authority* pp. 242–74
6 ibid. p. 255
7 S. Encel 'Cabinet and the Bureaucracy' in J. Wilkes (ed.) *Parliament, Bureaucracy, Citizens: Who Runs Australia?* Sydney: Angus and Robertson, 1972, p. 31
8 K. Mannheim *Freedom, Power and Democratic Planning* London: Routledge and Kegan Paul, 1950, p. 42
9 ibid. p. 44
10 M. Simms *A Liberal Nation: The Liberal Party and Australian Politics* Sydney: Hale and Iremonger, 1982, pp. 11–54
11 Encel 'Cabinet and the Bureaucracy' p. 32
12 ibid.
13 G. Caiden 'Administrative Reform' in Curnow and Wettenhall (eds) *Understanding Public Administration* pp. 183–5. See also G. Caiden *Commonwealth Bureaucracy* Melbourne University Press, 1967
14 Corbett argues that security of tenure is the prime cause of bureaucratic 'conservatism'. See D. Corbett 'Putting it Together and Keeping in

Together' in R. Smith and P. Weller (eds) *Public Service Inquiries in Australia* St. Lucia: University of Queensland Press, 1978, p. 66
15 Miliband *The State in Capitalist Society* pp. 119–20
16 *ibid.* p. 121
17 P. Wilenski 'Labor and the Bureaucracy', in Duncan *Critical Essays in Australian Politics* pp. 28–46
18 R. Berki *Socialism* London: Dent, 1975
19 Wilenski 'Labor and the Bureaucracy' pp. 36–43
20 M. Sexton *Illusions of Power: the Fate of a Reform Government* Sydney: George Allen and Unwin, 1979, p. 195. On the shortcomings of IDCs, see Spann *Government Administration in Australia* pp. 425–7
21 Wilenski 'Labor and the Bureaucracy' pp. 43–4
22 Sexton *Illusions of Power* p. 186
23 *The Times* 15 November 1976, cited e.g. in Sexton *Illusions of Power* p. 199
24 RCAGA: 10.1.1, p. 299
25 Specifically the proposal for a Department of Industries and the Economy. RCAGA:10.1.13-4, pp. 302–3
26 H. Stretton 'Capital Mistakes' in C. Bell and S. Encel (eds) *Inside the Whale: Ten Personal Accounts of Social Research* Sydney: Pergamon Press, 1978, p. 86
27 *ibid.*
28 This is referred to by Coombs. RCAGA: 11.3.13-4, pp. 369–70. See also Wilenski 'Labor and the Bureaucracy' p. 44
29 RCAGA: 2.3.2, p. 17
30 B. Hughes *Exit Full Employment: Economic Policy in the Stone Age* Sydney: Angus and Robertson, 1980
31 J. Edwards 'The Economy Game: Treasury and its Rivals' *Current Affairs Bulletin* Vol. LI, No. 12, May 1975, p. 6. See the discussion in P. Weller and J. Cutt *Treasury Control in Australia* Sydney: Ian Novak, 1976, pp. 44–6
32 Evidence before RCAGA, in Weller and Cutt *Treasury Control in Australia* p. 44
33 Stretton, 1978, 'Capital Mistakes' p. 85
34 RCAGA: 2.3.6, p. 18
35 See C. Hazelhurst and J. Nethercote (eds) *Reforming Australian Government: The Coombs Report and Beyond* Canberra: ANU Press, 1977; Smith and Weller (eds) *Public Service Inquiries in Australia*
36 Cited in R. Scott 'Towards a Professional Bureaucracy' in Smith and Weller (eds) *Public Service Inquiries in Australia* p. 193
37 RCAGA: 2.1.2-9, pp. 11–3; 4.2.1-17, pp. 59–67
38 *Review of Commonwealth Administration Report (RCA)* Canberra: AGPS, January 1983
39 RCAGA: 3.1.7, p. 32
40 RCAGA: 3.1.8, p. 32–3
41 RCAGA: 8.3.1-38, pp. 184–94
42 See M. Albrow *Bureaucracy* London: Pall Mall Press, 1970, pp. 62–6
43 RCAGA: 3.1.4, pp. 31–2

44 Albrow *Bureaucracy* p. 64
45 *ibid.*
46 RCAGA; 3.2.2, p. 33
47 Sir G. Vickers *The Art of Judgement* London: Chapman and Hall, 1965, p. 31. See the discussion in R. Smith 'Central Co-ordination and Control' in Smith and Weller (eds) *Public Service Inquiries in Australia* p. 179
48 Vickers *The Art of Judgement* p. 33, italics in original
49 RCAGA: 4.3.34-5, p. 78; 10.3.1-23, pp. 325-31; 10.1.40, pp. 299–310
50 RCAGA: 4.1.6, p. 59
51 Smith 'Central Co-ordination and Control' p. 184
52 R. Spann 'Ministers and Permanent Heads' in Smith and Weller (eds) *Public Service Inquiries in Australia* pp. 163–4
53 This was recognised by Coombs, (RCAGA: 4.2.17, p. 66). It was suggested that the situation could be partly remedied by fixed times for divisions.
54 RCAGA: 5.1.23-39, pp. 133–7
55 RCAGA: 5.1.28, pp. 114–5
56 RCAGA: 4.2.8-11, pp. 120–1
57 RCAGA: 5.2.12-6, pp. 121–2
58 RCAGA: 2.5.1, p. 26
59 RCAGA: 4.3.39, p. 78. Though interest in this was expressed in the health and social welfare areas: RCAGA: 10.3.17, p. 329. See also P. Self 'The Coombs Commission: An Overview' in Smith and Weller (eds) *Public Service Inquiries in Australia* p. 322
60 G. Hawker *Who's Master, Who's Servant* Sydney: George Allen and Unwin, 1981, pp. 77–84
61 Spann, *Government Administration in Australia* p. 115
62 M. Forrest 'Reporting and Review of Quangos' *Australian Journal of Public Administration* Vol. XLII, No. 1, March 1983, pp. 82–103
63 R. Wettenhall 'Quangos, Quagos and the Problems of Non-ministerial Organization' *ibid.* pp. 6–10
64 *ibid.* p. 26
65 Spann *Government Administration in Australia* pp. 118–20
66 Forrest 'Reporting and Review of Quangos' p. 90
67 Spann *Government Administration in Australia* pp. 120–49
68 *ibid.* p. 121
69 RCA: 3.70, p. 31
70 RCAGA: 4.4.1-42, pp. 81–95
71 RCA: 3.67-9, p. 30–1
72 Forrest 'Reporting and Review of Quangos' p. 90
73 RCAGA: 3.2.3-8, pp. 34–5
74 RCAGA: 3.2.9, p. 35
75 RCAGA: 3.3.1-15, pp. 36-42; 11.2.1-19, pp. 357–63
76 RCAGA: 9.1.12, pp. 242–3
77 RCAGA: 3.6.1-23, pp. 46–51; 11.3-4, pp. 363–79; 11.6.1-47, pp. 388–403
78 RCAGA: 11.4.1-33, pp. 379–88, especially 11.5.1-2, pp. 379–80. A

few innovations were proposed such as the establishment of a policy unit, and a co-ordinating unit for decentralisation
79 See Smith 'Central Co-ordination and Control' pp. 188–9
80 RCA: 8.2-7, pp. 75–6
81 Spann *Government Administration in Australia* p. 396
82 RCAGA: 11.3.1-21, pp. 36–74; 11.6.1-48, pp. 362–403
83 RCAGA: 3.6.7, p. 47
84 RCAGA: 3.6.5, p. 47
85 RCAGA: 10.1.13-14, pp. 302–3
86 B. Juddery 'What's In It For Us: The Public Service Response' in Hazelhurst and Nethercote (eds) *Reforming Australian Government* p. 168
87 L. Peres 'The Politics of Industrial Policy', in AIPS *Industrial Australia: 1975–2000, Preparing for Change:* Sydney: ANZ Book Co., 1974, pp. 151–2
88 RCAGA: 7.3.8-15, pp. 154–6
89 RCAGA: 7.5.1–7, pp. 161–3
90 RCA: 8.20-2, pp. 79–80
91 RCAGA: 3.4.7, p. 4. Recommendation 3
92 RCAGA: 4.3.12, p. 71. Recommendation 19
93 B. Schaffer Introduction to special issue on access *Development and Change* Vol. II. 1975, p. 3, cited in Smith 'Central Co-ordination and Control' p. 178
94 RCAGA: 7.2.7-8, pp. 150–1
95 RCAGA: 9.2.19-24, pp. 248–50
96 RCAGA: 4.5.8-23, pp. 98-103; 9.5.9-10, p. 273. RCA: 9.48, p. 100
97 RCA: 10.43-66, p. 117–23
98 This point is made by P. Samuel 'The Treasury and the Treasury Line' in Hazelhurst and Nethercote (eds) *Reforming Australian Government* pp. 147–53
99 RCA: 10.31-3, pp. 155–6
100 Coombs seems to see this as a behavioural rather than a structrual problem. RCAGA: 6.1.7, p. 26
101 RCAGA: 6.2.20, pp. 133–4
102 RCAGA: 6.1.8, pp. 126–7
103 M. Painter 'Access: The Public Service and the Public' in Smith and Weller (eds) *Public Service Inquiries in Australia* p. 242
104 RCAGA: 9.6.85-7, pp. 296–7
105 RCAGA: 6.3.12-4, p. 140
106 RCAGA: 4.4.39, p. 94. Recommendation 42
107 RCAGA: 10.4.1-29, pp. 335–42
108 As Coombs does. RCAGA: 6.1.6, p. 126
109 RCAGA: 6.2.4-5, pp. 129–30
110 Painter 'Access: The Public Service and the Public' p. 246
111 *ibid.* p. 242
112 RCAGA: 2.2.9, p. 15
113 See the various articles in *Australian Journal of Public Administration* Vol. XL, No. 2, June 1981, pp. 79–127

114 M. Kirby 'Towards the New Federal Administrative Law' in *ibid.* pp. 113-4. RCA: 5.19-40, pp. 45-50
115 B. Jinks 'The New Administrative Law: Some Assumptions and Questions' *Australian Journal of Public Administration* Vol. XLI, No. 3, Sept. 1982, pp. 212-3
116 Kirby 'Towards the New Federal Administrative Law' pp. 114-5
117 P. Duguit *Traité de Droit Constitutionel* '2nd edn' Paris: Boccard, 1927, p. 469, cited in *ibid.* p. 115
118 RCA: 5.28, p. 47
119 RCA: xv
120 RCA: 5.23, p. 46
121 See the discussion in Emy *The Politics of Australian Democracy*, 2nd edn, pp. 582-6, and RCA: 5.25, p. 46
122 See Hayek *Law, Legislation and Liberty*, Vol. II especially pp. 65-6
123 RCAGA: 8.3.1-38, pp. 184-94
124 RCAGA: 4.2.16, p. 66

Chapter 6

1 In the Australian Constitution there is some confusion as to when the term 'Commonwealth' refers to the central government and when it refers to the 'state as a whole'. It clearly refers to the latter in the preamble. See G. Sawer *Modern Federalism* Carlton: Pitman, 1976, p. 100 and G. Sawer *Australian Federalism in the Courts* Melbourne University Press, 1967, pp. 122-5
2 See the discussion in Sawer *Modern Federalism* pp. 51-75
3 J. Holmes and C. Sharman *The Australian Federal System* Sydney: George Allen and Unwin, 1977, p. 57
4 Sawer *Australian Federalism in the Courts* pp. 6-7
5 K. Wheare *Federal Government* London: Oxford University Press, 1953, pp. 32-3
6 Dworkin *Taking Rights Seriously*
7 McMillan, Evans and Storey *Australia's Constitution: Time For Change*
8 S. Clark 'Inter-governmental Quangos: The River Murray Commission' *Australian Journal of Public Administration* Vol. XLII, No. 1, March 1983, pp. 158-9
9 Dworkin *Taking Rights Seriously* pp. 266-78
10 H. Hart *The Concept of Law* Oxford University Press, 1961, pp. 77-96
11 McMillan, Evans and Storey *Australia's Constitution: Time For Change* pp. 94-5
12 *Weekend Australian* 2-3 July 1983
13 *Weekend Australian* 25-28 June 1983
14 C. Friedrich *Trends of Federalism in Theory and Practice* London: Pall Mall Press, 1968, p. 7
15 E. Mitchell *What Every Australian Ought to Know*, 1931, p. 7, cited in K. Foley 'Quangos and the Australian Loan Council' *Australian Journal of Public Administration* Vol. XLII, No. 1, March 1983, p. 147
16 Foley 'Quangos and the Australian Loan Council' p. 134

17 G. Sawer, cited in G. Reid 'Political Decentralization, Co-operative Federalism and Responsible Government' in R. Mathews (ed.) *Intergovernmental Relations in Australia* Sydney: Angus and Robertson, 1974, pp. 28–9
18 Sawer *Australian Federalism in the Courts* p. 174
19 *ibid*. p. 13
20 Spann *Government Administration in Australia* p. 239
21 *ibid*. pp. 215–6
22 Sawer *Australian Federalism in the Courts* p. 57
23 Cited in Crisp *Australian National Government* (1983) p. 58
24 *ibid* pp. 129–33
25 Sawer, *Modern Federalism* p. 52
26 Cited in A. Peachment and G. Reid *New Federalism in Australia: Rhetoric or Reality*? Adelaide: APSA Monograph No. 18, 1977
27 I. Radbone 'The Inter-state Commission' *Australian Journal of Public Administration* Vol. XLI, No. 4, December 1982, pp. 323–38
28 S. Clark 'Inter-governmental Quangos' p. 161
29 *Australian* 12 May 1973
30 T. Lewis 'Making Federalism Work: Problems of the States' in R. Mathews (ed.) *Making Federalism Work* Canberra: ANU, Centre for Research on Federal Financial Relations, 1976, pp. 212–3
31 Peachment and Reid *New Federalism in Australia* p. 52
32 *Weekend Australian* 2–3 July 1983
33 W. Riker 'Six Books in Search of a Subject or Does Federalism Exist and Does it Matter' *Comparative Politics* Vol. II, No. 1, Oct. 1969, p. 146
34 S. Davis *The Government of the Australian States* Melbourne: Longmans, Green, 1960, pp. 711
35 R. Hawke *The Resolution of Conflict* Sydney: Australian Broadcasting Commission, 1979
36 Much of the following is based on McMillan, Evans and Storey *Australia's Constitution: Time For Change*. See also N. Knight 'Federalism and Administrative Efficiency' in Mathews (ed.) *Intergovernmental Relations in Australia* pp. 43–56
37 G. Stevenson *Mineral Resources and Australian Federalism* Canberra: ANU, Centre for Research on Federal Financial Relations, *Research Monograph* No. 17, 1976, pp. 86–7
38 G. Crough 'The Ownership and Control of Australian Energy Resources' *The Journal of Australian Political Economy* No. 2, June 1978, p. 35
39 C. Flynn 'Bauxite Mining in Western Australia' *The Journal of Australian Political Economy* No. 5, July 1979, pp. 70–5
40 S. Encel 'The Constitution as a Social Document' in S. Encel, D. Horne and E. Thompson (eds) *Change the Rules: Towards a Democratic Constitution* Ringwood: Penguin Books, 1977, p. 43
41 C. Howard *Australia's Constitution* Ringwood: Penguin Books, 1978, p. 163
42 McMillan, Evans and Storey *Australia's Constitution: Time For Change* pp. 345–71
43 *ibid*. pp. 364–70

44 J. Quick and R. Garran *The Annotated Constitution of the Australian Commonwealth* Sydney: Angus and Robertson, 1901, p. 154
45 J. Bryce *The Amercian Commonwealth* 2 vols., London: Macmillan, 1889
46 *ibid.* Vol. I, p. 345
47 *ibid.* Vol. I, p. 334

Chapter 7

1 Schumpeter *Capitalism, Socialism and Democracy* p. 269
2 Pateman *Participation and Democratic Theory*
3 J. Rydon 'The Electorate' in J. Wilkes (ed.) *Forces in Australian Politics* p. 184
4 Cited in D. Horne, E. Thompson, D. Jaensch and K. Turner *Changing the System* Adelaide: *APSA Monograph* 25, 1981, p. 27
5 Davis *The Government of the Australian States* p. 565
6 D. Aitkin *Stability and Change in Australian Politics* Canberra: ANU Press, 1982, p. 1
7 *ibid.*
8 A. Campbell et al. *Elections and the Political Order* New York: John Wiley, 1966, p. 19
9 Kemp *Society and Electoral Behaviour in Australia*
10 R. Alford *Party and Society* London: John Murray, 1964
11 This is discussed in P. Reynolds 'Homogenisation and Embourgeoisement: A Consideration of Aspects of the Kemp Thesis' *Politics* Vol. XV, No. 1, May 1980, pp. 116–8
12 M. Berry 'Inequality' in A. Davies et al. *Australian Society* Melbourne: Longman Cheshire, 3rd edn, 1977, pp. 18–54
13 D. Kemp 'Class, Culture and Parties' *Meanjin* 2 1979, p. 168
14 See Reynolds 'Homogenisation and Embourgeoisement' p. 114
15 R. Connell and M. Goot 'The End of Class, Re-run' *Meanjin* 1 1979, p. 18
16 *ibid.* pp. 11–12
17 Poulantzas *Political Power and Social Classes*. Note Wright's criticism of this; E. Wright 'Class Boundaries in Advanced Capitalist Societies' *New Left Review* 98, July–Aug, 1976, pp. 3–41
18 Wright 'Class Boundaries in Advanced Capitalist Societies'
19 See Kemp's defence of this, in Kemp 'Class, Culture and Parties' p. 168
20 Aitkin *Stability and Change in Australian Politics* pp. 286–7
21 A. Campbell et al. *The American Voter* New York: John Wiley, 1960
22 *ibid.* pp. 24–32 and 39–115
23 H. Himmelweit, et al. *How Voters Decide* London: Academic Press, 1981
24 *ibid.* p. 11
25 *ibid.*
26 G. Pomper *The Voters' Choice* New York: Dodd Mead, 1975
27 Himmelweit *How Voters Decide* p. 8
28 *ibid.* p. 193

NOTES

29 Aitkin *Stability and Change in Australian Politics* pp. 36−7n
30 *ibid.* p. 288
31 Cited in D. Jaensch *An Introduction to Australian Politics* Melbourne: Longman Cheshire, 1984, p. 202
32 Pateman *Participation and Democratic Theory*
33 W. Morris Jones 'In Defence of Apathy: Some Doubts on the Duty to Vote' *Political Studies* Vol. II, No. 1, 1954, pp. 25−37
34 *Sun* 10 October 1969, cited in H. Mayer and H. Nelson (eds) *Australian Politics: A Third Reader* Melbourne: Longman Cheshire, 1973, p. 336
35 Australian Electoral Office *A Qualitative Analysis of Attitudes Towards Enrolment and Voting, Research Report* 1983

BIBLIOGRAPHY

Abercrombie, N., Hill, S. and Turner, B. *The Dominant Ideology Thesis* London: George Allen and Unwin, 1980
Aitkin, D. *The Country Party in New South Wales* Canberra: ANU Press, 1972
Aitkin, D. *Stability and Change in Australian Politics* Canberra: ANU Press, 1982
Albrow, M. *Bureaucracy* London: Pall Mall Press, 1970
Alford, R. *Party and Society* London: John Murray, 1964
Apter, D. *Choice and the Politics of Allocation* New Haven: Yale University Press, 1971
Austin, D. 'Ideology in Class Society: The Contribution of Max Weber' in Hiller (ed.) pp. 28–39
Australasian Federal Convention, 2nd Session *Official Debates* Sydney: Govt. Printer, 1897
Australian Electoral Office *A Qualitative Analysis of Attitudes Towards Enrolment and Voting, Research Report* 1983
Australian Financial Systems Inquiry (Campbell Committee) *Australian Financial System: Interim Report* Canberra: AGPS, May 1980
AIPS *Industrial Australia: 1975–2000, Preparing for Change* Sydney: ANZ Book Co. 1974
Bachrach, P. *The Theory of Democratic Elitism: A Critique* University of London Press, 1969
Bachrach, P. and Baratz, M. 'Two Faces of Power' in Castles *et al.* pp. 392–404
Bagehot, W. *The English Constitution* London: Fontana, 1963
Baily, J. 'Media Power—Is it Inevitable' in ANU Centre for Continuing Education *Power in Australia: Directions of Change* paper from the National Conference, Canberra, ANU, November, 1981, pp. 86–94
Bell, C. and Encel, S. (eds) *Inside the Whale: Ten Personal Accounts of Social Research* Sydney: Pergamon Press, 1978
Bell, R., Edwards, D. and Wagner, R. (eds) *Political Power: A Reader in Theory and Research* New York: The Free Press, 1969
Bellamy, E. *Looking Backward: 2000–1887* (1887) Boston: Houghton Mifflin, 1931

Berki, R. *Socialism* London: Dent, 1975
Berry, M. 'Inequality' in Davies et al. 1977, pp. 18–54
Block, F. 'The Ruling Class Does Not Rule: Notes on the Marxist Theory of the State' *Socialist Revolution* 33, 1977, pp. 6–28
Bolton, G. '1939–51' in Crowley (ed.) pp. 458–503
Bottomore, T. *Elites and Society* Harmondsworth: Penguin, 1966
Bowles, S. and Gintis, H. *Schooling in Capitalist America* New York: Basic Books, 1976
Broom, L. and Jones, F. *Opportunity and Attainment in Australia* Canberra: ANU Press, 1976
Brubaker, R. *The Limits of Rationality: An Essay on the Social and Moral Thought of Max Weber* London: George Allen and Unwin, 1984
Brugger, B. 'Classical British and European Liberalism and Democracy' in Wintrop (ed.) pp. 10–48
Bryce, J. *The American Commonwealth* 2 vols, London: Macmillan, 1889
Bulbeck, C. 'State and Capital in Tariff Policy' in Head (ed.) pp. 219–37
Burnham, J. *The Managerial Revolution*, (1941) Bloomington: Indiana University Press, Midland Books, 1973
Caiden, G. *Commonwealth Bureaucracy* Melbourne University Press, 1967
Caiden, G. 'Administrative Reform' in Curnow and Wettenhall (eds) pp. 175–91
Campbell, A. et al. *The American Voter* New York: John Wiley, 1960
Campbell, A. et al. *Electors and the Political Order* New York: John Wiley, 1966
Campbell E. *The 60 Rich Families Who Own Australia* Sydney: Current Book Distributors, 1963
Castles, F. et al. *Decisions, Organisations and Society* Harmondsworth: Penguin, 1976
Catley R. and McFarlane, B. *From Tweedledum to Tweedledee: The New Labour Government in Australia: A Critique of its Social Model* Sydney: ANZ Book Co., 1974
Catley, R. and McFarlane, B. *Australian Capitalism in Boom and Depression* Chippendale: APCOL, 1981
Chamberlain, C. *Class Consciousness in Australia* Sydney: George Allen and Unwin, 1983
Chambers, W. and Burnham, W. (eds) *The American Party Systems: Stages of Political Development* 2nd edn, New York: Oxford University Press, 1975
Childe, V. *How Labor Governs* (1923), Melbourne University Press, 1964
Clark, C. 'Parliamentarians by Lot' *Quadrant* Vol. XVIII, No. 3, May–June, 1974, pp. 48–57
Clark, M. (ed.) *Sources of Australian History* London: Oxford University Press, 1957
Clark, S. 'Inter-governmental Quangos: The River Murray Commission' *Australian Journal of Public Administration* Vol. XLII. No. 1, March 1983, pp. 154–72
Coleman, P. 'The Liberal and Country Parties: Platform, Politics and Performance' in Wilkes (ed.) 1963, pp. 1–17
Connell, R. *Ruling Class, Ruling Culture* Cambridge University Press, 1977

Connell, R., Ashenden, D., Kessler, S. and Dowsett, G. *Making the Difference: Schools, Families and Social Division* Sydney: George Allen and Unwin, 1982

Connell, R. and Goot, M. 'The End of Class, Re-run' *Meanjin* Vol. XXXVIII, No. 1, April, 1979, pp. 3–25

Connell, R. and Irving, T. *Class Structure in Australian History: Documents, Narrative and Argument* Melbourne: Longman, Cheshire, 1980

Connell, R. and Irving, T. 'A Working Paper Towards a Historical Theory of Class' in Hiller (ed.) pp. 10–27

Conybeare, J. 'Politics and Regulation: The Public Choice Approach' *Australian Journal of Public Administration* Vol. XLI, No. 1, March 1982, pp. 33–45

Cooksey, R. *Lang and Socialism: A Study in the Great Depression* Canberra: ANU Press, 1971

Corbett, D. 'Putting it Together and Keeping it Together' in Smith and Weller (eds) pp. 63–8

Crisp, L. *Australian National Government* Croydon: Longmans, 1965; Melbourne: Longman Cheshire, 1983

Crisp, L. *The Australian Federal Labor Party* Sydney: Hale and Iremonger, 1978

Crosland, A. *The Future of Socialism* London: Jonathan Cape, 1956

Crotty, W. (ed.) *Paths to Political Reform* Lexington Mass: Lexington Books, 1980

Crough, G. 'The Ownership and Control of Australian Energy Resources' *The Journal of Australian Political Economy* No. 2, June 1978, pp, 25–37

Crowley, F. (ed.) *A New History of Australia* Melbourne: Heinemann, 1974

Curnow, G. and Wettenhall, R. (eds) *Understanding Public Administration* Sydney: George Allen and Unwin, 1981

Dahl R. 'The Concept of Power' in Bell, Edwards and Wagner (eds) pp. 79–93

Davidson, A. *The Communist Party of Australia: A Short History* Stanford: Hoover Institution Press, 1962

Davies, A. and Encel, S. (eds) *Australian Society* 1st edn. Melbourne: Cheshire, 1963

Davies, A. et al. *Australian Society* Melbourne: Longman Cheshire, 3rd edn. 1977

Davis, S. *The Government of the Australian States* Melbourne: Longmans, Green, 1960

DeBats, D. 'Liberal-Democratic Theory in America' in Wintrop (ed.) pp. 49–82

Dicey, A. *Law of the Constitution* London: Macmillan, 1964

Dixson, M. *Greater than Lenin: Lang and Labor, 1916–1932, Melbourne Politics Monograph*, n.d.

Dow, G., Clegg, S. and Boreham, P. 'From the Politics of Production to the Production of Politics' *Thesis Eleven* 9, July, 1984, pp. 16–32

Duncan, G. (ed.) *Critical Essays in Australian Politics* Melbourne: Edward Arnold, 1978

Duncan, G. 'The A.L.P.: Socialism in a Bourgeois Society' in Duncan (ed.) pp. 77–96

Dworkin, R. *Taking Rights Seriously* Cambridge Mass: Harvard University Press, 1977
Ebbels, R. (ed.) *The Australian Labor Movement: 1850–1907, Extracts from Contemporary Documents* Melbourne: Cheshire, Landsdowne, 1966
Edwards, J. 'The Economy Game: Treasury and its Rivals' *Current Affairs Bulletin* Vol. L1, No. 12, May 1975, pp. 4–11
Emy, H. *The Politics of Australian Democracy* Melbourne: Macmillan, 1st. edn, 1974; 2nd edn, 1978
Emy, H. 'The Diffusion of Power' in Parkin, Summers and Woodward (eds) pp. 326–39 (excerpted from Emy, 1974)
Encel, S. 'Cabinet and the Bureaucracy' in J. Wilkes (ed.) 1972, pp. 30–57
Encel, S. *Equality and Authority: A Study of Class, Status and Power in Australia* Melbourne: Cheshire, 3rd edn. 1977
Encel, S., Horne, D. and Thompson, E. (eds) *Change the Rules: Towards a Democratic Constitution* Ringwood: Penguin, 1977
Encel, S. 'The Constitution as a Social Document' in Encel, Horne and Thompson (eds) pp. 43–53
Erikson, E. *Young Man Luther: A Study in Psychoanalysis and History* New York: Norton, 1962
Fine, B. and Harris, L. *Rereading Capital* New York: Columbia University Press, 1979
Fitzpatrick, B. and Wheelwright, E. *The Highest Bidder* Melbourne: Landsdowne, 1965
Flynn, C. 'Bauxite Mining in Western Australia' *The Journal of Australian Political Economy* No. 5, July 1979, pp. 70–5
Foley, N. 'Quangos and the Australian Loan Council' *Australian Journal of Public Administration* Vol. XLII, No. 1, March 1983, pp. 131–53
Forrest, M. 'Reporting and Review of Quangos' *Australian Journal of Public Administration* Vol. XLII, No. 1, March 1983, pp. 82–103
Foucault, M. *Power/Knowledge, Selected Interviews and Other Writings, 1972–1977* C. Gordon (ed.) Brighton: Harvester Press, 1980
Friedrich, C. *Trends of Federalism in Theory and Practice* London: Pall Mall Press, 1968
Freudenberg, G. *A Certain Grandeur: Gough Whitlam in Politics* Melbourne: Sun Books, 1978
Galligan, B. 'The Founders' Design and Intentions Regarding Responsible Government' in Weller and Jaensch (eds) pp. 1–10
George, H. *Progress and Poverty: An Inquiry into the Cause of Industrial Depressions and of Increase of Want with Increase of Wealth—The Remedy* London: Kegan Paul, Trench and Co., 1883
Giddens, A. *The Class Structure of the Advanced Societies* London: Hutchinson, 1973
Godwin, W. *Enquiry Concerning Political Justice and its Influence on Modern Morals and Happiness* (1789), Harmondsworth: Penguin, 1976
Gordon, R. (ed.) *The Australian New Left* Melbourne: Heinemann, 1970
Gouldner, A. *The Future of the Intellectuals and the Rise of the New Class* London: Macmillan, 1979
Graham, B. *The Foundation of the Australian Country Parties* Canberra: ANU Press, 1966

Grattan, C.H. *Introducing Australia* New York: John Day Co., 1942
Groenewegen, P. 'Consumer Capitalism' in Playford and Kirsner (eds) pp. 94–107
Habermas, J. *Legitimation Crisis* London: Heinemann, 1976
Hancock, K. *Australia* (1930) Sydney: Australasian Publishing Co., 1945
Hancock, K. *Country and Calling* London: Faber & Faber, n.d.
Harman, G. 'Pressure Groups and the Australian Political System' in Parkin, Summers and Woodward (eds) pp. 285–94 (originally in Mayer [ed.] 1973)
Hart, H. *The Concept of Law* London: Oxford University Press, 1961
Hawke, R. *The Resolution of Conflict* Sydney: Australian Broadcasting Commission, 1979
Hawker, G. *Who's Master, Who's Servant* Sydney: George Allen & Unwin, 1981
Hayek, F. *Law, Legislation and Liberty* Vol. II *The Mirage of Social Justice* London: Routledge and Kegan Paul, 1976
Hayek, F. 'Whither Democracy' in F. Hayek *Social Justice, Socialism and Democracy: Three Australian Lectures* Turramurra: the Centre for Independent Studies (CIS *Occasional Papers*, No. 2) 1979, pp. 33–45
Hazelhurst, C. and Nethercote, J. (eds) *Reforming Australian Government: The Coombs' Report and Beyond* Canberra: ANU Press, 1977
Head, B. (ed.) *State and Economy in Australia* Melbourne: Oxford University Press, 1983
Higley, J., Deacon D. and Smart, D. *Elites in Australia* London: Routledge and Kegan Paul, 1979
Hiller, P. (ed.) *Class and Inequality in Australia: Sociological Perspectives and Research* Sydney: Harcourt, Brace Jovanovich Gp., 1981
Himmelweit, H. et al. *How Voters Decide* London: Academic Press, 1981
Holloway, J. and Picciotto, S. (eds) *State and Capital: A Marxist Debate* London: Edward Arnold, 1978
Holmes, J. and Sharman, C. *The Australian Federal System* Sydney: George Allen and Unwin, 1977
Horne, D. *The Lucky Country, Australia in the Sixties* Ringwood: Penguin Books, rev. edn, 1967
Horne, D., Thompson, E., Jaensch, D. and Turner K. *Changing the System* Adelaide: *APSA Monograph* 25, 1981
Howard, C. *Australia's Constitution* Ringwood: Penguin Books, 1978
Hughes, B. *Exit Full Employment: Economic Policy in the Stone Age* Sydney: Angus and Robertson, 1980
Hughes, C. (ed.) *Readings on Australian Government* St. Lucia: University of Queensland Press, 1968
Hughes, C. *1977–83 Supplement* to *A Handbook of Australian Government and Politics 1965–1974* ANU, Research School of Social Sciences *Working Papers in Political Science* January 1984
Indyk, M. 'Making Government Responsible: The Role of Parliamentary Committees' in Weller and Jaensch (eds) pp. 93–109
Ionescu, G., and Gellner, E., (eds) *Populism: Its Meanings and Natural Characteristics* London: Weidenfeld and Nicolson, 1970

Irving, T. and Barzins, B. 'History ana the New Left: Beyond Radicalism' in Gordon (ed.) pp. 66–94
Jaensch, D. *The Australian Party System* Sydney: George Allen and Unwin, 1983
Jaensch, D. *An Introduction to Australian Politics* Melbourne: Longman, Cheshire, 1984
James, M. 'Sovereignty vs. Constitutionalism in Australian Political Thought' in L. Chipman et. al. *Constitutional Theory and Australian Practice* conference sponsored by the Centre for Independent Studies Turramurra, University of Sydney, 23 November, 1979
Janda, N. 'Primrose Paths to Political Reform: "Reforming" versus Strengthening American Parties' in Crotty (ed.) pp. 309–47
Jennings, I. *Parliament* 2nd edn, Cambridge University Press, 1957
Jessop, B. *The Capitalist State* Oxford: Martin Robertson, 1982
Jinks, B. 'The New Administrative Law: Some Assumptions and Questions' *Australian Journal of Public Administration* Vol. XLI, No 3, Sept, 1982, pp. 209–18
Johnson, N. *In Search of the Constitution: Reflections on State and Society in Britain* Oxford: Pergamon Press, 1977
Jones, W. 'In Defence of Apathy: Some Doubts on the Duty to Vote' *Political Studies* Vol. II. No. 1, 1954, pp. 25–37
Joske, P. *Sir Robert Menzies: 1894–1978, A New Informal Memoir* Sydney: Angus and Robertson, 1978
Juddery, B. 'What's In It For Us: The Public Service Response' in Hazelhurst and Nethercote (eds) pp. 165–73
Jupp, J. *Political Parties* London: Routledge and Kegan Paul, 1968
Kant, I. 'On the Common Saying: "This May Be True in Theory, But it Does not Apply in Practice"' in Reiss (ed.) pp. 61–92
Kemp, D. *Society and Electoral Behaviour in Australia* St. Lucia: University of Queensland Press, 1978
Kemp, D. 'Class, Culture and Parties' *Meanjin* Vol. XXXVIII, No. 2, July, 1979, pp. 166–72
Kerin, J. 'Parliament in Contemporary Society' in Mayer and Nelson (eds) 1976, pp. 384–6
King, A. 'Political Parties in Western Democracies: Some Sceptical Reflections' *Polity* Vol. II. No. 2, Winter, 1969, pp. 111–41
Kirby, M. 'Towards the New Federal Administrative Law' *Australian Journal of Public Administration* Vol. XL, No. 2, June 1981, pp. 103–16
Knight, N. 'Federalism and Administrative Efficiency' in Mathews (ed.) 1974, pp. 43–56
Kriegler, R. *Working for the Company, Work and Control in the Whyalla Shipyard* Melbourne: Oxford University Press, 1980
Lang, J.*Freedom and Independence for the Goldern Lands of Australia: The Right of the Colonies and the Interest of Britain and of the World* London: Longman, Brown, Green and Longman, 1852
Lewis, T. 'Making Federalism Work: Problems of the States' in Mathews (ed.) 1976, pp. 203–13
Loveday, P. 'Corporatist Trends in Australia' *Politics* Vol. XIX, No. 1,

May 1984, pp. 46–51

Lowi, T. 'Party, Policy and Constitution in America' in Chambers and Burnham (eds) pp. 238–76

Lukes, S. *Power: A Radical View* London: Macmillan, 1974

Lunn, H. *Joh: The Life and Political Adventures of Johannes Bjelke-Petersen* St. Lucia: University of Queensland Press, 1978

McFarlane, B. *Professor Irvine's Economics in Australian Labour History: 1913–1932* Canberra: Australian Society for the Study of Labour History, 1966

McFarlane, B. *Economic Policy in Australia* Melbourne: Cheshire, 1968

McGregor, C. *Profile of Australia* Ringwood: Penguin Books, 1968

McGregor, C. 'Patterns of Power' in Parkin, Summers and Woodward (eds) pp. 295–8 (abridged from McGregor, 1968).

McMichael, M. 'Australian Boards of Directors: Organisation and Functions' *The Australian Director* Aug. 1976, pp. 9–20

McMillan, J., Evans, G. and Storey, H. *Australia's Constitution: Time for Change* Sydney: George Allen and Unwin, 1983

McPherson, C. *The Life and Times of Liberal Democracy* Oxford University Press, 1977

McQueen, H. *Australia's Media Monopolies* Camberwell: Widescope, 1977

Maine, H. 'The Nature of Democracy' in H. Maine *Popular Government* London: John Murray, 1909

Mannheim, K. *Freedom, Power and Democratic Planning* London: Routledge and Kegan Paul, 1950

Marcuse, H. *One Dimensional Man, the Ideology of Industrial Society* (1964) London: Sphere Books, 1968

Mathews, R. (ed.) *Intergovernmental Relations in Australia* Sydney: Angus and Robertson, 1974

Mathews, R. (ed.) *Making Federalism Work* Canberra: ANU, Centre for Research on Federal Financial Relations, 1976

Matthews, T. 'Business Associations and the State, 1850–1979' in Head (ed.) pp. 115–49

Mayer, H. 'Some Conceptions of the Australian Party System, 1910–50' in Smith and Beever (eds) p. 217–40

Mayer, H. (ed.) *Australia's Political Pattern* Melbourne: Cheshire, 1973

Mayer, H. and Nelson, H. (eds) *Australian Politics: A Third Reader* Melbourne: Longman, Cheshire, 1973

Mayer, H. and Nelson, H. (eds) *Australian Politics: A Fourth Reader* Melbourne: Longman, Cheshire, 1976

Métin, A *Socialism Without Doctrine* (1901 and 1910) trans. R. Ward, Sydney: APCOL, 1977

Miliband, R. *The State in Capitalist Society* London: Weidenfeld and Nicolson, 1969

Mill, J.S. 'Representative Government' in J.S. Mill *Utilitarianism, Liberty, Representative Government* London: Dent, 1910, pp. 171–393

Mills, C.W. *The Power Elite* New York: Oxford University Press, 1959

Mills, R. *The Colonization of Australia, 1829–42* (1915) Sydney University Press, 1974

Murphy, D. *T.J. Ryan: A Political Biography* St. Lucia: University of Queensland Press, 1975
Murray, R. *The Split: Australian Labor in the Fifties* Melbourne: Cheshire, 1972
National Australasian Convention *Official Report of the National Australasian Convention Debates* Sydney: Govt. Printer, 1891
Newton, M. 'The Economy' in Davies and Encel (eds) 1963, pp. 230–52
O'Brien, P. 'Some Overseas Comparisons' in R. Gordon (ed.) pp. 219–34
O'Connor, J. *The Fiscal Crisis of the State* New York: St. Martins Press, 1973
O'Farrell, P. *The Catholic Church and Community in Australia: A History* Melbourne: Nelson, 1977
Offe, C. "'Crisis of Crisis Management". Elements of a Political Crisis Theory' *International Journal of Politics* Vol. VI, No. 3, Fall 1976, pp. 29–67
Page, E. *Truant Surgeon: The Inside Story of Fifty Years of Australian Political Life* Sydney: Angus and Robertson, 1963
Painter, M. 'Access: The Public Service and the Public' in Smith and Weller (eds) pp. 236–48
Palmer, V. *The Legend of the Nineties* Melbourne University Press, 1954
Parish, R. 'Preface' in Tullock et al. pp. vii–viii
Parker, R. 'Responsible Government in Australia' in Weller and Jaensch (eds) pp. 11–22
Parkin, A., Summers, J. and Woodward, D. (eds) *Government, Politics and Power in Australia* 2nd edn, Melbourne: Longman, Cheshire, 1980
Parkin, A. and Warhurst, J. (eds) *Machine Politics in the Australian Labor Party* Sydney: George Allen and Unwin, 1983
Pateman, C. *Participation and Democratic Theory* Cambridge University Press, 1970
Peachment, A. and Reid, G. *New Federalism in Australia: Rhetoric or Reality* Adelaide: *APSA Monograph*, 18, 1977
Peres, L. 'The Politics of Industrial Policy' in AIPS, pp. 148–65
Pettifer, J. (ed.) *House of Representatives Practice* Canberra: AGPS, 1981
Pike, D. *Paradise of Dissent: South Australia, 1829–1957* (1957) Melbourne University Press, 1967
Playford, J. 'Who Rules Australia' in Playford and Kirsner (eds) pp. 108–155
Playford, J. and Kirsner, D. (eds) *Australian Capitalism* Ringwood: Penguin Books, 1972
Polanyi, K. *The Great Transformation: The Political and Economic Origins of Our Time* (1944) Boston: Beacon Books, 1957
Pomper, G. *The Voters' Choice* New York: Dodd, Mead, 1975
Poulantzas, N. *Political Power and Social Classes* London: New Left Books, 1973
Pitman, R. *The Comparative Study of Political Elites* Englewood Cliffs, NJ: Prentice Hall, 1976
Quick, J. and Garran, R. *The Annotated Constitution of the Australian Commonwealth* Sydney: Angus and Robertson, 1901
Radbone, I. 'The Inter-state Commission' *Australian Journal of Public*

Administration Vol. XL1, No. 4, December 1982, pp. 323–38
Rand, A. *Capitalism: The Unknown Ideal* New York: Signet Books, 1967
Raskall, P. 'Who's Got What in Australia: The Distribution of Wealth' *The Journal of Australian Political Economy* No. 2, June 1978, pp. 3–16
Rawson, D. 'Who Wants Union Democracy' in ANU Centre for Continuing Education, pp. 143–50
Reid, G. 'Political Decentralization, Co-operative Federalism and Responsible Government' in Mathews (ed.) 1974, pp. 23–35 ·
Reid, G. 'Responsible Government and Ministerial Responsibility' in Curnow and Wettenhall (eds) pp. 39–55
Reiss, H. (ed.) *Kant's Political Writings* Cambridge University Press, 1970
Review of Commonwealth Administration (RCA), (Reid Report), Canberra: AGPS, January 1983
Reynolds, P. 'Homogenisation and Embourgeoisement: A Consideration of Aspects of the Kemp Thesis' *Politics* Vol. XV, No. 1, May 1980, pp. 114–18
Riker, W. 'Six Books in Search of a Subject or Does Federalism Exist and Does it Matter' *Comparative Politics* Vol. II, No. 1, Oct. 1969, pp. 135–46
Rose, R. *The Problem of Party Government* London: Macmillan, 1974
Rowse, T. *Australian Liberalism and National Character* Melbourne: Kibble Books, 1978
RCAGA *Report* Canberra: AGPS, 1976
Rydon, J. 'The Electorate' in Wilkes (ed.) 1963, pp. 167–204
Samuel, P. 'The Treasury and the Treasury Line' in Hazelhurst and Nethercote (eds) pp. 147–53
Sartori, G. *Parties and Party Systems: A Framework for Analysis* Cambridge University Press, Vol. 1, 1976
Sawer, G. *Australian Federalism in the Courts* Melbourne University Press, 1967
Sawer, G. *Modern Federalism* Carlton: Pitman, 1976
Schmitter, P. 'Still the Century of Corporatism?' *Review of Politics* Vol. XXXVI, No. 1, January, 1974, pp. 85–131
Schumpeter, J. *Capitalism, Socialism and Democracy* New York: Harper and Row, 1950
Scott, R. 'Towards a Professional Bureaucracy' in Smith & Weller (eds) pp. 193–202
Self, P. 'The Coombs Commission: An Overview' in Smith & Weller (eds) pp. 310–33
Sendy, J. *Comrades Come Rally! Recollections of an Australian Communist* Melbourne: Nelson, 1978
Serle, G. *From Deserts the Prophets Come: The Creative Spirit in Australia, 1788–1972* Melbourne: Heinemann, 1973
Sexton, M. *Illusions of Power: the Fate of a Reform Government* Sydney: George Allen and Unwin, 1979
Shann, E. *Bond or Free? Occasional Economic Essays* Sydney: Angus and Robertson, 1930
Simms, M. *A Liberal Nation: The Liberal Party and Australian Politics* Sydney: Hale and Iremonger, 1982

Smith, F. and Beever M. (eds) *Historical Studies: Selected Articles* Melbourne University Press, 1967
Smith, R. 'Central Co-ordination and Control' in Smith and Weller (eds) pp. 177–92
Smith, R. and Weller, P. (eds) *Public Service Inquiries in Australia* St. Lucia: University of Queensland Press, 1978
Snedden, B. 'Ministers in Parliament—A Speaker's Eye View' in Weller and Jaensch (eds) pp. 68–85
Snedden, B. 'Parliament: the Fulcrum of Democracy' in J. Holmes (ed.) *Televising Parliament, Working Papers On Parliament* No. 2, Melbourne University, Dept. of Political Science, in association with the Australasian Study of Parliament Gp., 1980
Spann, R. 'Ministers and Permanent Heads' in Smith and Weller (eds) pp. 154–76
Spann, R. *Government Administration in Australia* Sydney: George Allen and Unwin, 1979
Spence, W. *Australia's Awakening: Thirty Years in the Life of An Australian Agitator* Sydney: The Worker Trustees, 1909, reprinted 1961
Stevenson, G. *Mineral Resources and Australian Federalism* Canberra: ANU, Centre for Research on Federal Financial Relations *Research Monograph* No. 17, 1976
Stewart, A. 'The Social Roots' in Ionescu and Gellner (eds) pp. 180–96
Stretton, H. 'Capital Mistakes' in Bell and Encel (eds) pp. 67–92
Tawney, R. *Equality* (1931) London: Unwin Books, 1964
Theophanous, A *Australian Democracy in Crisis* Melbourne: Oxford University Press, 1980
Thompson, E. 'The Washminster Mutation' in Weller and Jaensch (eds) pp. 32–40
Triado, J. 'Corporatism, Democracy and Modernity' *Thesis Eleven* 9, July 1984, pp. 33–51
Tullock, G. et al. *The Economics of Bureaucracy and Statutory Authorities* St. Leonards, NSW: The Centre for Independent Studies *C.I.S. Policy Forums* 1, 1983
Uhr, J. 'Parliamentary Reform in Canberra' *The Australian Quarterly* Vol. LIV, No. 3, Spring 1972
UNESCO, *Transnational Corporations in World Development: A Reexamination* New York UNESCO, Commission on Transnational Corporations, 4th. Session, 15–26 May 1978
Vickers, G. *The Art of Judgement* London: Chapman and Hall, 1965
Wakefield, E. *A Letter from Sydney and Other Writings* London: Dent, 1929
Ward, J. *James MacArthur: Colonial Conservative, 1798–1867* Sydney University Press, 1981
Ward, R. *The Australian Legend* Melbourne: Oxford University Press, 1965
Waterson, D. *Squatter, Selector and Storekeeper: A History of the Darling Downs* Sydney University Press, 1968
Webb, L. 'The Australian Party System' in Hughes (ed.) 1968, pp. 321–43
Webb, S. & B. *A Constitution for the Socialist Commonwealth of Great Britain* 2nd. edn, Cambridge University Press, 1975

Weber, M. *Economy and Society* 2 Vols, Berkeley: University of California Press, 1978
Weller, P. and Cutt, J. *Treasury Control in Australia* Sydney: Ian Novak, 1976
Weller, P., and Jaensch, D. (eds) *Responsible Government in Australia* Richmond: Drummond, 1980
Wertheim, W. *Evolution and Revolution: The Rising Waves of Emancipation* Harmondsworth: Penguin, 1974
Wettenhall, R. 'Quangos, Quagos and the Problems of Non-ministerial Organization' *Australian Journal of Public Administration* Vol. XLII, No, 1, March 1983, pp. 5–52
Wheare, K. *Federal Government* London: Oxford University Press, 1953
Wheelwright, E. *Ownership and Control of Australian Industry* Sydney: Law Book Co., 1957
Wheelwright, E., and Miskelly, J. *Anatomy of Australian Manufacturing Industry* Sydney: Law Book Co., 1967
White, D. *The Philosophy of the Australian Liberal Party* Melbourne: Hutchinson, 1978
Wickham, G. 'Power and Power Analysis: Beyond Foucault' *Economy and Society* Vol. XII, No, 4, November, 1983, pp. 468–96
Wild, R. *Social Stratification in Australia* Sydney: George Allen and Unwin, 1978
Wilenski, P. 'Labor and the Bureaucracy' in Duncan (ed.) pp. 28–46
Wilkes, J. (ed.) *Forces in Australian Politics* Sydney: Angus and Robertson, 1963
Wilkes, J. (ed.) *Parliament, Bureaucracy, Citizens: Who Runs Australia* Sydney: Angus and Robertson, 1972
Williams, C. *Open Cut: The Working Class in an Australian Mining Town* Sydney: George Allen and Unwin, 1981
Windschuttle, K. and E. *Fixing the News: Critical Perspectives on the Australian Media* North Ryde: Cassell, 1981
Wintrop, N. (ed.) *Liberal Democratic Theory and its Critics* London: Croom Helm, 1983
Wolfsohn, T., Contribution to 'A Symposium of Power in Australia' *Arena* 6, 1965, pp. 8–10
Wright, E. 'Class Boundaries in Advanced Capitalist Societies' *New Left Review* 98, July–August 1976, pp. 3–41; expanded in E. Wright *Class Crisis and the State* London: Verso, 1979, pp. 30–110

INDEX

Aborigines 4, 14, 40, 57, 158, 162, 172
Abortion 219
AIDC 188
Aitkin, D. 215, 220, 221, 222
Alford, R.A. 217
ANZAC 24
Apathy 199
Apter, D. 78
Arbitration 17, 44
Australian Assistance Plan 182
Australian Broadcasting
  Commission 150
Australian Dairy Corporation 150
Australian Democrats 97, 98, 99, 100,
  101, 113, 117, 121, 204, 205, 212
Australian Institute of Political
  Science 36
Australian Medical Association 63
Australian Patriotic Association 4
Australian Socialist Party 21, 27
Australian Workers Union 18

Bagehot, W. 87, 91, 105, 111
Bank Nationalisation 67
Barwick, G. 178
Bednall, C. 68
Bellamy, E. 13, 18
Bentham, J. 6, 91, 200
Berki, R. 137, 138
Bicameralism 117–23 *passim*, 201
Bill of Rights 93
Bjelkemander 211
Bjelke-Petersen, J. 49, 98, 183, 191,
  211
Blackburn Convention 23
Boyer Lecture 186

Bryce, J. 194, 195
Bulbeck, C. 66
Bureaucracy 64
Burke, E. 3, 92, 112, 127

Caiden, G. 135
Cain, J. 210
Cairns, J. 139
Campbell Committee 185
Catholic Action 34, 41, 48
Catholic Social Studies Movement 41
Catley, R. 50
Centre for Independent Studies 82, 93
Chamberlain, C. 69
Chifley, J.B. 39
Childe, V.G. 23
Clark, C. 115
Class 65–70 *passim*
Class Analysis 65, 66
Commonwealth Employment
  Service 145
Committee System 109, 110, 118, 122
Communist Can 134
Communist Party of Australia 27, 28,
  37, 41, 44
Communist Party of Australia
  (M–L) 45, 98, 199
Compulsory Voting 202, 203, 207
Conciliation and Arbitration
  Commission 150
Coneybeare, J. 82
Connell, R.W. 66, 68, 69, 81, 218
Connor, R. 47
Constitution 33, 92, 93, 94, 112
Constitutional Convention 92, 123,
  179, 183

255

Conventions 91, 92
Coombs, H.C. 137, 140
Co-operative Federalism 164, 188
Co-ordinate Federalism 164, 165–70 passim
Corporatism 74–8 passim
Country Party See National Party
Crisp, L.F. 87, 115
Crosland, A. 56
CSIRO 179

Dahl, R.A. 60
Davis, S.R. 185
Deakin, A. 17, 19, 120, 166
Democratic Centralism 114
Democratic Labor Party 41, 48, 96, 98, 99, 100, 101, 102, 121, 204, 205, 207, 212
Department of Urban and Regional Development 138, 155, 176, 182
Depression 35
de Toqueville, A. 32
Discipline (party) 114
Dixon, O. 176, 177, 178
Dixson, M. 26
Douglas Credit 34
Duncan, W.G.K. 36
Dunstan, D.A. 45, 46, 50, 210, 212
Durkheim, E. 15
Duverger, M. 204, 205

Economic Planning and Advisory Council 76
Edwards, J. 141
Electoral Commission 214
Elites 71–4 passim
Embourgeoisment 216, 217
Emy, H. 58, 95
Encel, S. 64, 80, 130, 132, 134, 190
Essentialism 79
Ethnicity 219
Eureka Stockade 8, 10, 44
Evans, G. 168
Evatt, H.V. 41
Everidge, E. 43

Fabianism 19
Fascism 24, 25
Federal Court 160
Federation 164
Feminism 58, 70, 71
First Past the Post 207
Fixed Term 123–7 passim
Franklin Dam 151, 168, 169, 186, 188

Fraser Island 188
Fraser, J.M. 47, 102, 181, 184
Freedom of Information 92
Freeth, G. 100
Free Trade 20
Freud, S. 40
Fusion (1909) 20

Gairmander 211
Garran, R. 192
Gerrymander 208
Giddens, A. 72, 80
Goot, M. 218
Gorton, J. 42
Gouldner, A. 78
Gourlay, R. 5
Governor General 121, 123
Grattan, C.H. 36, 37
Great Depression 31
Green, T.H. 15, 32

Hancock, K. 32, 33, 34, 36, 50, 130, 222
Hawke, R.J. 51, 76, 102, 185
Hawker, G. 148, 149
Hayden, W. 139
Hegemony 68
Higgins, Justice 31
High Court 68, 94, 113, 151, 168, 169, 171, 176, 177, 178, 182, 187, 211
Higley, J. 72, 73, 74
Himmelweit, H. 221, 222
Holmes, J. 164, 179
House of Representatives 120
Howard, C. 190
Hughes, B. 141
Hughes, W.M. 17, 20, 23, 29, 30
Human Rights Commission 161

Ideology 16
Industrial Workers of the World 11, 21, 22
Industries Assistance Commission 150
Inequality 55, 56
Irvine, R.F. 32
Irving, T. 66, 68, 69
Isaacs, I. 177

James, M. 91
Jupp, J. 127

Kemp, D. 78, 216, 217, 218, 219
Keynes, J.M. 32, 134, 141, 142
Killen, J. 49

INDEX

King, A. 127
Koowarta 167, 169, 171
Kriegler, R. 69

Labor Party 11, 17, 18, 20, 21, 23, 27, 28, 29, 34, 35, 37, 39, 45, 46, 47, 49, 50, 51, 61, 95–103 *passim*, 106, 113, 114, 115, 116, 121, 122, 123, 133, 134, 172, 176, 180, 189, 206, 214, 215, 217
Labour Movement 11, 12, 13, 25
Lane, W. 11, 13
Lang, J. 25, 26, 27, 32, 34, 48, 49, 178
Lang, J.D. 7, 8, 9, 35
Lang Labor 25, 27, 34, 38
Lawson, H. 13
Lenin, V.I. 26, 27
Leninism 26, 27, 28
Lewis, T.L. 183
Liberalism 6
Liberal Party 17, 38, 42, 43, 47, 75, 79, 95–103 *passim* 113, 114, 116, 117, 123, 133, 134, 140, 173, 178, 180, 183, 206, 214, 215
Loan Council 169, 170, 179, 185, 188
Local Government 174–6 *passim*
Locke, J. 9, 90
Long Boom 9, 41
Loveday, P. 75, 76, 77
Lowi, T. 103
Lukes, S. 60, 138

MacArthur, J. 3, 4
McFarlane, B. 50, 76
McMichael, M. 56
MacPherson, C. 103
McQueen, H. 208
Madison, J. 127, 166
Malapportionment 208, 209, 210, 212
Mann, T. 11
Mannheim, K. 37, 133, 134, 151
Marijuana Party 59
Marxism 65–70 *passim*, 83, 200
Mayer, H. 50
Media 68, 69
Menzies, R.G. 38, 41, 42, 43, 134, 178
Mercantilism 5
Michels, R. 127
Miliband, R. 73, 136, 137
Mill, J.S. 9, 18, 32, 77, 103, 159
Mills, C.W. 68, 78
Mitchell, E. 170
Mosca, G. 133
Murphy, L. 109, 178

Nationalist Party 22
National Party 10, 29, 30, 35, 43, 46, 48, 79, 95–103 *passim*, 113, 115, 123, 173, 180, 183, 206, 212, 214
Neutrality 111
New Australians 40
New Federalism 181, 182, 184, 185, 189
New Guard 24, 25
New Protection 13
New States 174
Nuclear Disarmament Party 97, 212

Odgers, J.R. 109
Offe, C. 83
Ombudsman 92, 159, 160
One Big Union 23
One Vote One Value 208
Organic Federalism 164
Owen, R. 18

Painter, M. 157
Parker, R.S. 88, 89, 104
Parkes, H. 35, 171
Parliament 87–95 *passim*
Parsons, T. 60
Party Identification 216
Party System 95–103 *passim*
Pateman, C. 200, 223
Peachment, A. 184
Peacock, A. 103
Playford, J. 69, 72
Pledge 116
Pluralism 58–61 *passim*, 75
Plurality 206, 207
Pomper, G. 221
Populism 4, 7–14 *passim*, 15, 25, 29
Power, defined 57
Powers Referendum 39
Preferential Vote 206, 207
Premiers' Conference 179
Premiers' Plan 34
Pressure Group 59, 60
Prices Justification Tribunal 150
Privy Council 176
Proportional Representation 205, 207
Protectionist Liberals 17
Public Service 59, 111, 150
Public Service Board 148, 150, 152, 153

Quango 59, 149, 150
Quick, J. 192

Racial Discrimination Act 168

Racial Purity   19
Racism   14, 40
Rawson, D.W.   76
RCAGA   137, 139, 142–8 *passim*, 150–9 *passim*, 162, 163
Reid Report   145, 146, 147, 150, 151, 154, 155, 159, 160, 161, 163
Reid, R.L.   184
Referendum   172, 173, 190, 191, 194
Representative Government   112–7 *passim*
Republic   193
Republicanism   8
Responsible Government   6, 10, 89, 104–12 *passim*
Responsible Party   105, 126
Reynolds, P.   217
Ricardo, D.   13
Right to Vote   202, 203
River Murray Agreement   182
Rowse, T.   33, 36
Rydon, J.   202

Sartori, G.   98
Sawer, G.   165, 170, 171, 179
Schools Commission   150, 182
Schumpeter, J.   42, 200, 223
Senate   94, 109, 110, 117–23 *passim*, 179, 204, 212
Shann, E.   31
Sharman, C.   164, 179
Simms, M.   133, 134
Smith, A.   5, 60
Smith, R.F.I.   146
Snedden, B.M.   107, 122
Snowy Mountains Scheme   179
Snyder, C.   18
Socialism   14, 15, 20–3 *passim*
Socialist Labor Party   21
Socialist Party of Australia   45, 199
Social Liberalism   14–19 *passim*, 20, 36
Sovereignty   90
Spann, R.   147, 174
Speaker   122, 123
Spence, C.H.   204
Spence, W.G.   17, 21
Spencer, H.   171
State's Rights   164
Status   62
Statute of Westminster   34
Statutory Authority   149, 150

Stevenson, G.   187, 188
Stone, J.   141
Stretton, H.   140, 142
Swinging Voter   107
Syndicalism   22

Tariff   13
Tawney, R.   56
Theophanous, A.   69
Thompson, E.   89
Torrens, R.R.   5
Trades Unions   11
Transnational Corporations   188, 191
Treasury   152, 153

Uniform Tax Case   178
Uranium   82
United Australia Party   28, 37, 134
Universal Declaration of Human Rights   94
Utilitarianism   4, 7, 31

Vickers, G.   146
Victorian Socialist Party   11, 21, 22, 27
Vietnam   44, 108, 217

Wakefield, E.G.   6
Wakefield Scheme   5, 7
Ward, J.   4, 16
Washminster Mutation   90
Webb, L.   128
Weber, M.   62–5 *passim*, 83, 89, 145, 146, 149
Wentworth, W.C.   5, 35
Wertheim, W.F.   16
Westminster Model   88, 89, 94, 95, 104, 105, 108, 111, 117, 118, 121, 132, 141, 143, 147, 148, 152, 154, 160, 161, 163, 178
Wheare, K.C.   165, 169
Wheelwright, E.   56
White Australia Policy   40
Whitlam, E.G.   50, 137, 181, 189, 194, 211
Wild, R.   69, 72, 80
Wilenski, P.   138
Wilson, H.   139
Windschuttle, K.   69
Wolfsohn, T.   61
Workers Educational Association   15
Wran, N.   210